"I can think of no one in the world better qualifie[d to write on iner]rancy than my lifelong friend Vern Poythress. Se[veral Gospels say] there are differences between accounts of the sa[me events in Matthew] and John, and no responsible reader can simpl[y sweep them under the] rug. But can all of the accounts still be reconcile[d with one another?] In this book, Poythress provides an outstanding resource that carefully analyzes every important Gospel passage where an inconsistency or a contradiction has been alleged. He draws on the rich resources of centuries of church history and his own remarkable wisdom in analyzing human linguistic communication to provide a sure-footed, thoughtful, humble, and even spiritually challenging guide to these key passages. This is the best book I know of for dealing with Gospel difficulties. It is profoundly wise, insightful, and clearly written, and it will surely strengthen every reader's confidence in the trustworthiness of the Bible as the very words of God."

Wayne Grudem, Research Professor of Theology and Biblical Studies,
Phoenix Seminary

"Shall we defend biblical inerrancy with arguments that are naïve and unconvincing? Or shall we assume that discrepancies among the Gospels cannot be resolved? Vern Poythress shows us that we need not make such a choice. Clear, convincing, accessible, and practical, *Inerrancy and the Gospels* is everything we need in a book on this topic. While sharpening readers' skill at harmonization, Poythress also develops a thoughtful, God-honoring foundation for addressing Gospel difficulties and the spiritual challenges that accompany them. I want every student, every pastor, and every skeptic I know to read this book—and recommend it to their friends."

C. D. "Jimmy" Agan III, Associate Professor of New Testament,
Director of the Homiletics Program, Covenant Theological Seminary

"When Vern Poythress has chosen to write on a particular subject, the resulting book has always been (in my memory) the best book on that subject. This one is about the inerrancy of Scripture, dealing particularly with problems in the Gospel narratives, and I know of nothing better in the field. It is fully cogent, very helpful, linguistically sophisticated, and, above all, faithful to the Scriptures as the word of God."

John M. Frame, J. D. Trimble Chair of Systematic Theology and Philosophy,
Reformed Theological Seminary, Orlando, Florida

"It is all too common today to bemoan harmonization, but there is value in pursuing the real possibility that differences in the Gospels can and should be seen as complementing one another in their presentation of truth. Vern Poythress's *Inerrancy and the Gospels* uses a self-authenticating approach to Scripture to argue that harmonization does give insight in how the Gospels work. This is a study well worth reading and considering, regardless of whether one accepts the self-authenticating model or not."

Darrell L. Bock, Executive Director of Cultural Engagement, Center for Christian Leadership; Senior Research Professor of New Testament Studies,
Dallas Theological Seminary

"Vern Poythress has the unique ability to make a complex subject understandable to anyone. In this book he tackles head-on the age-old issue of how to harmonize the four Gospels. In so doing, he helps us understand how they should be not only harmonized, but also appreciated for their unique and vital witness to the truths of the person and work of our incarnate Savior. This is an excellent introduction to the study of the Gospels."

S. M. Baugh, Professor of New Testament, Westminster Seminary California

"Vern Poythress's *Inerrancy and the Gospels* is of perennial value, but is especially timely given both the popularization of critical theories about the Gospels and the migration of some scholars from evangelical to critical approaches. He exemplifies his forebear Ned Stonehouse's engagement with critical scholarship by not only playing defense, but also gleaning positive insights from synoptic comparisons. The hermeneutical principles that he articulates are in keeping with Scripture's self-authenticating character and demonstrate a knowledge of contemporary developments in hermeneutics. The examples he uses to illustrate those principles are varied while including the typically most challenging harmonizations. Scholars and pastors alike who wish to understand and proclaim the unity and variety of the Evangelists' witness will want to thoroughly digest what Dr. Poythress provides here."

Michael J. Glodo, Associate Professor of Biblical Studies,
Reformed Theological Seminary, Orlando, Florida

"Let's be honest. Bible-believing Christians sometimes struggle to understand apparent discrepancies in the Gospels. Poythress's book *Inerrancy and the Gospels* is now on the top of my list to recommend to students who are seeking a biblically faithful resource on this issue. It is up-to-date, balanced, and historically informed. I plan to adopt *Inerrancy and the Gospels* as a required textbook for my New Testament survey course."

Robert L. Plummer, Associate Professor of New Testament Interpretation,
The Southern Baptist Theological Seminary

"In this work, Vern Poythress, one of evangelicalism's leading proponents and defenders of inerrancy, traverses the difficult terrain of Gospel harmonization. With theological acumen and exegetical sensitivity, Poythress equips the reader with the categories, distinctions, and reading strategies needed to study the Gospels in the way that God has intended. The result is magnificent—Poythress shows us how a proper understanding of harmonization enhances our appreciation of the rich unity and diversity of the Gospels. I warmly commend this work to students, pastors, and scholars alike."

Guy Prentiss Waters, Professor of New Testament,
Reformed Theological Seminary, Jackson, Mississippi

INERRANCY

AND

THE GOSPELS

Other Crossway Books by Vern Sheridan Poythress

Redeeming Science: A God-Centered Approach
In the Beginning Was the Word: Language—A God-Centered Approach
Redeeming Sociology: A God-Centered Approach
Inerrancy and Worldview: Answering Modern Challenges to the Bible

INERRANCY

AND

THE GOSPELS

A God-Centered Approach
to the Challenges of harmonization

VERN SHERIDAN POYTHRESS

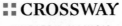

WHEATON, ILLINOIS

Inerrancy and the Gospels: A God-Centered Approach to the Challenges of Harmonization
Copyright © 2012 by Vern Sheridan Poythress
Published by Crossway
        1300 Crescent Street
        Wheaton, Illinois 60187

Cover design: Studio Gearbox
Cover image: Dover
Interior design and typesetting: Lakeside Design Plus

First printing 2012
Printed in the United States of America

Unless otherwise indicated, Scripture quotations are from the ESV® Bible (*The Holy Bible, English Standard Version*®), copyright © 2001 by Crossway. Used by permission. All rights reserved.

Scripture quotations marked KJV are from the *King James Version* of the Bible.

Scripture quotations marked NASB are from *The New American Standard Bible*®. Copyright © The Lockman Foundation 1960, 1962, 1963, 1968, 1971, 1972, 1973, 1975, 1977, 1995. Used by permission.

Scripture quotations marked NIV are from the *Holy Bible, New International Version*®. Copyright © 1973, 1978, 1984 Biblica. Used by permission of Zondervan. All rights reserved. The "NIV" and "New International Version" trademarks are registered in the United States Patent and Trademark Office by Biblica. Use of either trademark requires the permission of Biblica.

Scripture references marked NKJV are from *The New King James Version*. Copyright © 1982, Thomas Nelson, Inc. Used by permission.

All emphases in Scripture quotations have been added by the author.

Trade paperback ISBN:	978-1-4335-2860-6
ePub ISBN:	978-1-4335-2863-7
PDF ISBN:	978-1-4335-2861-3
Mobipocket ISBN:	978-1-4335-2862-0

Library of Congress Cataloging-in-Publication Data
Poythress, Vern S.
    Inerrancy and the Gospels : a God-centered approach to the challenges of harmonization / Vern Sheridan Poythress.
      p. cm.
    Includes bibliographical references (p.   ) and indexes.
    ISBN 978-1-4335-2860-6 (tp)
    1. Bible. N.T. Gospels—Harmonies—History and criticism. 2. Bible. N.T. Gospels—Criticism, interpretation, etc. 3. Bible. N.T. Gospels—Evidences, authority, etc. I. Title.
BS2562.P69 2012
226'.013—dc23   2012017161

Crossway is a publishing ministry of Good News Publishers.

VP	24	23	22	21	20	19	18	17	16	15	14	13	12
14	13	12	11	10	9	8	7	6	5	4	3	2	1

I am grateful for my teachers
at Westminster Theological Seminary,
who taught me to honor and submit to God's Word,
and set an example of submission themselves;
and I am grateful for generations before them,
who fought the good fight of faith.

CONTENTS

PART ONE

THE CHALLENGE
OF HARMONIZATION

1

DIFFICULTIES IN THE GOSPELS

In the centuries after the Bible was written, the church recognized that it was the word of God and treated its contents as trustworthy.[1] But in modern times some people have come to question that conviction. Moreover, there are difficulties in some of the details in the Bible. For example, comparisons between accounts in the four Gospels, Matthew, Mark, Luke, and John, turn up a large number of differences, some of which are easy to appreciate positively, but others more difficult. In this book we are going to look at a sampling of these difficulties, with the goal of treating them in harmony with the conviction that the Bible is God's word.

We are looking at this topic partly because we can often learn more from the Bible if we consider difficulties carefully and do not merely skirt around them. But we will also try to lay out some principles for dealing with difficulties. Other books have considered the broad question of the historical reliability of the Gospels.[2] Still other books have discussed the general issue of the authority of the Bible, and some of these books have done a very good job indeed.[3]

---

[1] See, for example, John D. Woodbridge, *Biblical Authority: A Critique of the Rogers/McKim Proposal* (Grand Rapids: Zondervan, 1982). The Jewish recognition that the Old Testament was the word of God laid the foundation for Christians' understanding of the Old and New Testaments together.

[2] On defending historical reliability, see chap. 11 below.

[3] I think of Benjamin B. Warfield, *The Inspiration and Authority of the Bible* (repr., Philadelphia: Presbyterian and Reformed, 1967); Archibald A. Hodge and Benjamin B. Warfield, *Inspiration*, with introduction by Roger R. Nicole (repr., Grand Rapids: Baker, 1979); *The Infallible Word: A Symposium by the Members of the Faculty of Westminster Theological Seminary*, 3rd ed., ed. N. B. Stonehouse and Paul Woolley (Philadelphia:

The Inspiration and Authority of the Bible

Without re-covering the ground of these books, we may briefly summarize the teaching of the Bible on the subject of inspiration.[4] The Bible is the word of God, God's speech in written form. What the Bible says, God says. Two classic texts summarize the meaning of inspiration.

> All Scripture is *breathed out by God* and profitable for teaching, for reproof, for correction, and for training in righteousness, that the man of God may be complete, equipped for every good work. (2 Tim. 3:16–17)

> For no prophecy was ever produced by the will of man, but men *spoke from God* as they were *carried along by the Holy Spirit.* (2 Pet. 1:21)

In addition, Jesus testifies to the authority of the Old Testament in his explicit statements, in the ways that he quotes from and uses it, and in the way that he understands his own life as the fulfillment of it.

> Do not think that I have come to abolish the Law or the Prophets; I have not come to abolish them but to fulfill them. For truly, I say to you, until heaven and earth pass away, *not an iota, not a dot,* will pass from the Law until all is accomplished. (Matt. 5:17–18)

> Scripture cannot be broken. (John 10:35)

> Do you think that I cannot appeal to my Father, and he will at once send me more than twelve legions of angels? But how then should *the Scriptures* be fulfilled, that *it must be so*? (Matt. 26:53)

If we claim to be followers of Christ, we should submit to his teaching.

Many aspects of Scripture testify to its divine origin. But it is through the Holy Spirit working inwardly in the heart that people become fully convinced that it is the word of God.[5]

Presbyterian and Reformed, 1967); Richard B. Gaffin Jr., *God's Word in Servant-Form: Abraham Kuyper and Herman Bavinck on the Doctrine of Scripture* (Jackson, MS: Reformed Academic, 2008); Woodbridge, *Biblical Authority*; Herman Bavinck, *Reformed Dogmatics*, vol. 1, *Prolegomena*, ed. John Bolt, trans. John Vriend (Grand Rapids: Baker, 2003), 353–494; D. A. Carson and John D. Woodbridge, eds., *Scripture and Truth* (Grand Rapids: Zondervan, 1983); John M. Frame, *The Doctrine of the Word of God* (Phillipsburg, NJ: P&R, 2010). Readers should also note the principial qualifications with respect to presuppositions and method in Cornelius Van Til's "Introduction" to the 1967 edition of Warfield, *Inspiration*, 3–68.

[4]See also the summary in John Murray, "The Attestation of Scripture," in *The Infallible Word*, 1–54.

[5]"We may be moved and induced by the testimony of the Church to an high and reverend esteem of the Holy Scripture. And the heavenliness of the matter, the efficacy of the doctrine, the majesty of the style, the consent of all the parts, the scope of the whole (which is, to give all glory to God), the full discovery it makes of the only way of man's salvation, the many other incomparable excellencies, and the entire

Dealing with Difficulties

When we have become convinced that the Bible is God's word, we can consider the implications. We can ask, How should we proceed in particular cases of difficulty when we come to the Bible with the conviction that it is God's speech to us?

My primary challenge in accomplishing this task is myself. I am a finite, fallible human being. I am also affected by remaining sin. And sin affects biblical interpretation. So I cannot be an ideal example. Of course, neither can anyone else subsequent to the apostles. God designed the church, the people of God, to work together. We strive together, "with all the *saints*," to comprehend "what is the breadth and length and height and depth, and to know the love of Christ that surpasses knowledge, that you may be filled with all the fullness of God" (Eph. 3:18). We help one another. In particular, any contribution I may make builds on the insights of others before me. And if I do a good job, my contribution becomes in turn a source of help for others after me. So you must understand that this book represents part of a path toward a future fullness of knowledge, when we will know God "even as [we] have been fully known" (1 Cor. 13:12).

Foundations

Because I am building on what others have done, I will not repeat the work of other people who have argued for the authority of the Bible as the word of God. Nor will we revisit the issues covered in my earlier book *Inerrancy and Worldview*.[6] There I indicate ways in which an understanding and acceptance of the biblical worldview contributes to understanding the Bible positively and honoring its authority.

If we reckon with the fact that God is personal and that he rules the world personally, we have a *personalistic* worldview that has notable contrasts with the *impersonalism* that characterizes a lot of modern thinking.[7] The robust personalism of the Bible helps to dissolve some difficulties that trouble

---

perfection thereof, are arguments whereby it doth abundantly evidence itself to be the Word of God: yet notwithstanding, our full persuasion and assurance of the infallible truth and divine authority thereof, is from the inward work of the Holy Spirit bearing witness by and with the Word in our hearts" (Westminster Confession of Faith 1.5).

[6]Vern S. Poythress, *Inerrancy and Worldview: Answering Modern Challenges to the Bible* (Wheaton, IL: Crossway, 2012).

[7]We may note that the personal God of the Bible is distinct from spirits and gods postulated in other religions. Animistic religion believes in many personal spiritual beings. But since it does not acknowledge one personal Creator, the deepest roots for the world still end up being impersonal. Islam believes in one Allah, but its adherents follow rules without having a personal relationship to him. So even a monotheistic religion can be characterized by an impersonalistic atmosphere in practice.

modern people if they read the Bible against the background of modern impersonalism. This contrast between personalism and impersonalism is important when we deal with the Gospels. I will draw on the contrast when necessary, but will not repeat in detail the reasoning in the earlier book.

In addition, both this book and *Inerrancy and Worldview* rely on a broader understanding of God, science, language, history, and society, an understanding informed by the Bible and at odds with modern thinking.[8] When we take biblical teaching seriously, it certainly leads to a revised approach to how we understand the Bible. But it also leads us to revise how we analyze virtually all modern ideas, including ideas about meaning and interpretation. We will draw on this understanding when needed, without reviewing the entire territory.

---

[8]See Vern S. Poythress, *God-Centered Biblical Interpretation* (Phillipsburg, NJ: P&R, 1999); Poythress, *Redeeming Science: A God-Centered Approach* (Wheaton, IL: Crossway, 2006); Poythress, *In the Beginning Was the Word: Language—A God-Centered Approach* (Wheaton, IL: Crossway, 2009); Poythress, *Redeeming Sociology: A God-Centered Approach* (Wheaton, IL: Crossway, 2011).

I cannot within this book enter into extended discussion of modern critical approaches to the Bible. I offer only the following summary: we should practice humility and self-critical awareness about our assumptions; we should take seriously the fallibility of human sources outside the Bible. But we should not endorse modernity. One of the points in my books is that a whole spectrum of assumptions and interpretive frameworks belong to the modern world, and that critical interpreters within our modern situation are not nearly critical enough of these frameworks. They cannot be, because they have no solid place to stand from which to engage in criticism. They have not been willing to accept the Bible as a secure guide on the basis of which they can sift through the good and bad in the world of ideas.

2

An Example:
The Centurion's Servant

We begin with an example. Matthew 8:5–13 and Luke 7:1–10 contain accounts about Jesus's healing a centurion's servant. How do we deal with the differences? Here are the two accounts,[1] side by side:

Matthew 8:5–13	Luke 7:1–10
[5] When he had entered Capernaum, a centurion came forward to him, appealing to him, [6] "Lord, my servant is lying paralyzed at home, suffering terribly."	[1] After he had finished all his sayings in the hearing of the people, he entered Capernaum. [2] Now a centurion had a servant who was sick and at the point of death, who was highly valued by him. [3] When the centurion heard about Jesus, he sent to him elders of the Jews, asking him to come and heal his servant. [4] And when they came to Jesus, they pleaded with him earnestly, saying, "He is worthy to

[1] In this book I use the English Standard Version (ESV). If we use the original Greek text, we can now and then see further small similarities and differences not fully visible in English. But many of the most important differences come through well enough in English. So, for simplicity, we will customarily use English. I will refer directly to the original languages only at times when a significant extra feature needs to be noticed.

John 4:46–54 has an account of healing at a distance, showing some similarities to the accounts in Matthew and Luke. But it concerns an official's "son," which indicates that it is a different event from the one narrated in Matthew and Luke (Luke 7:2 has "servant, slave," [Greek *doulos*], which contrasts with being a son; see R. T. France, *The Gospel of Matthew* [Grand Rapids: Eerdmans, 2007], 312).

Matthew 8:5–13	Luke 7:1–10
	have you do this for him, [5] for he loves our nation, and he is the one who built us our synagogue." [6] And Jesus went with them. When he was not far from the house, the centurion sent
[7] And he said to him, "I will come and heal him." [8] But the centurion replied, "Lord,	friends, saying to him, "Lord, do not trouble yourself, for
I am not worthy to have you come under my roof,	I am not worthy to have you come under my roof. [7] Therefore I did not presume to come to you.
but only say the word, and my servant will be healed. [9] For I too am a man under authority, with soldiers under me. And I say to one, 'Go,' and he goes, and to another, 'Come,' and he comes, and to my servant, 'Do this,' and he does." [10] When Jesus heard this, he marveled and said to those who followed him, "Truly, I tell you, with no one in Israel have I found such faith. [11] I tell you, many will come from east and west and recline at table with Abraham, Isaac, and Jacob in the kingdom of heaven, [12] while the sons of the kingdom will be thrown into the outer darkness. In that place there will be weeping and gnashing of teeth." [13] And to the centurion Jesus said, "Go; let it be done for you as you have believed."	But say the word, and let my servant be healed. [8] For I too am a man set under authority, with soldiers under me: and I say to one, 'Go,' and he goes; and to another, 'Come,' and he comes; and to my servant, 'Do this,' and he does it." [9] When Jesus heard these things, he marveled at him, and turning to the crowd that followed him, said, "I tell you, not even in Israel have I found such faith."
And the servant was healed at that very moment.	[10] And when those who had been sent returned to the house, they found the servant well.

The most notable difference between the two accounts lies in the role of the "elders of the Jews" and the centurion's "friends" in Luke 7. There the elders and the friends serve as intermediaries; Luke does not indicate that the centurion meets Jesus face to face. By contrast, in Matthew 8 there is no mention of intermediaries. What do we say about this difference?

The Possibility of Multiple Events

In any case that deals with parallel passages we have to ask whether they recount the same incident or two different incidents. In this case there are many similarities between the two accounts. The centurion's speech given in Matthew 8:9 is almost identical to Luke 7:8. We can safely conclude that we are dealing with two accounts of one event. So there is a genuine difficulty.

A Solution by Several Stages of Events

We can profit from the insights of previous generations. Consider one solution that has been offered. Norval Geldenhuys and others have put forward the idea that there were several stages in the encounter between Jesus and the centurion.[2] The centurion first sent elders of the Jews (Luke 7:3–5), then sent friends (Luke 7:6–8), then came in person and repeated some of what had been said earlier (Matt. 8:5–9). Geldenhuys gives this explanation:

> When we bear in mind the parallel account in Matthew viii. 5–13, we must picture to ourselves that after the centurion had sent his friends to Jesus he also went to Him himself. Owing to the seriousness of the circumstances and his inner urge to go to Jesus himself, notwithstanding his feeling of unworthiness, he overcame his initial hesitation. Luke emphasises the fact that the centurion sent friends, while Matthew only states that the centurion went to Jesus. And so the two Gospels supplement each other.[3]

This possibility results in a clean explanation in which Matthew and Luke each mention a complementary portion of the total interaction. Such an explanation is customarily called a *harmonization*, because it attempts to show that the two passages are in harmony.

Geldenhuys recognizes that there is still a minor difficulty. In Luke, the centurion states explicitly that he is unworthy (7:6), and that is why he has sent others instead: "Therefore I did not presume to come to you" (7:7). Yet, according to Geldenhuys, the centurion nevertheless changed his mind and *did* come in the end for a face-to-face meeting. On the surface, his coming in person appears to be in tension with his expressed plan *not* to come. But Geldenhuys supplies possible motivations by reminding us of the "seriousness of the circumstances," by postulating an "inner urge" to come to Jesus, and by labeling his original attitude "initial hesitation" rather than a firm resolve not to come because of his unworthiness. Is all this possible? It is. Human motivations and decision making are complex and often include some wavering or change of mind.

Geldenhuys's picture of the events also results in a certain notable repetition. In Luke 7:6–8 the friends give a speech expressing the centurion's request and his reasoning about authority. The same speech occurs in Matthew 8:8–9, using almost identical words. Geldenhuys's reconstruction interprets these accounts as records of two distinct speeches, one by the friends and one by the centurion in person. This too is possible since the friends were sent

---

[2]Norval Geldenhuys, *Commentary on the Gospel of Luke* (Grand Rapids: Eerdmans, 1950), 220; likewise Gleason L. Archer, *Encyclopedia of Bible Difficulties* (Grand Rapids: Zondervan, 1982), 322.
[3]Geldenhuys, *Commentary on the Gospel of Luke*, 220.

by the centurion, and the centurion told them what to say. In Geldenhuys's picture of the event, the centurion repeated in person what he had said to his friends earlier. We may ask why the centurion thought he had to repeat his speech, since his friends had already delivered it. But human motivations are complex. Particularly in a situation of distress, such as the emotional turmoil the centurion experienced, he might in spite of himself repeat what he knew had already been said.

So Geldenhuys's reconstruction of the events is possible. Is it the only possibility? Augustine and Calvin have offered another explanation.

Representatives Acting on Behalf of the Centurion

Saint Augustine in about AD 400 wrote *The Harmony of the Gospels*, in which he discussed a large number of difficulties.[4] He believed that the Gospels have divine authority,[5] and he consistently tried to show that the differences between the Gospels were not due to error but exhibited harmony. His work has formed the background for many later attempts.[6] When comparing Matthew 8:5–13 and Luke 7:1–10, Augustine explains:

> How can Matthew's statement that there "came to Him a certain centurion," be correct, seeing that the man did not come in person, but sent his friends? The apparent discrepancy, however, will disappear if we look carefully into the matter, and observe that Matthew has simply held by a very familiar mode of expression. . . . This [the practice of using a representative or intermediary], indeed, is a custom which has so thoroughly established itself, that even in the language of every-day life . . . [we call men] *Perventores* who . . . get at the inaccessible ears, as one may say, of any of the men of influence, by the intervention of suitable personages. If, therefore access [to another person's presence] itself is thus familiarly [in everyday speech] said to be gained by the means of other parties, how much more may an approach be said to take place, although it be by means of others.[7]

John Calvin offers a similar explanation:

> Those who think that Matthew and Luke give different narratives, are led into a mistake by a mere trifle. The only difference in the words is, that Matthew

---

[4]Augustine, *The Harmony of the Gospels*, in vol. 6 of *A Select Library of the Nicene and Post-Nicene Fathers of the Christian Church*, ed. Philip Schaff (repr., Grand Rapids: Eerdmans, 1979), 65–236. Augustine's text is hereafter cited in *NPNF1* by book, chapter, and paragraph.

[5]Ibid., 2.12.28: "that word of God which abides eternal and unchangeable . . . the most exalted height of authority"; see also elsewhere throughout the work.

[6]See, for example, M. B. Riddle, introduction to Augustine, *The Harmony of the Gospels*, 67–70.

[7]Augustine, *The Harmony of the Gospels*, 2.20.49.

says that *the centurion came to him,* while Luke says that he sent some of the Jews to plead in his name. But there is no impropriety in Matthew saying, that the centurion did what was done in his name and at his request. There is such a perfect agreement between the two Evangelists in all the circumstances, that it is absurd to make two miracles instead of one.[8]

A more recent scholar, R. T. France, writes as follows:

His [Matthew's] omission of the *means* of the centurion's approach to Jesus is a valid literary device to highlight the message of the incident as he sees it (on the principle, common in biblical and contemporary literature, that a messenger or servant represents the one who sent him to the point of virtual identity).[9]

As a further illustration of the principle, Craig Blomberg points to Matthew 27:26 and Mark 15:15.[10] Both verses report that Pilate scourged Jesus; but, given the social and military protocol of the Roman world, Pilate would not have taken up the scourge in his own hands. The verses mean that Roman soldiers would have physically handled the scourge, acting on Pilate's orders. That is to say, the Roman soldiers represented Pilate because they acted under his authority. Pilate *did* scourge Jesus, though he did not do it "in person" but through representatives acting on his behalf. Likewise, the centurion really *did* address Jesus, but he did it by means of persons acting under his authority and on his behalf—the elders and friends represented him.

Is such a reconstruction of the events possible? According to Augustine and Calvin, it is. In fact, they obviously prefer it to a more elaborate reconstruction such as Geldenhuys offered. They regard their simpler reconstruction as more likely. Both Augustine and Calvin are vigorous defenders of the divine authority of the Bible. They express no doubts about the accounts being truthful and correct. Rather, they show that they assume each account to be true when they undertake to give an explanation that harmonizes the two. The main difference they have in comparison with Geldenhuys is that they consider the possibility that the centurion acted through representatives.

Though Augustine and Calvin think that their reconstruction is likely, it is still tentative. So is the reconstruction by Geldenhuys. We have the accounts in Matthew and Luke, which are inspired by God. They are what God says and are therefore trustworthy. That is the conviction we have and the basis on which we work. But we do not have a third account, also inspired, to tell

---

[8]John Calvin, *Commentary on a Harmony of the Evangelists, Matthew, Mark, and Luke,* 3 vols., trans. William Pringle (Grand Rapids: Eerdmans, n.d.), 1:378.
[9]Richard T. France, "Inerrancy and New Testament Exegesis," *Themelios* 1 (1975): 17.
[10]Craig L. Blomberg, *The Historical Reliability of the Gospels,* 2nd ed. (Downers Grove, IL: InterVarsity, 2007), 176.

us exactly how the original two accounts fit together. We make our own reasoned guesses, but they are fallible. We do not have complete information. Our reconstruction, though it may be plausible, is subordinate to the Gospel accounts as we have them.

Positive Role of Differences

We can also ask what positive contribution each Gospel record makes in its distinctiveness. The Gospel of Matthew offers a simpler account in some ways. It does not require the additional linguistic complexity that arises when an account makes explicit the roles of the elders of the Jews and the friends that the centurion sends. For example, the material in Luke 7:3–5 about the Jewish elders does not need to be present in Matthew's version, and Luke 7:6, which mentions the friends, finds a simpler analogue in Matthew 8:7. The statement in Luke 7:7, "Therefore I did not presume to come to you," is also not in Matthew. By omitting some details, Matthew puts greater concentration on the main point: Jesus has power to heal at a distance, merely by speaking a word.

Though Matthew's account is shorter, it does contain one significant piece that does not occur in Luke, namely Matthew 8:11–12: "I tell you, many will come from east and west and recline at table with Abraham, Isaac, and Jacob in the kingdom of heaven, while the sons of the kingdom will be thrown into the outer darkness. In that place there will be weeping and gnashing of teeth." A similar saying occurs in Luke 13:28–30, in the context of a different episode.

> In that place there will be weeping and gnashing of teeth, when you see Abraham and Isaac and Jacob and all the prophets in the kingdom of God but you yourselves cast out. And people will come from east and west, and from north and south, and recline at table in the kingdom of God. And behold, some are last who will be first, and some are first who will be last.

In both passages Jesus warns hearers about religious presumption. In Matthew 8:5–13 the centurion's faith contrasts with the lack of faith within Israel (8:10). This contrast makes it appropriate for Jesus to warn Israelites not to presume on enjoying messianic salvation merely because they are Israelites, apart from faith on their part. Similarly, Luke 13:22–30 warns Israelites not to depend on the mere fact that Jesus ministered among them (13:26) or that they see themselves as heirs of the patriarchs (13:28).[11]

---

[11] Thus, I see the parallels between Matt. 8:11–12 and Luke 13:28–30 as due to the fact that Jesus said similar things in similar circumstances. We leave this issue to one side in order to concentrate on the more notable difficulty, which has to do with the relation between Matt. 8:5–13 and Luke 7:1–10.

Matthew shows repeated concern for the unique role of the Jews and the issue of Jewish rejection of Jesus. Matthew alone has the expression "sons of the kingdom": "the sons of the kingdom will be thrown into the outer darkness" (Matt. 8:12). These "sons of the kingdom" are Jews who are resisting his ministry. They have the privilege of having a certain nearness to "the kingdom," that is the kingdom of God, and yet, tragically, they "will be thrown into the outer darkness." Matthew alone includes the pointed threat, "Therefore I tell you, the kingdom of God will be taken away from you and given to a people producing its fruits" (Matt. 21:43). Matthew, more than the other Gospels, emphasizes the Jewishness of Jesus (Matt. 1:1–17). Twice Jesus emphasizes his ministry "to the lost sheep of the house of Israel" (Matt. 10:6; 15:24). But Jews who presume on their heritage are in danger of being left out.[12]

This theme is important to Matthew. It comes out pointedly in our first passage, Matthew 8:5–13, because Jesus commends the centurion for his faith and contrasts this commendation with the failure in Israel: "Truly, I tell you, with no one in Israel have I found such faith" (Matt. 8:10). The centurion was a Roman soldier, not a Jew. His Gentile character comes more starkly to the foreground in that Matthew does not mention "elders of the Jews" as intermediaries.

Luke, by contrast, explicitly mentions the Jewish intermediaries. The intervention of the intermediaries is not the final reason why Jesus answers the centurion's request. It is the centurion's faith, not the merit of the Jews, that leads to blessing (Luke 7:9). But Jews who wanted to rely on their privileges might nevertheless be tempted to overlook this point and take refuge in the special role that the centurion appears to create for them. The passage in Matthew helps to remove this mistaken notion. All in all, Luke and Matthew do not disagree in substance about the role of the centurion's faith or the role of Jewish religious privileges. They do differ in *emphasis*. And that difference in emphasis has practical value when Matthew is addressing a Jewish sense of privilege.

Now let us turn to Luke. What kind of emphasis do we find when we read the account in Luke? Like Matthew, Luke makes the point that Jesus has the power to heal at a distance. In addition, the fact that the centurion is a Gentile still comes out in Luke 7:9. The Gospel of Luke as a whole, together with Acts, has a theological interest in the theme that salvation is going out to the nations (Luke 24:47; Acts 1:8). This theme is confirmed when we see Jesus ministering to the centurion. Matthew and Luke agree in this respect.

But does Luke have, in addition, some distinctive emphasis? By mentioning the Jewish elders, Luke makes plainer the centurion's humility. The elders say prominently, "He is *worthy* to have you do this for him" (7:4). The centurion himself, by contrast, states plainly that he is "not worthy" (7:6). That is, he

---

[12]See France, *Gospel of Matthew*, 310–11.

means that he is not worthy of having Jesus perform a healing for him, which is why he sent the elders of the Jews, whom he considers more worthy than himself. And in addition, he is not even "worthy to have you come under my roof" (7:6)! "Therefore," he says, "I did not presume to come to you" (7:7), which again expresses his humility.

The Gospel of Luke has humility as a theme. "He [the Lord] has brought down the mighty from their thrones and exalted those of humble estate" (Luke 1:52). "For everyone who exalts himself will be humbled, but the one who humbles himself will be exalted" (Luke 18:14; see 14:11). Luke devotes attention to social outcasts and marginalized people: women, the poor, the sick, tax collectors, Gentiles (Luke 4:18; 7:21–23). Luke 7:1–10, by explicitly including the role of the intermediaries and by including the contrast between "worthy" (7:4) and "not worthy" (7:6), has highlighted the theme of humility and of Jesus's mercy to the "unworthy."

In addition, Luke indicates that Jesus's compassion extends even to people who are not directly present in front of him. He takes the trouble to answer a request from someone whom he has never met face to face.

In sum, Matthew and Luke have distinctive emphases; Matthew emphasizes the centurion's *Gentile* status, and Luke emphasizes his *humility*. Both of these emphases say something significant about the kingdom of God and Jesus's ministry. First, the kingdom of God will include Gentiles and all who come to Jesus in faith. Jews who do not trust in Jesus are excluded. Second, those who enter the kingdom must come in humility, recognizing that they do not deserve the benefits that God offers.

Both emphases are valid. Both are actually exemplified in the incident with the centurion's servant. In fact, at a deep level the two emphases imply one another. If God welcomes the humble, it implies that people do not receive God's kingdom and his salvation because of their supposed qualifications or worthiness. Therefore, Jews cannot depend on their privileged religious position. Conversely, if Jews do not enter the kingdom of God on the basis of their religious privileges, it implies that not only they but everyone else must enter in humility. In coming to God, no one may take pride in himself or his alleged worthiness; everyone must humble himself.

It is worthwhile to think about how the two emphases harmonize in the two accounts of the same episode. It is important that we respect the trustworthy character of the Gospels. But it is also valuable to acknowledge their distinctiveness. We are richer by having the two Gospels draw attention to distinct aspects of the meaning of the events and the meaning of the kingdom of God. We can appreciate what God is doing more deeply than if we just had one account, or if we just paid attention to our reconstructed idea of the events and not to the Gospels' distinctive ways of explaining the events.

PART TWO

PRINCIPLES
FOR HARMONIZATION

3

INITIAL PRINCIPLES
FOR HARMONIZATION

By working through one example about the centurion's servant, we have already illustrated several principles with broader applicability. Let us pause to consider them.

Inspiration: The Trustworthiness of the Bible

The Bible is God's speaking in written form. Because God is trustworthy and true, so is the Bible. Because God knows everything and is all-powerful, he will not fail in the way that human beings can fail through misinformation or lapse of attention.

Our assumptions about the Bible and about God play a central role in how we understand and study the Bible. These assumptions are so important that they deserve much more discussion than we can give them here—they deserve whole books. Accordingly, I am referring readers to books that have already done a good job, such as the foundational work of Benjamin B. Warfield, *The Inspiration and Authority of the Bible*.[1]

---

[1]Benjamin B. Warfield, *The Inspiration and Authority of the Bible* (repr., Philadelphia: Presbyterian and Reformed, 1967). See also Archibald A. Hodge and Benjamin B. Warfield, *Inspiration*, with introduction by Roger R. Nicole (Grand Rapids: Baker, 1979); Richard B. Gaffin Jr., *God's Word in Servant-Form: Abraham Kuyper and Herman Bavinck on the Doctrine of Scripture* (Jackson, MS: Reformed Academic, 2008); John D. Woodbridge, *Biblical Authority: A Critique of the Rogers/McKim Proposal* (Grand Rapids: Zondervan, 1982);

Our assumptions about truth also make a difference. We will have occasion to reflect on the nature of truth and true communication later on. But we may at this early point make a clarification. When we say that God speaks truthfully and that his speech can be trusted, we are including all of his speech. His speech includes instances where he makes specific assertions, but also other kinds of speech.

People sometimes use the word *true* in a narrow sense to describe the truth of *assertions*, in distinction from commands, requests, questions, wishes, and longer, complex discourses.[2] For example, Jill may say, "The door is open." In this context, "The door is open" is an assertion. It is true or false, depending on the position of the door. But suppose Jill says, "Please open the door." We would not normally say that her request is "true." Nevertheless, requests, questions, and longer discourses usually also imply commitments on the part of the speaker to various related statements. Jill implies that the door is not yet open, or at least not fully open. Consider the command "You shall not steal" in Exodus 20:15. Though not an assertion, it implies a number of assertions. It implies (1) that stealing is wrong, (2) that God says, "You shall not steal," and (3) that God does not approve of stealing. All of these implications are true.

Longer discourses like the Gospels contain parables of Jesus, and these have to be received for what they are—as parables—if we are going to appreciate their truth properly. Parables imply truths about the kingdom of God, but such implications must be sought out by appreciating how parables do their job. When we say that God's speech is always truthful, we should endeavor to preserve the richness of his speech and not insist that only some kinds of discourse or only some pieces within a discourse have authority over us.[3]

Help from the Past

We can receive help from other people who have thought about difficulties in the Bible. The four Gospels have been with us since the first century. The church through the centuries has had much opportunity to think about them and compare them. We should remember that apparent discrepancies we

---

Herman Bavinck, *Reformed Dogmatics*, vol. 1, *Prolegomena*, ed. John Bolt, trans. John Vriend (Grand Rapids: Baker, 2003), 353–494; John M. Frame, *The Doctrine of the Word of* God (Phillipsburg, NJ: P&R, 2010).

[2]On speech acts, see Vern S. Poythress, *In the Beginning Was the Word: Language—A God-Centered Approach* (Wheaton, IL: Crossway, 2009), appendix H.

[3]Frame, *Doctrine of the Word of God*, makes clear that God's authority belongs to all aspects of his speech, including questions and commands as well as statements. Ps. 119:151 says, "All your commandments are true," applying the word "true" to commandments, not merely assertions. This kind of use shows the appropriateness of using the word "true" with respect to communications of other kinds besides assertions. See also, "Your law is true" (Ps. 119:142); "Your word is truth" (John 17:17).

find have been around for a long time, and people before us have trusted in God's Word while knowing about these difficulties. Not all proposed harmonizations will be equally attractive. But by consulting many sources we may often find one or more that offer reasonable explanations.

Here are some older sources that I have found helpful:

Alford, Henry. *The Greek Testament* . . . . Vol. 1. 7th ed. London: Longmans, Green, 1898.

Andrews, Samuel J. *The Life of Our Lord upon the Earth: Considered in Its Historical, Chronological, and Geographical Relations.* Grand Rapids: Zondervan, 1954.

Archer, Gleason L. *Encyclopedia of Bible Difficulties.* Grand Rapids: Zondervan, 1982.

Augustine. *The Harmony of the Gospels.* In vol. 6 of *A Select Library of the Nicene and Post-Nicene Fathers of the Christian Church.* Series 1, edited by Philip Schaff, 65–236. Reprint, Grand Rapids: Eerdmans, 1979. This work is sometimes also called *Harmony of the Evangelists.*

Bengel, Johann A. *Gnomon of the New Testament.* 2 vols. Philadelphia: Perkinpine and Higgins, 1860.

Calvin, John. *Commentary on a Harmony of the Evangelists, Matthew, Mark, and Luke.* 3 vols. Translated by William Pringle. Grand Rapids: Eerdmans, n.d.

——— . *The Gospel according to St John.* 2 vols. Translated by T. H. L. Parker. Edited by David W. Torrance and Thomas F. Torrance. Grand Rapids: Eerdmans, 1959.

Hendriksen, William. *A Commentary on the Gospel of John.* London: Banner of Truth, 1959.

——— . *Exposition of the Gospel according to Luke.* Grand Rapids: Baker, 1978.

——— . *Exposition of the Gospel according to Mark.* Grand Rapids: Baker, 1975.

——— . *Exposition of the Gospel according to Matthew.* Grand Rapids: Baker, 1973.

McClellan, John Brown. *The New Testament of Our Lord and Saviour Jesus Christ, a New Translation* . . . . Vol. 1. London: Macmillan, 1875.

Stonehouse, Ned B. *The Witness of the Synoptic Gospels to Christ: One Volume Combining the Witness of Matthew and Mark to Christ and the Witness of Luke to Christ.* 2nd ed. Grand Rapids: Baker, 1979.

More might be added to this basic list. Not all of these sources are of equal value for harmonization questions; some of the harmonizations are less plausible than others. But these sources regularly address harmonization questions and try to make contributions to understanding.

In addition, many commentaries written by evangelicals address harmonization questions at least some of the time. These commentaries are too numerous to mention.[4] Among recent works we should also mention the *ESV Study Bible*,[5] whose notes regularly address questions of harmonization.[6]

Accounts of Two Distinct Events

Sometimes differing accounts have to do with two distinct incidents. In the case of the centurion's servant, Calvin quickly dismisses that possibility.[7] The number of similarities between the two accounts shows that we are dealing with the same event. But other cases are not so clear-cut. Jesus traveled around, especially in Galilee. Given the variations in location and audience, he would have repeated himself in his teaching. So similar-sounding teaching may sometimes derive from two or more distinct incidents. Jesus also engaged in a ministry of healing and exorcism wherever he went. In various places there were bound to be similar cases of leprosy, blindness, and demon possession.

Omission of Detail

One account may legitimately omit a detail included in another. In the case of the centurion's servant, Matthew does not mention the intermediaries, either the elders of the Jews or the friends of the centurion. In addition, he does not mention that the centurion says, "Do not trouble yourself" (Luke 7:6). Luke does not mention that Jesus talks about many coming "from east and west" (Matt. 8:11–12). However, the difficulty does not merely consist in various small omissions. Matthew, by completely omitting the intermediaries, has left out a detail in a way that may trouble some people because they wonder whether the result of the omission is satisfactory with respect to its truthfulness. Augustine, Calvin, and R. T. France answer this concern by pointing out that the intermediary acts on behalf of the one he represents, and so the two are identified. We will address this concern further in some of our later principles.

---

[4]Craig L. Blomberg, *The Historical Reliability of the Gospels*, 2nd ed. (Downers Grove, IL: InterVarsity, 2007), 309n48, provides a useful starting list.

[5]*ESV Study Bible: English Standard Version* (Wheaton, IL: Crossway, 2008).

[6]Note also Blomberg, *Historical Reliability*, 152–95. For side-by-side comparison, see one of the "harmonies" with parallel columns for each Gospel. The standard source is Kurt Aland, ed., *Synopsis quattuor evangeliorum*, 5th ed. (Stuttgart: Württembergische Bibelanstalt, 1967).

[7]John Calvin, *Commentary on a Harmony of the Evangelists, Matthew, Mark, and Luke*, 3 vols., trans. William Pringle (Grand Rapids: Eerdmans, n.d.), 1:378.

Considering the Environment of the Gospels

God gave us the Gospels within the environment of the first century. In doing so, God took into account the assumptions, expectations, and mind-set of the time and setting in which the Gospels were originally written. We should avoid merely imposing our own modern expectations.

Note R. T. France's comment.

> His [Matthew's] omission of the *means* of the centurion's approach to Jesus is a valid literary device to highlight the message of the incident as he sees it (on the principle, common in biblical and contemporary literature, that a messenger or servant represents the one who sent him to the point of virtual identity).[8]

France appeals to a "principle, common in biblical and contemporary literature." Purely individualistic thinking from a modern setting may bring mistaken expectations to the Bible. The human authors who wrote biblical books, and those who first read them, had an appreciation for corporate wholes such as a family or a nation. They understood that a representative took the place of the one he represented. France then implies that an ancient reader, who understood the expectations within the environment in which Matthew was written, would not have been disturbed in the same way as would a modern, individualistic thinker.

We may make the same point by considering the divine author of Matthew, not merely the human author. Consistent with his character, God speaks within contexts, contexts that he himself controls. The meaning of a particular speech takes into account such contexts and interacts with them.[9] God as Creator established the principle of representation in the first place. Adam represented the whole human race when he fell into sin. God has also established representatives in other, more specialized cases. The high priest represented the whole nation when he came before God (Lev. 16:5, 15, 16, 21). The king of Israel represented the whole people and led them. A father represents his family. God has also established a world in which human beings can appoint representatives of a temporary sort. Jeroboam appears to have headed up the delegation that came to Rehoboam (1 Kings 12:3, 12). Joab represented Absalom's case to David (2 Sam. 14:33).

These structures of representation—ordained by the sovereignty of God—were already in the background when the centurion undertook to have the elders of the Jews present his petition. God in writing the Gospel of Matthew

---

[8]Richard T. France, "Inerrancy and New Testament Exegesis," *Themelios* 1 (1975): 17.
[9]Vern S. Poythress, *Inerrancy and Worldview: Answering Modern Challenges to the Bible* (Wheaton, IL: Crossway, 2012), chap. 11; Poythress, *In the Beginning Was the Word*, especially chaps. 7 and 11.

took into account the structures of representation that he ordained. And he shaped the hearts of people in those times to appreciate the meaning of representation. God took account of the fact that, in the first century environment, he was writing to people who understood the "virtual identity" between an intermediary and the one whom he represents.

Theological Emphasis

Each Gospel may highlight particular theological emphases through the way in which it presents its account of an episode. As we have observed, Matthew emphasizes the centurion's status as a Gentile and the danger of Jews not having faith in the Messiah. Luke emphasizes the centurion's humility. These two emphases fit into larger theological themes, the themes of salvation by faith, open to Gentiles, and the theme of humility. Both of these themes have a positive role within biblical doctrine. And they both become manifest in the episode with the centurion.

Thus, the *differences* between the Gospels are an integral and significant part of the Gospels. The differences are there for a purpose: they help us. All the Gospels are talking about events that actually happened; they are not "making it up." But they are telling about the events in ways that help us to grasp their significance and their theological implications. We do not need to feel as if we have to "roll back" the significance and the implications in order to get to "bare" events.

The Gospels, since they are written with God's authority, deserve our ultimate allegiance and trust. They are therefore *more ultimate* and *more reliable* accounts of the events of the life of Christ than is any humanly constructed harmonization, which would try to figure out "what really happened." It is legitimate for us to try to see how the various Gospel accounts fit together into a larger picture. But this larger picture should include everything that the Gospels give us, rather than only a minimum core in the form of our modern human reconstruction of what happened.

Human reconstructions can help, but when reconstructions of the events go into all the details, they often contain a certain amount of guesswork. The guesswork means that our own fallibility and the incompleteness of our information come into play. If we are honest, we have to admit that we cannot be sure about everything in our reconstruction. By contrast, we can be sure about the Gospels themselves. Their differences, as well as the areas they hold in common, belong to the Bible, which God intended to function as the foundation in our religious instruction and, indeed, in our whole life.

4

History, Theology, and Artistry

We can add some other principles to the ones we have just listed. But first we take up a larger issue, the issue of how history, theology, and literary artistry relate to one another. Let us begin by focusing primarily on history and theology. Later we will consider literary artistry as well.

Bare Facts

Some people think that history means just "bare facts." They think that any theological significance has to be treated as an afterthought. According to this way of thinking, the meaning or emphasis of any historical writer becomes something that the individual writer pastes onto the facts merely on the basis of his subjective judgments and interests. In other words, according to this view "the *real* thing" in history consists in the bare events. All interpretation, selection, and comment are human additions. Theology, literary elegance, and personal meaning are human inventions.

This view of the relation between history and theology, though it may seem "natural" to many modern ears, is deeply at odds with the Bible's understanding of history and theology. We touch here on the issue of how *worldviews* and assumptions affect our interpretation of the Bible. The issue of worldview receives fuller discussion in the companion book *Inerrancy and*

Worldview.[1] We need to pick up some of the same issues here, drawing also on the relation of history to language and society.[2]

Multiple Perspectives

First, the involvement of persons and their perspectives in knowledge does not in itself undermine the validity of knowledge. An impersonalist worldview may suggest that truth must ultimately be impersonal. But God is the ultimate standard for truth, and he is personal. We may express this reality by saying that truth is what God knows. So personal involvement, namely *God's* involvement, is necessary for the existence of truth. And of course human persons must become involved *as persons* when they come to know something true. This involvement takes place according to the design of God. It is not innately alien or corrupting.

Second, God is one God in three persons. Matthew 11:27 indicates the involvement of persons of the Trinity in knowledge: "All things have been handed over to me by my Father, and no one knows the Son except the Father, and no one knows the Father except the Son and anyone to whom the Son chooses to reveal him." Each person of the Trinity has his distinct personal perspective on knowledge. God the Father knows all things by being the Father, and in being the Father he knows the Son. The Son as Son knows the Father, and in doing so knows all things. Similarly, the Holy Spirit knows all things in connection with his distinctive role in searching "the depths of God" (1 Cor. 2:10; see also 2:11). Personal perspectives are therefore inherent in knowledge at the deepest level, the divine level. By implication, personal, perspectival knowledge of truth among human beings belongs to the very character of the truth; it is not a distortion of an original allegedly *impersonal* truth.

This perspectival character of the truth has implications for our attitude toward the Gospels. When they wrote, the human authors—Matthew, Mark, Luke, and John—brought to their writing their own distinct human perspectives on the life, death, and resurrection of Jesus. These perspectives belong integrally to the account and must not be viewed as "imposed" on originally impersonal facts.

These perspectives have their effect on the whole of each Gospel. Each Gospel invites us to read it as a unified story, setting forth events in the life

---

[1]The issue of history and theology receives discussion in Vern S. Poythress, *Inerrancy and Worldview: Answering Modern Challenges to the Bible* (Wheaton, IL: Crossway, 2012), chaps. 11 and 26.
[2]See Vern S. Poythress, *In the Beginning Was the Word: Language—A God-Centered Approach* (Wheaton, IL: Crossway, 2009); and Poythress, *Redeeming Sociology: A God-Centered Approach* (Wheaton, IL: Crossway, 2011).

of Jesus and leading up to his death and resurrection. Moreover, because God is the divine author of each Gospel, each Gospel represents not only a distinct *human* perspective, but also a distinct *divine* perspective. God speaks not only what is common to the Gospels—some kind of "core"—but what is distinct in each one. God raised up the four Evangelists: Matthew, Mark, Luke, and John. He shaped each of their personalities and backgrounds according to his design, and through the Holy Spirit he empowered them to write exactly what they wrote. All of it is God's word.[3]

Testimony from Irenaeus and Augustine

Observations about the distinctiveness of each Gospel go back at least as far as Irenaeus. He compared the four Gospels to the four winds and to the four-faced character of the cherubim in Revelation 4:7.[4] The four "living creatures" or cherubim in Revelation 4:7 have four distinct faces, like a lion, an ox, a man, and an eagle. Irenaeus underlined his claim about the Gospels by attempting to indicate ways in which each of the Gospels corresponds in its particular emphasis and approach to one of the faces of the cherubim: Matthew corresponds to the human face, Mark to the eagle, Luke to the ox, and John to the lion.

Augustine made similar points. In his book *The Harmony of the Gospels* he noted that the Gospel of John is distinct in character from the other three Gospels (1.4.7; 1.5.8). He saw distinctive emphases in the other three as well (1.3.5–6; 1.6.9). He alluded to earlier interpreters who tried to see a connection between the four Gospels and the four living creatures of Revelation 4:7. Augustine preferred the correlation that links Matthew with the lion, Mark with the man, Luke with the ox, and John with the eagle.[5]

All the attempts at linkages show that early Christians were aware of important differences between the Gospels. By correlating the differences with the living creatures, interpreters were also indicating that the differences had a heavenly and not merely human origin. God authorized the differences, as well as the similarities.

Does each Gospel really imitate one of the four living creatures? The ancients differed in their opinions about which Gospel should be linked with which living creature. The differing opinions show that the idea of each

---

[3]Archibald A. Hodge and Benjamin B. Warfield, *Inspiration*, with introduction by Roger R. Nicole (repr., Grand Rapids: Baker, 1979), 11–29; Vern S. Poythress, *Symphonic Theology: The Validity of Multiple Perspectives in Theology* (repr., Phillipsburg, NJ: P&R, 2001); Poythress, *Inerrancy and Worldview*, chap. 11.
[4]Irenaeus, *Against Heresies*, in *The Ante-Nicene Fathers: Translations of the Writings of the Fathers down to A.D. 325*, vol. 1, ed. Alexander Roberts and James Donaldson (Grand Rapids: Eerdmans, 1979), 3.11.8.
[5]Augustine, *The Harmony of the Gospels*, in vol. 6 of *NPNF1*, 1.6.9.

Gospel having a specific linkage to exactly one living creature is doubtful. But the ancient writers still recognized important truths, namely, that the four Gospels offer diverse points of view, that this diversity comes from God, and that it honors God, just as the living creatures praise God continually (Rev. 4:8).

These ancient Christian reflections agree with what we ourselves can see in the Gospels. The Gospels are intrinsically in harmony, but also complementary. No one Gospel says everything that could be said. Each one is completely true in what it presents about Christ and his life. If we had access to only one Gospel out of the four, it would give us knowledge of God in Christ, and we would be saved by trusting in Christ as he is presented in that Gospel. We would have true knowledge. But it would not be all the knowledge we could ever have. We learn more when we read a second Gospel because it brings out aspects of Christ that were not so much in the foreground in the first. The four Gospels together give us greater riches than any one alone. They harmonize in a symphony rather than giving a unison performance.[6] This symphonic harmony agrees magnificently with the very character of God, who is magnificently rich, and with the character of Christ, who reveals God to us in his fullness. The richness is inexhaustible. The differences among the Gospels make known the manifold wisdom of God (Eph. 3:10).

Theological Meaning of Events

Now let us consider the relation of historical facts to theological meaning. Luke 24:44–47 indicates that the suffering, death, and resurrection of Christ were planned by God beforehand, and that they were anticipated in the Old Testament. These events that Christ accomplished are at the heart of redemption. But more broadly, the entirety of history takes place according to God's plan (Eph. 1:11; see also Isa. 46:9–11; Lam. 3:37–38). God's plan has meaning within his mind. Divine meaning actually precedes the events themselves. God had planned all of history even before he created the world. From the beginning, there was meaning. God has purposes in all events, but especially in the central events of redemption: the life, death, and resurrection of Christ. So these central events had meaning beforehand.

The central events in redemption also received interpretation afterward as the apostles looked back on the life, death, and resurrection of Christ, and on the Old Testament history that led up to his coming. Because the apostles were officially commissioned by Christ (Acts 1:8), their interpretation is not merely human but divine interpretation. Historical events, according to the

---

[6]Poythress, *Symphonic Theology*, especially chap. 5.

Bible's worldview, are not "bare events," "brute facts," but events with meaning according to the plan of God. They have *theology* inherent in them. Therefore the theological significances highlighted in the Gospels and in other places in the Bible are not arbitrary additions to bare events. There is actually no such thing as a bare event. That idea is a figment produced by antibiblical assumptions.[7] The Gospels draw out meanings and implications that God's plan assigned to the events from before the foundation of the world.

The realization that theological meaning is inherent in events dissolves many difficulties that are produced when modern people try to dig underneath the theological significance and theological interpretation in the Gospels in order to obtain "reality." What this digging actually obtains is not reality, but a reflection of erroneous assumptions about history.[8]

Having the Right Foundations

Many modern scholars look at matters differently from what I have just described. My approach may seem dogmatic and naive to them—I am just accepting what the Bible says and what the Gospels say. Yes, I do that. I do it because I think that response is what the Bible deserves; it is God's word. We will discuss matters concerning our attitudes at a later point (see part three). Trust is neither "dogmatic" nor "naive"—pejorative words—but rather the appropriate response.

Dogmatic is the label that proponents of modern worldviews give to those who do not accept their assumptions.[9] We can respond not only by positively explaining the appropriateness of trusting the Bible, but also by questioning the alternative. Modern worldviews have their own assumptions. And those assumptions turn out to have a flimsy basis—really no basis at all. The Bible gives good reasons for doubting them.

God does not intend for us to function with ourselves as the final authority, pretending to be autonomous in our judgments. He intends that we follow his instruction. When we do so, we can learn a great deal from the Gospels, including those parts that challenge us with difficulties. Showing how that

---

[7]See Poythress, *Inerrancy and Worldview*, chaps. 11 and 26; Cornelius Van Til, *A Christian Theory of Knowledge* (Philadelphia: Presbyterian and Reformed, 1969), 34–37.

[8]See Poythress, *Inerrancy and Worldview*, chaps. 5–7. Of course, there is an opposite error where reality is radically subjectivized. In a subjectivistic view, "reality" is only what each person decides to make it. God's Word gives us the standard by which we ought to reject such deviant views.

[9]For example, people may judge that simple trust in the Bible is "unfalsifiable." But in practice people will worry about falsifiability only when they have doubts about truth. We discuss doubts in chap. 11, and the worldviews that include assumptions about truth and history in Poythress, *Inerrancy and Worldview*. A biblically based worldview includes distinctive attitudes toward life in general and intellectual life in particular (see chap. 11–15 in this book and chaps. 27–35 of Poythress, *Inerrancy and Worldview*).

process of learning works out in practice is one goal of this book. Debating the fundamental assumptions of worldview belongs to my previous book, *Inerrancy and Worldview*, and to many other books on apologetics. I am sorry to disappoint readers who at this point may expect a fuller discussion of fundamental assumptions. But here I want to build on assumptions that are already in place.

Principles about History and Theology

We may now summarize basic principles about the relation of history to theological interpretation.

1. Divine meaning in events

God as Lord of history gives meaning to events. Because in the plan of God the events themselves have meaning and purpose, theological interpretation is not a biased imposition on "neutral" or "brute" events but, when soundly based, an exposition of what the events themselves actually meant.

2. Theological selectivity

Because the events are rich in meaning within the total plan of God, all theological exposition of the events is necessarily selective in emphasis. The difference between the emphasis on inclusion of Gentiles in Matthew 8:5–13 and the emphasis on humility in Luke 7:1–10 offers an example of this type of selective emphasis.

3. Harmony between history and theology

We do not put theological significance and history in opposition to one another, because God himself has placed the two in harmony. He is Lord of both.

Artistry

Now let us consider the topic of literary artistry. God employs rich speech. How do we know that? We can see it concretely by looking at the poetry in the Psalms and the Old Testament Prophets. We can also see that it is consistent with his character. When God speaks, his speech expresses the richness of his character and his plan.

We have spoken of history and theology. They both belong to aspects of God's speech. There are other dimensions as well. For example, God means to engage us and to change us. When he speaks, he provides information.

But he also gives us communion with himself and he works to transform us. God is beautiful in his character. So his speech expresses his beauty. And sometimes his speech may exhibit literary artistry as one means that underlines his beauty and the beauty of his thoughts. The artistry may also draw us in, moving us and fascinating us. It becomes a means that God uses in the process of transforming us. Artistry is not in competition with history or theology—all three serve the same end, each reinforcing, complementing, and pointing to the others. God is truthful, beautiful, and sovereign over history. The three go together.

We may therefore formulate these additional principles:

4. Literary artistry

God employs literary artistry. He speaks in harmony with his own beauty and wisdom. He uses adornment, metaphor, allusions, patterns for narratives, and many other resources of languages when he communicates to us. These enhance communication and show us the richness of his character rather than creating tension with truthfulness.

5. The Gospels as literary wholes (narratives)

All three aspects—historical, theological, and literary—work together in each Gospel as a complete book. Theological emphases, historical selectivity, and literary sensitivity are present in each Gospel as a unified narrative. Each Gospel is designed by God to be read as a literary whole that tells the history of Jesus's life, death, and resurrection and shows us the theological significance of his life and work. Distinctive theological emphases appear not only when we compare a single passage with parallel passages in other Gospels, but also when we consider how a passage contributes to the overall message of the Gospel in which it lies. Each individual passage within a Gospel needs to be read as part of the larger narrative to which it belongs.

5

THE HISTORICAL CLAIMS OF THE GOSPELS

We must consider what sort of books the Gospels claim to be. Since they are God's own word, they will be wholly truthful, just as God is true. But that fact, by itself, leaves wide scope for what types of communication God may choose. God, having given us language, possesses in himself full capability for using all its resources, including the resources of various genres and types of communication.[1]

Genres

The Bible as a whole contains many kinds of discourse. We have the book of Proverbs, songs and prayers in the book of Psalms, prophecies, riddles, historical records, and more. Jesus told parables, which are stories that do not claim to be accounts of events that actually happened at one particular time. No one is troubled by their fictional character, because parables do not claim to be anything else. God can use fiction for his purposes. But we know that he does not present fiction as if it were fact, for that would be inconsistent with his truthfulness. It is therefore important to consider what sort of claims the Gospels make about what they present.

---

[1]See Vern S. Poythress, *In the Beginning Was the Word: Language—A God-Centered Approach* (Wheaton, IL: Crossway, 2009), especially chap. 23 on genre.

We cannot explore all the dimensions of these questions without radically expanding our discussion and producing a very long book. We must be content with a beginning. We will summarize principles that have been more fully developed in commentaries and book-length discussions of the character of the Gospels.

The Gospel of Luke

The Gospel of Luke begins with a "prologue," the first four verses.

> [1] Inasmuch as many have undertaken to compile a narrative of the things that have been accomplished among us, [2] just as those who from the beginning were eyewitnesses and ministers of the word have delivered them to us, [3] it seemed good to me also, having followed all things closely for some time past, to write an orderly account for you, most excellent Theophilus, [4] that you may have certainty concerning the things you have been taught. (Luke 1:1–4)

Several features in this passage indicate that Luke is concerned to tell us about what really happened. He refers to "the things that have been accomplished among us" (1:1). He is talking about events, things that have taken place. He mentions "eyewitnesses" (1:2), indicating that he is aware of the value of eyewitness testimony in contrast to second-hand or third-hand reports. He indicates that he has "followed all things closely for some time past" (1:3). He has given concentrated attention to the topic. And he aims to give Theophilus and other readers "certainty" (or "the exact truth," 1:4, NASB).

In addition, this passage in Luke corresponds in several of its themes to Flavius Josephus's prologue to his *Jewish War*.[2] Even some particular key words correspond. Luke's prologue has looser associations with some other writings of the time: 2 Maccabees 2:19–31; Diodorus of Sicily, *The Library of History* 1.3.2; 4.1; 6.2; and Dionysius of Halicarnassus, *Roman Antiquities* 1.5.4. It thus ranges itself within the broad category of history writing in the Hellenistic world.[3]

But there is more. Beginning with Luke 1:5 the Greek style shifts to a style imitating the Septuagint, the Greek translation of the Old Testament. By so doing, the Gospel of Luke links itself to the pattern of history writing in the Old Testament. Luke refers to "the things that have been accomplished

---

[2] Flavius Josephus, *The Jewish War*, with English translation by H. St. J. Thackeray (London: Heinemann; Cambridge: Harvard University Press, 1967), 1.1.1–3.

[3] Joel B. Green, *The Gospel of Luke* (Grand Rapids: Eerdmans, 1997), 1–6; Darrell L. Bock, *Luke*, vol. 1, *1:1–9:50* (Grand Rapids: Baker, 1994), 51–67. See also Loveday C. A. Alexander, "Luke-Acts in Its Contemporary Setting with Special Reference to the Prefaces (Luke 1:1–4 and Acts 1:1)" (DPhil diss., Oxford University, 1977).

among us" (1:1). These accomplished events continue the redemptive line of acts and words of God that goes through the course of history laid out in the Old Testament. Luke therefore orients its narrative to *divine* acts, which involve theological significance, and in this respect it takes a viewpoint distinct from more "secular" Hellenistic histories.

Darrell Bock comments:

> Many [commentators] suggest that the use of a literary convention in the prologue to make claims about accuracy proves nothing about the real historical character of Luke's work. . . . It must be noted, however, that the goal of what Luke wishes to accomplish, assurance, is greatly affected by his accuracy. Also, unlike many of the historians to whom Luke is compared, his writing is virtually contemporary to the events he describes. As a result, his ability to be careless with the facts is limited. . . .
>
> One could also question the morals of a writer who believes in a religion that stresses the telling of the truth, and who yet misrepresents the history he describes. Such religious constraints did not exist for many ancient secular writers.[4]

When we combine these human considerations with the reality of divine authorship of Luke, we may be confident that Luke not only aimed at truth but achieved it.

Other Gospels

We can now consider briefly the other Gospels. Broadly speaking, they clearly belong to the same genre, "Gospel," as does Luke.[5] Hence, they too are giving us historical accounts of real events. I thus disagree with those who think that the strong theological interests in the Gospel of John move it away from historical reality. And I disagree with M. D. Goulder's theory that the Gospel of Matthew offers us nonhistorical midrash in imitation of Jewish midrash.[6]

---

[4]Bock, *Luke*, 1:66–67.

[5]Richard T. France, *Matthew: Evangelist and Teacher* (Downers Grove, IL: InterVarsity, 1989), 123–27.

[6]M. D. Goulder, *Midrash and Lection in Matthew: The Speaker's Lectures in Biblical Studies, 1969–71* (London: SPCK, 1974); similarly, Robert Gundry, *Matthew: A Commentary on His Literary and Theological Art* (Grand Rapids: Eerdmans, 1982). See responses in D. A. Carson, "Gundry on Matthew: A Critical Review," *Trinity Journal* 3 (1982): 71–91; R. T. France and David Wenham, eds., *Studies in Midrash and Historiography*, Gospel Perspectives 3 (Sheffield: JSOT, 1983); France, *Matthew: Evangelist and Teacher*, 202–5; Craig L. Blomberg, *The Historical Reliability of the Gospels*, 2nd ed. (Downers Grove, IL: InterVarsity, 2007), 75–87. It should be noted that among the Jews midrashic practice took place in a context where Jewish tradition anchored itself in a previously fixed, centuries-old, inspired text that was recognized by all the Jews being addressed. The Gospels of course allude to the preceding prophecies in the Old Testament. But, unlike Jewish midrash, they give us accounts of *new* events. R. T. France observes, "Fulfilment and history are not in conflict; rather the fulfilment takes place in the history. Indeed it is not easy to see quite what 'fulfilment' might mean if there is no actual history in which the pattern is fulfilled. Matthew's

We need to consider briefly what it means for the Gospels to belong to a genre, in this case the "Gospel" genre. Consider first the general concept of a "genre." Roughly speaking, a genre is a grouping of materials that have commonalities recognized by people belonging to a particular culture and language group. It is an "insider's" category within a culture or language. All genres throughout all cultures are sovereignly controlled by God. Any genre has aspects of (1) contrast and identification, (2) variation, and (3) distribution (in larger literary and cultural contexts).[7] The aspect of *contrast and identification* implies that it is a distinct grouping, with features that distinguish it from other genres. *Variation* means that there is a range of possibilities, or variant manifestations, of a genre. Each instance of a genre is different from other instances, without being outside the genre. For example, the genre of Hellenistic history writing presents us with a range of works. It includes different instances. At the same time, it contrasts with other kinds of literature, such as Hellenistic works of philosophy, astronomy, and mathematics.

Now consider the Gospels as a genre. The genre "Gospel" belongs to God in a special, direct way, because he brought the genre into being in composing the four Gospels. God created the genre according to his wisdom. He took into account the people he was addressing. People in the first century could recognize this genre and see that it was similar in some ways to secular history writing, but that it differed as well, both in its divine authority and in the redemptive uniqueness of the events on which it focused.

This genre of "Gospel," like other genres that God has ordained, includes a range of instances—what we call "variation." Each Gospel is different from the others. And the differences may include differences in historical focus and selectivity. We must not too quickly decide that writing history can take place in only one way, or with only one set of expectations. We will return to consider this issue in greater detail after we have talked at greater length about expectations for truth in writing history.

Principles concerning Genre

In the meantime, we may formulate the following principles:

---

undoubted enthusiasm for discovering patterns of fulfilment, and the subtlety of the interpretative methods he has employed to draw attention to them, which has led to the comparison of his work with some aspects of later 'midrash,' should be seen not as weakening his sense of historical responsibility, but rather as demanding a careful record of the facts on which the whole claim to fulfilment depends" (France, *Matthew: Evangelist and Teacher*, 205).

[7] Poythress, *In the Beginning Was the Word*, chaps. 19 and 23.

1. The genre of Gospel

The four Gospels have recognizable common features and concerns that imply they belong to a common group of literature, the genre "Gospel."

2. Gospel as a distinct genre

The genre "Gospel" is distinct from other genres in its time. God brought into being this specialized genre in the context of the early church, without any exact parallels preceding it, because the events and their meaning were unparalleled. It has some similarities to Hellenistic history writing, to Hellenistic biographies, and to Old Testament history writing. But the genre "Gospel" is also distinctive.

3. The genre of history writing

Luke's prologue places Luke in the larger generic category of Hellenistic history writings.

4. Other Gospels in comparison with Luke

The other Gospels, though varying in focus, technique, and theological emphasis, have obvious similarities with Luke. God has thereby shown readers that the other Gospels are doing something similar to Luke.

5. Fulfillment in history

The Gospels' concern for fulfillment demands that the events discussed actually happened.[8]

---

[8]France, *Matthew: Evangelist and Teacher*, 205.

6

THE AUTHORITY OF THE GOSPELS

We have already discussed the fact that the Gospels as part of the Bible are the word of God and therefore have special authority. As God's speech, they have God's truthfulness. Let us draw out some implications.

God's Word Exercising Authority over Us

Because God is true, the Gospels speak truly. But we can say more. God's speech about historical events is not only truthful, but *definitive* in its account of events. A merely human account of events can sometimes turn out to be wholly truthful. But if it is merely human, it is never definitive. It never occupies a kind of "top level," by which it would become determinative for every other account. But God's Word, as the word of the Creator and as the absolute authority, has a definitive role. It *defines* the character of events rather than being merely a secondary account in dependence on events. We may say that it is *ontologically definitive*.

God's Word is also *epistemologically definitive*. People should be building their knowledge, and the foundations of their knowledge, on God's instruction as the secure starting point. Of course, we do not understand God's Word infallibly. But often our understanding is sound, and it should play a basic role, not merely an ancillary role, as we sift through modern claims about knowledge. The Bible testifies both directly and indirectly to its character as the word of God. The Holy Spirit opens human hearts to pay attention to this testimony, and so people have *divine* confirmation, not merely human confirmation, for the epistemological role that God designed the Bible to play.[1]

A person awakened by the Holy Spirit is weighing many questions and many claims in his mind. Such a person will not always immediately believe everything said in the Gospels. The process of clearing out sin, including sinful predispositions in the mind, may be a gradual one. But the correct goal for this path of growth in knowledge is a firm trust in God, which includes firm trust in what God says. Hence, as a person continues to grow in faith, the Gospels and all the other parts of the Bible increasingly take a central role in sifting claims for truth and claims for knowledge in every area of life.

Finally, God's Word is *ethically definitive*. God is the ultimate standard for what is right. God's Word always shows ethical purity. So it becomes a model for our own ethical thinking, not merely when it directly proclaims moral standards ("You shall not steal"), but everywhere it speaks, because it is always an upright example of ethically pure speech. This exemplary character of God's Word has implications for how we react to it. If God's Word *seems* to us ethically deficient, it is *we*, not God, who are in the wrong and who must change.

Depending on what kind of difficulty we confront, we may have to change in more than one way. Sometimes the difficulty is merely that we have misunderstood a particular verse or portion within the Bible. Sometimes we have misunderstood the context. Sometimes we misunderstand how God's character is in harmony with what we read. Sometimes we have distorted moral standards ourselves, internally, and those distortions are meant to be undone through the work of God's Word and God's Spirit on us.

Principles for Interpretation

We may summarize our findings in the following principles:

1. The Bible as the word of God

The Gospels, like other canonical writings, are the word of God: they are what God says.

2. God's Word as ontologically definitive

The Word of God presents ontologically definitive description and interpretation of the events it presents.

---

[1] See 1 Thess. 1:5; 2:13; 2 Tim. 3:16; 2 Pet. 3:16; 1 John 2:20–21; Rev. 22:18–19; and the discussion on the internal testimony of the Holy Spirit, John Murray, "The Attestation of Scripture," in *The Infallible Word: A Symposium by the Members of the Faculty of Westminster Theological Seminary*, 3rd ed., ed. N. B. Stonehouse and Paul Woolley (Philadelphia: Presbyterian and Reformed, 1967), 1–54, esp. 42–54.

3. Ultimacy of Gospel accounts

The Gospels, not hypothetical reconstruction of events behind them, are ultimate representations.

4. The Gospels as epistemological foundation

God wants us to trust the Gospels and receive guidance from them as we sift claims about knowledge and truth.

5. Possibility of harmonization

Harmonization is possible because God is consistent with himself.

6. Harmonization as meaningful

Harmonization is a significant and meaningful endeavor because God really did act to save us through events that took place in space and time.

Harmonization work in past centuries, including the work of Augustine and Calvin, frequently had an apologetic focus. It aimed to defend the Bible against charges of inconsistency and error. This goal is legitimate since being faithful to God includes trusting what he says. Harmonization efforts could influence both Christian believers and those who do not yet believe. These efforts may help believers overcome doubts, and they may help non-Christians consider seriously the claims of the Christian faith.

7. Secondary importance of harmonization

Harmonization is of secondary importance because we already have definitive accounts in the Gospels themselves.

8. Keeping the text in view

Because of the primacy of the Gospels as we have them, harmonization may not be done at the cost of violence to the text.

9. Adjustment in our standards

God's Word is always ethically pure and is a standard for the purity of our speech and our thoughts. Our standards of error and correct speech, not the text's, must sometimes undergo adjustment. But the total adjustment of our standards must bring them more in line with the totality of Scripture and the character of God. We should not interpret one piece of Scripture in a way that creates disharmony with some other piece.

7

A MENTAL-PICTURE THEORY

In our discussion of the episode of the centurion's servant (chap. 2), we saw that Matthew does not mention the intermediaries who came to Jesus on behalf of the centurion. In his account we do not hear about either the Jewish elders (Luke 7:3–4) or the centurion's friends (Luke 7:6). To some people these omissions seem troubling. Some may boldly claim that Matthew has "committed an error" and say that he has not truthfully represented the facts.

But Matthew is completely true. The difficulty actually lies in fallible human expectations about Matthew and the other Gospels. People have expectations as to what, in their minds, constitutes a trustworthy account. These expectations may sometimes go astray and create an unnecessary difficulty. People may find themselves disappointed and their expectations frustrated when they hear that the centurion sent elders and friends. So we need to think about these expectations and ask ourselves carefully what the Gospels claim to give us and what they do not claim to give us.

Developing a Mental Picture

As we read Matthew 8:5–13, we may try to form a mental picture of the scene. We may populate our mental picture with the things that Matthew 8:5–13 tells us. Suppose we try it. In our mind's eye we imagine what it would be like when Jesus entered Capernaum (8:5). We picture the centurion and his servant at the centurion's home (8:6). We picture the centurion coming to Jesus (8:5). When the centurion comes near to Jesus, he addresses Jesus (8:6), and Jesus responds (8:7).

In this process, we picture the centurion as standing in Jesus's presence. We have no picture of elders or friends. The picture that we derive from Matthew therefore does not correspond exactly to the actual location of the centurion as we might infer it from Luke's account. And it does not correspond to a reality in which other people are in the picture, namely, the elders and later the friends. Our picture omits these people; it has, as it were, a blank space in the mental "photograph" where the elders would appear in a one-to-one picture.

A "mental-picture" theory of truth expects that a true account will produce in readers a mental picture in direct correspondence to the actual events. Ideally, such a picture would enjoy a one-to-one correspondence. Each participant in the events would correspond to a person present in the mental picture. The sequence of events would correspond in one-to-one fashion to a sequence of mental pictures. The positions of the persons would correspond to the positions in the mental picture. And so on. If we push expectations far enough in this direction, we might call the result a "video-recording" concept of truth. A "true" narrative, according to this theory, produces a mental picture equivalent to a video recording of the entire episode.

But this conception is unworkable. A literal video recording of reasonable quality provides massive detail about colors, textures, shapes, and positions of every person and object in a scene, all the motions of the various persons and objects, and all the sounds audible within the scene (including, for example, the sound of a dog barking in a neighboring yard). Verbal communication does not equal a video recording. Verbal communication is "sparse." It does not mention all the colors or all the positions of all the persons and objects. Typically, it does not mention all the bystanders in a scene. Were some of the apostles present when the centurion sent elders? Which ones? What were the expressions on their faces? We simply do not know. In our mental pictures we may, if we wish, begin to fill out in our imagination many of these details. But neither Matthew nor Luke gives us massive details. Even if they did, they would still fall short of a video recording.

And even a video recording presents a difficulty. Modern video recording takes place from a particular camera location and camera angle, with particular lighting, a specific placing of microphones, a particular focus for the lens, a particular speed for shooting the individual frames, and specific sensitivities to brightness and colors in the light-detecting surface within the video camera. Do we require multiple cameras, multiple camera angles, and multiple microphones? Do we require multiple perspectives? No one spatial perspective produces *the* definitive video recording of the episode.

Ordinary people know intuitively that verbal communication does not supply all this detail. People may still sometimes choose to form a detailed mental picture of the events on the basis of verbal communication. That is their option. But they know tacitly that they are adding detail in their imagination, and that they cannot hold the original reporter responsible for what they add.

What has gone wrong with the mental-picture theory of truth? It does not respect the nature of verbal communication as *sparse*. We may wonder whether it is contaminated with a desire for complete and even absolute knowledge—divine knowledge. In an approach like this, anything short of exhaustive divine knowledge might be regarded as defective.

Is human knowledge defective? God's knowledge is indeed complete; it is exhaustive. Ours is not. But that does *not* mean that our knowledge is somehow defective. In creating us, God designed us to have limited knowledge. It is a good and wise design, not a defect (Gen. 1:31). We can still know many truths, including the things that God tells us in his accounts of the centurion's servant.

So the demand for human beings to have divine knowledge results in an unbiblical notion of truth. We may suspect that this notion is contaminated with the desire for autonomy, the desire for a human being to have a position such that he can be the ultimate standard. In this case, he wants to be the ultimate standard for making pronouncements about the episode. Human beings end up trying to displace the unique role of God, who simultaneously knows, for example, how everything looks from every possible camera angle at every possible moment.

Truth in a Statement

We may further illustrate the difficulties with the mental-picture approach by considering an ordinary human scene. Suppose Carol and Donna are sitting in the living room of Carol's house. Carol says to Donna, "On my kitchen floor there is a triangle drawn with ink." Now Donna tries to picture in her mind the situation that Carol has described. Let us suppose that she comes up with the mental picture in figure 1. Does Donna's mental picture exactly match what she would actually find if she went into the kitchen?

In figure 2 we see some possibilities for what might actually be there. In the first row of figure 2, the first triangle is similar to what Donna pictures, but upside-down. The second triangle is an obtuse triangle, a different shape.

Figure 1. Mental picture of a triangle

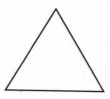

The third has a different orientation. The fourth is very thin. In the second row, the first (no. 5) is very small. Triangle 6 has thick edges. Triangle 7 is filled in black. Number 8 is freehand, and so the edges are not exactly straight. Number 9 is a triangle covered up by a rectangular rug! In the last row, 10 has a circle as well as a triangle. Triangle 11 is drawn not directly on the floor but on a piece of paper on the floor. Number 12 has a person standing on the triangle. Thirteen has a triangle with one of its corners going under the wall at one edge of the kitchen floor. Any of these pictures might represent that actual situation that Carol's words described.

The lesson should be clear. Mental pictures do not correspond to verbal language in a neat way. Language is sparse. Mental pictures can fail to match language in many ways. This failure in match is not a failure in language or in truth. God gave us language that operates with this sparseness. The failure

Figure 2. Possible drawings of a triangle

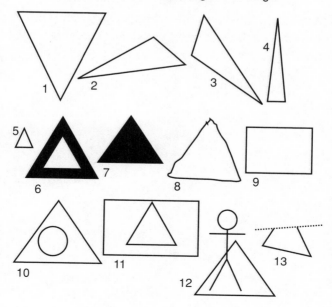

is the failure of the mental-picture *theory* of what it means for language to express truth.

Principles regarding Mental Pictures

We may summarize our findings in the following principles:

1. Sparseness in language

Human verbal accounts of events are sparse. They inevitably leave out much detail.

2. Mental pictures as supplementing

Mental pictures of events derived from a verbal account fill out detail.

3. Lack of correspondence in mental pictures

Mental pictures do not correspond exactly to the events. Reasonable people do not expect them to.

4. God's wise use of language

God in describing events in the Bible offers description in harmony with the way in which he has ordained language to function, as sparse description.

5. God's not endorsing mental pictures

God does not guarantee that our mental pictures of events described in the Bible will precisely match those events. God *does* guarantee that everything he says is true.

8

Truth in a Biblical Worldview

If a mental-picture theory of truth is inadequate, what alternatives do we have? We want to let God be God. And we should let the Gospels be the Gospels, to communicate to us in the way they choose rather than what our distorted expectations might dictate.

God as the Standard for Truth

Ultimately God defines truth. And God is inexhaustible. So we can continue to learn and continue to adjust and deepen our expectations about God as we come to know him more deeply throughout this life. This life is not the end, but leads to a consummation in which "I shall know fully, even as I have been fully known" (1 Cor. 13:12). So none of us within this life can provide the absolutely fullest answers about truth.

But we can make a beginning. The Bible has much to say about truth and its origin in God. Christ is "the truth" (John 14:6).[1] Starting with God himself, we may make progress in our expectations.

A Triad of Perspectives: Contrast, Variation, and Distribution

As part of a way to help, I propose using a perspectival triad about meaning that has been more fully developed in an earlier book.[2] This approach

---

[1]See Vern S. Poythress, *In the Beginning Was the Word: Language—A God-Centered Approach* (Wheaton, IL: Crossway, 2009), chap. 35; Poythress, *Redeeming Science: A God-Centered Approach* (Wheaton, IL: Crossway, 2006), chap. 14.

[2]Poythress, *In the Beginning Was the Word*, chap. 19.

to meaning says that unified pieces of personal action, including verbal communication, can be characterized by contrast, variation, and distribution. These three interlocking features apply in particular to truth in communication.

True communication has contrast, variation, and distribution. Let us take these aspects one at a time. First, the word *distribution* indicates that words, sentences, and speeches occur in regular ways within larger contexts. They are "distributed" within contexts. For example, Carol's speech to Donna in the previous chapter talks about "my kitchen floor." Donna uses the context in order to understand Carol. Since Carol is the speaker, "my kitchen floor" must mean *Carol's* kitchen floor. Donna must also use her knowledge that she is in Carol's house. And if Carol also owns a vacation cabin, Donna must infer from the context whether Carol is talking about the vacation cabin or the house in which they are sitting.

Second, the word *contrast* serves as a shorthand label to indicate that what we say always has contrasts with other expressions that we could have chosen instead. It also indicates that we are saying something definite. If Carol says there is a triangle, that statement contrasts with her saying that there is a pentagon or a landscape painting. If she says the triangle is in the kitchen, that contrasts with saying that it is in one of the bedrooms. Specific meanings do belong to what we say.

Third, the word *variation* indicates that words and sentences cover a range of instances. Just as each dog is a variation of the dog species, so each use of a word or a sentence is a variation on the range of its possible uses. Variation is needed in an account of truth, because it is another way of looking at the fact that pieces of language do not communicate by using infinite sharpness; they do not directly say everything that could possibly be said. Carol says that there is a triangle on the kitchen floor. That leaves open many details about the shape, orientation, size, thickness, and environment of the triangle. That is, it allows *variation* in the specifics with respect to the triangle.

Variation

Variation is essential to human language. A word that could designate only one very specific object or specific situation could never be reused. For practical purposes it would be worthless. And since it would never be reused, it would not be learned by a new generation. Even if hypothetically such a word existed, it would drop out of the language in the next generation.

With the number of words available in one human language, people can produce many, many short sentences. But none of these sentences can be infinitely specific because there are only so many choices of words. Fortunately, we can become more and more specific by writing a longer sentence and expanding a discourse into many sentences and paragraphs. But this takes time. We confront here aspects of human finiteness.

Is variation then a "concession" to human finiteness? Analysis of the origin of language in God and in God's speech indicates that variation in human discourse reflects an aspect in God's own Trinitarian character. How is this so?

God's character does not change (Mal. 3:6). He does not "vary" in that sense. So what do we mean? God is three persons. The word *God* has a range of application. It applies to God the Father, God the Son, and God the Spirit. These three applications of the word show its variation. In addition, contrast, variation, and distribution in communicating truth reflect the application of particle, wave, and field views on language, and these views in turn reflect the Father, the Son, and the Holy Spirit.[3] Human beings are finite and God is infinite; but human beings made in the image of God reflect in their finiteness God in his infinitude.

Thus variation and the sparseness that goes with it are not in themselves defects or failures in truthfulness. Range of application or range of possible reference does not mean error, but flexibility.

Contrast

Then what *does* constitute a failure in truth? Truth *contrasts* with error. If Carol says there is a triangle on her kitchen floor when there is *not*, she is deceiving Donna. There is a contrast between her claim and the actual truth that there is no triangle there.

Of course, as finite human beings we can fail in other ways besides deliberately lying. In everyday human communication we sometimes see errors due to ignorance. Perhaps Carol says there is a triangle there, but does not know that it has been cleaned up since the last time she looked. What she says, she says in all moral innocence, but still there is a contrast between the two statements—that there is a triangle on the floor and that there is not. Because God is all-knowing, he does not fail because of ignorance. Because

---

[3]Ibid., chap. 7, pp. 56–57; chap. 19, pp. 154–57. See also Poythress, "Reforming Ontology and Logic in the Light of the Trinity: An Application of Van Til's Idea of Analogy," *Westminster Theological Journal* 57, no. 1 (1995): 187–219.

God is a God of truth, he does not lie, and so he does not fail us by lying. So whenever he speaks, what he says contrasts with error.

Contrasts come up not only with respect to the main point or the obvious points that a passage in the Bible makes. Contrasts exist in the details as well. No detail should be ignored. It is there because God wanted it there. It contrasts with other things that he could have said (including omitting a particular detail).

How does this principle work with the Gospels? In the story about the centurion's servant, Matthew 8:5–13 does not specify exactly how the centurion's request reached Jesus. In the context of the first century, where the culture sometimes used representatives or mediators to carry communication, Matthew's account leaves open the possibilities. It permits *variation* in the way the communication was actually realized. It is in that respect vague or nonspecific, but not in error. But Matthew still says something definite. That is, the account still produces contrasts. According to Matthew, the centurion told Jesus that his servant was sick, and indicated that he was unworthy to have Jesus come to his house. The centurion did actually communicate to Jesus these thoughts and intentions, just as Matthew says he did.

Luke's account provides greater detail. The centurion sent elders of the Jews, and then sent friends. These details contrast with lack of detail and with other possibilities, such as sending Jews who were not elders, or sending the centurion's wife, or sending a detachment of soldiers, or sending friends first and then the elders of the Jews. We would rightly feel that Luke has misled us if, hypothetically, we were to find that he had simply invented the part about the elders out of thin air in order to make the theological point that the centurion was humble and deferential.

An Example of Variation

We can use the same principles in other situations. For example, all three Synoptic Gospels—Matthew, Mark, and Luke—contain an account of the healing of a demoniac in which the demons afterward go into a herd of pigs (Matt. 8:28–34; Mark 5:1–20; Luke 8:26–39). Matthew says that "two demon-possessed men met him [Jesus]" (Matt. 8:28), while Mark and Luke both mention only one. So how many were there? Is this an error?

In a mental-picture theory of truth, a person's mental picture must have either two men or one. The mental picture fills in details in its imagination. But neither Mark nor Luke does this filling in. Each mentions one demoniac. They do not, however, say explicitly that there was *only* one. If they had said there was only one, that claim would have *contrasted* with two. But only mentioning one leaves open the possibilities. It leaves variation. The language that they use leaves open the possibility that there might have been only one; it also leaves open the possibility that one may have been representative for more than one. This range of possibilities is *variation*. On the other hand, when Matthew says that there were two, that *contrasts* with one. So there were two—at least two.

Mark and Luke omit this detail. But omission is not error. Calvin comments:

> There is probability in the conjecture of *Augustine*, who thinks that there were two, but accounts for not more than one being mentioned here by saying, that this one was more generally known, and that the aggravation of his disease made the miracle performed on him the more remarkable. . . . The circumstance of their [Mark and Luke] holding up to commendation one singular instance of Christ's divine power is not inconsistent with the narrative of Matthew, in which another, though less known man, is also mentioned.[4]

Diagramming Contrast and Variation

We can represent the information given in the different Gospels diagrammatically. Matthew chooses to specify how many demoniacs were healed. Mark and Luke choose to focus on one. This choice of two possible foci can be represented along a horizontal axis (fig. 3).

Figure 3. Focus options: one versus many

Focus on One	Specify How Many

On a second, vertical axis we can plot the alternatives as to what is communicated about how many were actually healed. The result is figure 4.

Figure 4. How many healed? (grid)

	Focus on One; Mention One	Specify How Many
Indicate two healed		
At least one healed		
Indicate only one healed		

---

[4]John Calvin, *Commentary on a Harmony of the Evangelists, Matthew, Mark, and Luke*, 3 vols., trans. William Pringle (Grand Rapids: Eerdmans, n.d.), 1:428–29; Augustine, *Harmony of the Gospels*, in vol. 6 of *NPNF*1, 2.24.56.

Figure 5. How many healed?

	Focus on One; Mention One	Specify How Many
Indicate two healed	0	✓
At least one healed	✓	✓
Indicate only one healed	0	✓

variational range;
no contrast

contrast

If the focus is on one demoniac, the text will not tell us that this one *con-trasts* with some other number. Variation allows several possibilities. On the other hand, if Matthew specifies that there were two, this does contrast with one. We can represent the possibilities in the diagram. The viable combinations of possibilities with figure 4 can be marked with a check mark ✓ to indicate that the combination is viable, while the symbol 0 indicates that a particular combination is not really an option.

A filled-in diagram will then appear as in figure 5. Two instances of 0 appear. The combination of a narrative decision to focus on one and a specific assertion that there was exactly one is not viable (0 in lower left). Neither is the combination of a narrative decision to focus on one and a specific assertion that there were two (0 in upper left). So when Mark and Luke choose to focus on one demoniac (as in the left-hand column of fig. 5), they are not making any statement that *contrasts* with the possibility that there were two demoniacs.

Round Numbers

Similar principles apply to the evaluation of round numbers. A round number is vague rather than erroneous. Suppose an ordinary human writer uses the number 600 as a round number. He does not intend this number to contrast with 602. The number 600 faithfully represents the truth by indicating that the actual figure is around 600.

Such an approach could apply to 1 Corinthians 10:8. Paul mentions that "twenty-three thousand fell in a single day." He is presumably alluding to the event in Numbers 25:9, but the verse in Numbers says "twenty-four thousand." Was the precise number halfway between, at 23,500? Charles Hodge comments: "Both statements are equally correct. Nothing depended on the precise number. Any number between the two amounts may, according to

Figure 6. Round numbers

	Choice to Use Round Number	Choice to Use Exact Number
599	0	✓
600	✓	✓
602	0	✓

variational range; no contrast

contrast

common usage, be stated roundly as either the one or the other."[5] Hodge speaks of what happens "according to common usage." People in a variety of cultures have understood the use of round numbers. These people understand because it is "common usage."

We may represent the working of round numbers in figure 6. If a writer decides to use 600 as a round number, 600 does not contrast with 599 or 602. There is no error if we find out later that the exact figure was 602. On the other hand, if he undertakes to give an exact figure, 600 does contrast with 599, 602, and every other number in the vicinity.

Our discussion of contrast and variation does not alter the common understanding of round numbers in any fundamental way, but simply explains more explicitly what has been going on all along in many cultures and languages.[6] It puts the practice of using round numbers within a broader context of the operation of language. People tacitly understand that language is flexible. God made it that way. And in many situations, outside of contexts where we have an expectation for special exactitude, round numbers are one instance of this flexibility.

Hodge adds, "Nothing depended on the precise number." That statement seems to be Hodge's way of indicating that in the context of Paul's communication, no positive evidence appears that would indicate that God is deviating from common communicative needs. In the absence of such a special context, we cannot rightly expect God to give us something more exact than what normally belongs to a round number in common usage. People do not need

---

[5] Charles Hodge, *An Exposition of the First Epistle to the Corinthians* (New York: Robert Carter & Brothers, 1882), 178.

[6] The "Chicago Statement on Biblical Inerrancy" agrees: "We further deny that inerrancy is negated by Biblical phenomena such as a lack of modern technical precision, irregularities of grammar or spelling, observational descriptions of nature, the reporting of falsehoods, the use of hyperbole and *round numbers*, the topical arrangement of material, variant selections of material in parallel accounts, or the use of free citations" (italics mine; from article 13; accessed July 12, 2011, http://www.bible-researcher.com/chicago1.html).

Figure 7. Brevity

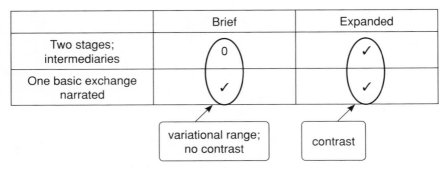

to know an exact number of fatalities, and therefore God does not offer to supply it. He supplies what readers need in order to know what incident in the Old Testament is being referred to and that about 23,000 died. He also indicates that the occurrence has meaning and implications for the attitude of the Corinthians as the people of God.

Contrast and Variation in Matthew 8:5–13

We can give the same kind of analysis and diagrammatic representation for the situation in Matthew 8:5–13. Anyone writing an account of the episode had to make decisions as to what to include and what to omit. Matthew decided to be brief and to concentrate on the essentials. He also decided to highlight that Jesus was being gracious to a *Gentile*. Having made those decisions, he could not simultaneously enter into every detail of the events. It would have become distracting to bring in explicitly the information about the Jewish elders and the friends. We can see the choices made in two dimensions. One dimension was the choice to be brief rather than expansive. The other was the choice of whether to include the specific actions by the elders and the friends (see fig. 7).

Having decided for brevity, Matthew was in a situation where mention of the extra stages was not a realistic option. His account does not have a specific contrast between elders and no elders. It would have a contrast if he had mentioned the elders or if he had said that there was no intermediary.

Principles of Contrast, Variation, and Distribution

We may therefore suggest the following principles about contrast, variation, and distribution:

1. Truth as contrastive

Truth contrasts with error.

2. God's claims for truth

God makes definite claims for truth whenever he speaks to us in the Bible. Those claims contrast with other things that theoretically could have been said instead.

3. God's use of variation

God's writings in the Bible show the linguistic feature of flexibility or *variation*, which means that the language employed covers a *range* of possibilities or "variants." We ought not to expect that such language would enable us to choose confidently and explicitly *within* the range of possibilities that it covers.

4. Variation versus error

Flexibility or range of variation in itself is not error.

5. Round numbers

Round numbers and omissions of detail are instances that allow a range of possibilities with respect to the details that are not mentioned.

6. The influence of context

The context or distribution of words, sentences, and acts of communication helps us to determine what kinds of contrasts and variations are being employed in a particular case. The context often allows us to decide between two possible meanings and indicates whether information is intended to be minutely precise or to cover a larger range.

9

Truthfulness versus Artificial Precision

The principle of flexibility or "variation" in language is important. It steers us away from expecting or demanding artificial precision when we come to the Bible. In the previous chapter we included quotes from Augustine, Calvin, and Hodge. These saints—and many others—have understood that the Bible speaks according to what Hodge called "common usage." God knows completely the resources of language, since it is his gift to human beings. He has fashioned language with contrasts and with flexibility. He speaks using those resources. That means that according to his own infinite wisdom he may speak truth and still choose not to adopt a kind of *pedantic precision*. He gives us truth that is indeed fully true without giving *all* truth. He is omniscient while we are not.

It is worthwhile to underline this principle with some further quotes from past generations of saints. These quotes, of course, are not themselves infallible. They are nevertheless valuable because they reexpress in a variety of words the fact that the Bible is infallible and at the same time not *precisionistic*.

Reflections from Ned B. Stonehouse

In his book *Origins of the Synoptic Gospels* Ned B. Stonehouse discusses at some length difficulties about the incident with the rich young ruler.[1] In that

---

[1]Ned. B. Stonehouse, *Origins of the Synoptic Gospels: Some Basic Questions* (Grand Rapids: Eerdmans, 1963), chap. 5, pp. 93–112. Stonehouse was president of the Evangelical Theological Society in 1957. See also the discussion of the rich young ruler in chap. 27 of the present volume.

context he offers broader principles for dealing with difficulties. His words are worth quoting at length.

Various tendencies in the history of harmonization of the Gospels may be recalled. One tendency, that is both conservative and simple, has been to join divergent features and to seek to weave them together into a harmonious whole. Where, however, the divergent elements are exceedingly difficult to combine in that way, it is insisted that the narratives must be regarded as reporting different events or different sayings. This approach is indeed one that I regard as fundamentally unobjectionable in principle; and at times its application leads to satisfactory results. And in general it certainly is to be preferred to the tendency, which seems to be characteristic of many modern writers, to cry "discrepancy!" at the presence of even minor linguistic differences. Or in the same spirit it may be declared dogmatically, without the benefit of any objective evidence, that two highly divergent narratives or records of teaching necessarily must be envisioned as the result of radical editorial modifications of a single source. Nevertheless, there is, in my judgment, a sounder attitude to most problems of harmonization than that which was characterized above as conservative and simple. It is marked by the exercise of greater care in determining what the Gospels as a whole and in detail actually say as well as greater restraint in arriving at conclusions where the available evidence does not justify ready answers. In particular, there is the possibility of genuine progress if one does not maintain that the trustworthiness of the Gospels allows the evangelists no liberty of composition whatsoever, and does not insist that in reporting the words of Jesus, for example, they must have been characterized by a kind of notarial exactitude or what Professor John Murray has called "pedantic precision." Inasmuch as this point seems constantly to be overlooked or disregarded in the modern situation it may be well to stress again that orthodox expositors and defenders of the infallibility of Scripture have consistently made the point that infallibility is not properly understood if it is supposed that it carries with it the implication that the words of Jesus as reported in the Gospels are necessarily the *ipsissima verba* [exact words]. What is involved rather is that the Holy Spirit guided the human authors in such a way as to insure that their records give an accurate and trustworthy impression of the Lord's teachings.[2]

Reflections of John Murray

We continue by quoting from the footnote that Stonehouse appends to the quotation just given.

John Murray, *Calvin on Scripture and Divine Sovereignty* (Grand Rapids: Baker, 1960), p. 30, declares: "It must be emphatically stated that the doctrine of bibli-

---

[2]Ibid., 109–10.

cal inerrancy for which the church has contended throughout history, and for which a great many of us still contend, is not based on the assumption that the criterion of meticulous precision in every detail of record or history is the indispensable canon of biblical infallibility. To erect such a canon is utterly artificial and arbitrary and is not one by which the inerrancy of Scripture is to be judged . . . . The Scripture abounds in illustrations of the absence of the type of meticulous and pedantic precision which we might arbitrarily seek to impose as the criterion of infallibility. Every one should recognize that in accord with accepted forms of speech and custom a statement can be perfectly authentic and yet not pedantically precise. Scripture does not make itself absurd by furnishing us with pedantry." Quoted by permission.

The view presented here is that which has been maintained by leading Reformed theologians. *Cf., e.g.* Murray, *ibid.*, pp. 11ff., 29ff., 35ff.; B. B. Warfield, *Revelation and Inspiration* (New York: Oxford, 1927), pp. 205f., 420; *Christology and Criticism*, pp. 108f.; A. Kuyper, *Encyclopaedie der Heilige Godgeleerdheid*, 2nd ed. (Kampen: Kok, 1909), II, 505f. (Eng. trans., *Principles of Sacred Theology* [Grand Rapids: Eerdmans, 1954], p. 550); H. Bavinck, *Gereformeerde Dogmatiek*, 3rd ed. (Kampen: Kok, 1918), I, 469ff.; L. Berkhof, *Introduction to the New Testament* (Grand Rapids: Eerdmans-Sevensma, 1915), p. 42. Particular attention may also be directed to the statement of A. A. Hodge and B. B. Warfield, in their famous article on "Inspiration" in *The Presbyterian Review*, II (April, 1881): "There is a vast difference between exactness of statement, which includes an exhaustive rendering of details, an absolute literalness, which the Scriptures never profess, and accuracy, on the other hand, which secures a correct statement of facts or principles intended to be affirmed" (p. 238; *cf.* pp. 229ff., 237, 242, 244ff.). Cf. also A. Kuyper's conclusion, *loc. cit.*, "When in the four Gospels Jesus, on the same occasion, is made to say words that are different in form of expression, it is impossible that He should have used these four forms at once. The Holy Spirit, however, merely intends to make an impression on the Church which wholly corresponds to what Jesus said."[3]

Stonehouse comments further on the issue of harmonization.

We confess that much that has been attempted in the interest of demonstrating the unity of the gospels has been extreme and far-fetched, not because of any positive proof of actual disunity, but because it has proceeded from a fundamentally false conception of the aim of the evangelists and the distinctive character of the gospels. To make this confession is, to be sure, not a late and regretful acknowledgment of the faults of all orthodox scholars in the past, for no less an exponent of the authority and unity of the Scriptures than John

---

[3]Ibid., 110n17.

Calvin protested in his day against the faulty approach of Osiander.[4] If the evangelists aimed to compose a history or biography of Christ, as complete in detail as possible, with scrupulous attention to itinerary and chronological sequence, and to report the words of Jesus with stenographic accuracy, there would be very little in one gospel that could be regarded as finding its counterpart in any other. Since, however, none of these features is supported by the evidence, and since particularly none of the evangelists aims to supply a complete historical framework [chronologically] of the life of Christ, it follows that much of the disparagement of "harmonistics" is based upon radically erroneous conceptions of the character of the gospels. The defender of the truth and authority of the gospels does not face the necessity of fitting all the details of the records into a continuous [chronological] framework. The evangelists do not provide sufficient data for such an effort, and did not intend to do so.[5]

I agree with Stonehouse's sentiments. Others must judge how well I succeed in carrying them out in my own reflections on harmonization.

---

[4]Stonehouse adds a footnote here: "*E.g.*, in his comment on Mt. 20:29" (Ned B. Stonehouse, *The Witness of the Synoptic Gospels to Christ: One Volume Combining The Witness of Matthew and Mark to Christ and The Witness of Luke to Christ*, 2nd ed. [Grand Rapids: Baker, 1979], 163n5).

[5]Ibid., 163–64.

10

Variations in Writing History

Language exhibits flexibility not only at the level of words or numbers, but also at the level of genres. Historical writing represents a genre in a broad sense. Within this broad genre, there are many variations. A human account of historical events can be detailed or sparse, colloquial or in high style, true or false or partly both. It can have a variety of purposes: moral, religious, social, or legal. Genres are not infinitely precise, so even someone who immediately recognizes the genre of a particular text must still adjust within that broad genre to the particularities of the one text he is studying. And authors may choose to "stretch" the boundaries of an existing genre or combine genres.[1] Readers coming from other cultures may sometimes not be familiar with all the ins and outs of a genre specific to one culture. But commonalities of human nature help understanding. People in every culture have the capability for producing narratives about what happened.[2]

We have already concluded that the Gospels are historical accounts (chap. 5). The claims in Luke's prologue (Luke 1:1–4) and the similarities between Luke and the other three Gospels tell us that all four Gospels narrate what happened rather than inventing events or overlaying fact with fiction. But the broad genre "Gospel" still allows variations in point of view and emphasis (chap. 4). In principle, these variations in viewpoint may include variations in the *way* in which each Gospel describes the events.

---

[1]Vern S. Poythress, *In the Beginning Was the Word: Language—A God-Centered Approach* (Wheaton, IL: Crossway, 2009), 188.
[2]See, for example, Robert E. Longacre, *The Grammar of Discourse* (New York: Plenum, 1983), 3–6.

So we may consider the four Gospels one by one. What does each one indicate about its approach to writing the history of the events?

Luke's Approach

Because the Gospel of Luke includes a prologue in Luke 1:1–4, we can understand its claims more directly. As we have seen (chap. 5), it places itself alongside the Old Testament historical writings and also shows analogies to Hellenistic historical writings. At the same time, it links itself with the theological interest in promise and fulfillment. Luke 1:1 speaks about "the things that have been accomplished among us," hinting at the relation to Old Testament promises that have now been brought to realization by what has "been accomplished." The idea of fulfillment becomes explicit especially at the end of Luke.

> And he said to them, "O foolish ones, and slow of heart to believe all that the prophets have spoken! Was it not *necessary* that the Christ should suffer these things and enter into his glory?" And beginning with Moses and all the Prophets, he interpreted to them in all the Scriptures the things *concerning himself.* (Luke 24:25–27)

> Then he said to them, "These are my words that I spoke to you while I was still with you, that everything written about me in the Law of Moses and the Prophets and the Psalms must be *fulfilled.*" Then he opened their minds to understand the Scriptures, and said to them, "*Thus it is written, that* the Christ should suffer and on the third day rise from the dead, and that repentance and forgiveness of sins should be proclaimed in his name to all nations, beginning from Jerusalem. (Luke 24:44–47)

In addition, Luke 1:5 makes a sudden transition from the elegant Greek of 1:1–4 to a style like the Septuagint, reminding readers of its relation to the Old Testament. Because Luke is inspired by God, it belongs with the Old Testament writings—it is authoritative and canonical. On the issue of historical claims, Luke shows that it is describing real events, as is underlined by its relationship both to Old Testament historical writings and to what Hellenistic historians *claimed* to offer. At the same time, these events fit into the plan of God for redemption. History and theology thus go together (chap. 5).

Matthew's Approach

Now consider the Gospel of Matthew. Matthew opens with a genealogy. Actually, it gives us two genealogical lists. The first is a summary: "The book of the genealogy of Jesus Christ, the son of David, the son of Abraham" (Matt. 1:1). Then follows an extended list: "Abraham was the father of Isaac, and Isaac the father of Jacob, and Jacob the father of Judah and his brothers, and Judah the father of Perez and Zerah by Tamar, and Perez the father of Hezron, and Hezron the father of Ram, and Ram . . ." (Matt. 1:2–4). These genealogies call to mind the genealogies in Genesis 5, 10, and 11:10–32, the larger genealogical structure of the history in Genesis (e.g., 2:4; 5:1; 6:9; 11:27), and the genealogies in 1 Chronicles 1–9. In this respect, as well as others, Matthew has more of a Jewish feel, and probably had especially in mind Jewish and Jewish-Christian readers. The genealogy immediately connects it with Old Testament histories.

The opening genealogical list in verse 1 offers only a summary. Jesus Christ is the son of David, the son of Abraham. The expression "son of" in this context does not mean narrowly that one person is the first-generation direct male descendant of the other, as we commonly use the word *son* in English.[3] The underlying word in Greek (*huios*) has flexibility or variation. It can cover not only first-generation descent but any number of generations.[4] The expanded genealogy in Matthew 1:2–16 fills in many of the intermediate generations, but not all. A comparison with the Old Testament list of kings of Judah shows that Matthew 1:8 is compressed. For example, Matthew reads, "Joram the father of Uzziah." Kings and Chronicles give more complete records: Joram (or "Jehoram") fathered Ahaziah, who fathered Joash (or "Jehoash"), who fathered Amaziah, who fathered Uzziah (also called "Azariah"). When we compare Matthew 1:8 with Kings and Chronicles, we see that Matthew 1:8 omits Ahaziah, Joash, and Amaziah and skips from Joram directly to Uzziah. The detailed wording in Matthew 1:8 in Greek actually gives us the expression "Joram *begat* [Greek *egennēsen*] Uzziah." The Greek word for "begat" includes variation: it may denote either one-generation immediate descent or descent over a span of more generations. Hence, Matthew is using the key word *begat* flexibly, in accord with its normal meaning, and not erroneously.

Both Matthew and his Jewish readers would have known the Old Testament list of the kings of Judah. By using a case where the facts were already known, and by using the summary list in Matthew 1:1, Matthew indicates clearly that he is comfortable with compression.

The compression that Matthew uses is not a random operation. Consider first the summary list in Matthew 1:1. It includes Abraham, David, and Jesus Christ. Why these three? Christ as the endpoint of the genealogy is

---

[3]Somewhat less commonly, perhaps, than in Greek or Hebrew, English also attests the use of "son" for "male descendant" with possible intermediate generations (*Merriam-Webster's Collegiate Dictionary*, 11th ed. [Springfield, MA: Merriam-Webster, 2008], "son," 1c).

[4]See Frederick William Danker, ed., *A Greek-English Lexicon of the New Testament and Other Early Christian Literature*, 3rd ed. (Chicago: University of Chicago Press, 2000), under υἱός ("son"), 1c.

clearly the climax. David is included because God's promise to David (2 Sam. 7:5–16) guarantees a line of kings descending from David, and later prophetic promises indicate that the Messiah is to come from this line. Abraham is included because he is the father of the whole Jewish nation. God's promise to Abraham (Gen. 12:1–3 and elsewhere) laid the foundation for the distinctive blessings and privileges that came to the Jewish people.

This kind of selectivity indicates that Matthew has thought carefully about what he includes in the genealogies. (And of course God as divine author has ordained what is written.) Once we understand the care in Matthew, we can notice other details that doubtless have subtle significance. For example, Matthew includes in the expanded genealogy the names of five women: Tamar, Rahab, Ruth, Bathsheba, and Mary (1:3, 5, 6, 16). These were famous women. But we also know that all came to play a role as mothers in the Messianic line in unusual ways. Tamar pretended to be a prostitute and became pregnant through her father-in-law Judah (Genesis 38). Rahab was a prostitute before coming to faith in God (Josh. 2:1); Ruth was a Moabite (Ruth 1:4); Bathsheba became David's wife in connection with adultery and murder (2 Samuel 11); Mary conceived as a virgin (Matt. 1:18, 23). Moreover, all except Mary seem to have had Gentile ancestry. Bathsheba is mentioned not by her own name but as "the wife of Uriah" (1:6), who was a Hittite (2 Sam. 11:3). And the expression "the wife of Uriah" reminds readers of the sordid story of David's adultery and murder. The inclusion of these women subtly reminds us about the grace of God in the gospel. God brings good out of evil. He includes people who do not have special human privileges.

Matthew's Subtleties

Matthew plainly provides the central facts about Jesus's ancestry. But the text also includes subtleties. It invites reflection on the significance of details like the inclusion of the women. Once we have noticed some subtleties, others come to our attention.

Matthew groups the genealogy into three sections of fourteen generations each (Matt. 1:17). The number fourteen for the middle group (Matt. 1:6–11, from David to Jechoniah) has been produced only by omitting some of the kings of Judah. This intentional compression indicates that the point is not that we have literally fourteen generations with no omissions, but that some theme is being emphasized. What theme? It is not immediately clear; the point is subtle. Fourteen is twice seven, the number symbolizing completeness. In addition, the key number fourteen is possibly related to the fact that if one adds up the numerical values associated with the letters in

David's name in Hebrew, the total comes to fourteen. (The Jews of the first century were familiar with this practice of "gematria," in which one added up the numerical values of letters.) If this is part of the point of the number fourteen, Matthew is underlining further the importance of David, and so recalls the Old Testament promises about the coming of the Messiah in the line of David (see Matt. 2:6). The grouping into three sets of fourteen also draws attention to the middle group, which consists of the kings of Judah during the monarchy period. These kings anticipated the coming of the Messiah as the great king (see Matt. 2:2, 6).

We also find that two of the names in the list of kings have unusual spellings. Amon the son of Manasseh is spelled "Amos" (Matt. 1:10); Asa the son of Abijah is spelled "Asaph" (Matt. 1:7–8). Some Greek manuscripts have the more usual spellings "Amon" and "Asa." Scribes making copies of a manuscript have a tendency to smooth out irregularities such as an unusual spelling. They look at the word they are copying, and their memory of the common spelling interferes with their immediate memory of the unusual spelling on the copy in front of them. That interference sometimes leads to substituting the more common spelling. So the unusual spellings almost certainly represent the original spelling in the autograph of Matthew.[5]

What significance do these unusual spellings have? In the first place, an unusual spelling is not an error. Technically speaking, a variation of this kind is a graphological variation that preserves the correct referent and therefore preserves the correct genealogical relations. It is all the more harmless because all the names represent transliterations from Hebrew, and systematic phonemic and graphological differences between Hebrew and Greek mean that there is no *one* way to accomplish transliteration. Transliteration allows variation.

But in Matthew's case there may be something more. Like many other aspects of the genealogy, it is subtle. By spelling "Asa" as "Asaph," Matthew refers to king Asa, the son of Abijah; at the same time, on top of this main connection, it creates a literary allusion to or reminiscence of Asaph, of the tribe of Levi, the head of the Levitical singers (1 Chron. 25:1). This allusion subtly suggests that Jesus is not only literally the heir to the kingly line of David, through king Asa, but figuratively and spiritually heir to the Levitical line of priestly activity. By spelling "Amon" as "Amos," Matthew refers to king Amon, the son of Manasseh and at the same time creates a literary allusion

---

[5]In addition, some of the key manuscripts with the unusual spellings are of better quality and earlier.

to Amos the prophet. It suggests that Jesus is spiritually the heir to the Old Testament prophets.

Matthew's genealogy offers us an advantage for interpretation because we have access to the Old Testament genealogical records. We can see both that Matthew is faithfully following and affirming these records and that Matthew engages in highlighting and compression in order subtly to draw attention to some thematic connections and theological truths. Matthew thereby invites us to expect the same sort of thing throughout the Gospel.

We summarize with the following principles:

1. Real events in Matthew

Matthew recorded what happened in the life of Jesus, just as he recorded the actual genealogy, as previously recorded in the Old Testament.

2. Compression

Matthew used compression in recounting the events. We see an instance of compression in Matthew 8:5–13, the story of the centurion's servant. Matthew leaves out all mention of the Jewish elders and the centurion's friends, who served as intermediaries. The narrative gets compressed by omitting these extra personages and extra stages.

Similarly, Matthew 9:18–26 compresses the story of the healing of Jairus's daughter. In comparison with Mark 5:22–43, Matthew omits the mention of two stages in the development, in the first of which Jairus's daughter is at the point of death, and in the second of which messengers come to Jairus to announce that his daughter has just died. In Matthew, the events are compressed: the daughter has died, and Jesus brings her to life.[6]

3. Highlighting of themes

Matthew thematically highlights themes and theological significances as he tells about the events. In Matthew 8:10–12, the centurion's Gentile origin is highlighted, and it underlines Matthew's larger point that Gentiles are now being admitted to the kingdom of God, while Jewish unbelievers are left out.

---

[6]See chap. 28 for a further discussion of the incident with Jairus's daughter. Another instance of compression occurs in Matt. 21:18–22, which is discussed in chap. 20. See also Craig L. Blomberg, *The Historical Reliability of the Gospels*, 2nd ed. (Downers Grove, IL: InterVarsity, 2007), 177–80.

Mark's Approach

We need to say only a little about the distinctive approach in the Gospel of Mark. Mark begins with the announcement, "The beginning of the gospel of Jesus Christ, the son of God" (Mark 1:1). After this opening there follows a quotation from the Old Testament (Mark 1:2–3). And then we plunge into action. Mark is a Gospel of action.

But Mark's beginning indicates that this action has theological significance. First, Mark's Gospel reveals Jesus as the "Christ," "the Son of God," indicating that he is fulfilling the Old Testament promises concerning the coming of the Messiah. Second, it is the "gospel," the good news of salvation as prophesied in Old Testament passages like Isaiah 52:7–10. Third, the actions that Mark records correspond to specific prophecies.

For example, in Mark 1:2–3 the Old Testament quotations come from two different prophets, Malachi 3:1 and Isaiah 40:3. In introducing the quotations Mark mentions only Isaiah: "As it is written in Isaiah the prophet" (1:2).[7] Is this a problem? Isaiah is the more prominent of the two prophets, and the verse in Malachi 3:1, written later than Isaiah, may actually allude to the verse in Isaiah 40:3. Whether or not Malachi offers a definite allusion, the two prophecies are organically related, because both prophecies promise the coming of a messenger in preparation for the coming of God. Mark has grouped the two together for good reason and has further underlined their unity by mentioning only Isaiah as the earlier and more prominent prophet.

This kind of citation should be seen as an instance of flexibility, that is, of variation. Mark's mention of Isaiah indicates that at least a portion comes from Isaiah, and that one can find the main thrust there. Moreover, Mark's mention of Isaiah *contrasts* with various theoretically possible alternatives, such as mentioning Amos or Jonah, whom he decides not to quote. At the same time, Mark's citation is not precisionistic; it allows the flexibility that other material can also be included. And of course reasonable readers who know their Old Testament would understand Mark and would get the point. Mark chooses flexibility here because he is focusing on main points.

By contrast, a pedantic, precisionistic approach, interested only in setting forth the most thorough information about every source, would insist on mentioning explicitly both sources, Malachi and Isaiah. But Mark's purposes and his genre, his manner of communication, have other foci. We may represent this in figure 8.

---

[7] The different manuscript copies of the Gospel of Mark show a variation in wording here. Copies belonging to the Byzantine family of texts have the wording, "As it is written in the prophets." This wording eliminates all difficulty. But the best manuscripts have the wording with "Isaiah." And we know that scribes who copied manuscripts tended to introduce changes that smooth out difficulties like this one. So we infer that the autograph of Mark had the wording referring to Isaiah.

Figure 8. Citation

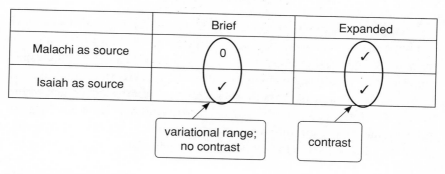

John's Approach

The Gospel of John begins not with the earthly life of Jesus, but with theological reflections that go back to creation and to eternity. "In the beginning was the Word . . . " (John 1:1). Later it announces, "the Word became flesh and dwelt among us, and we have seen his glory . . . " (John 1:14). John, like the other Gospels, is interested in telling us what happened in space and time—in the "flesh." Like 1 John, it is against "docetism" and all forms of religion that evaporate materiality (1 John 1:1–2; 4:1–3; note John 19:34–36; 20:25, 27). It promises to give us real history, events in space and time.[8] At the same time, it gives us deep theological interpretation of the significance of the events. The disciples understood the significance of events only partially when the events were happening. Jesus indicates that the coming of the Holy Spirit will bring a decisive advance in understanding: "I have said these things to you in figures of speech. The hour is coming when I will no longer speak to you in figures of speech but will tell you plainly about the Father" (John 16:25).

When Jesus gives the gift of the Holy Spirit, the Spirit will guide them in understanding.

> I still have many things to say to you, but you cannot bear them now. When the Spirit of truth comes, he will guide you into all the truth, for he will not speak on his own authority, but whatever he hears he will speak, and he will declare to you the things that are to come. He will glorify me, for he will take what is mine and declare it to you. (John 16:12–14)

In the light of these promises, John's prologue (John 1:1–18) suggests that John is going to expound theological significance. He speaks as one to whom the Holy Spirit has come. So John is looking at the events of Jesus's earthly

---

[8]See F. F. Bruce, "The Trial of Jesus in the Fourth Gospel," in *Gospel Perspectives: Studies of History and Tradition in the Four Gospels*, vol. 1, ed. R. T. France and David Wenham (Sheffield: JSOT, 1980), 18.

life retrospectively, from the standpoint of one to whom the Spirit has given further understanding.

Of course the same is true in a general way for all four Evangelists. All four wrote under the inspiration of the Holy Spirit, the Spirit who had been given in a fuller way after Jesus's resurrection and ascension. All four Gospels communicate to Christians who live after the resurrection of Christ and Pentecost. At the same time, the Gospel of John by its introduction gives more emphasis to interpreting in theological depth. And that emphasis helps to explain some of the many differences between it and the other three Gospels.[9]

We therefore have the following summary principles:

1. Real events in John

The Gospel of John talks about real events.

2. Theological significance in John

The Gospel of John unveils the theological significance of events, and the full depth of this unveiling belongs to the time after the giving of the Holy Spirit at Pentecost.

Differences between the Gospels

Each of the four Gospels gives us the truth about the life of Jesus. No one Gospel is exhaustive, nor does it claim to be—each is selective. And each makes choices about how it is going to tell the history. Each is interested in highlighting theological significances and relationships to the Old Testament. Matthew is noteworthy for his Jewishness, for his compression, and for the introduction of subtle hints of extra significance. Mark is noteworthy for action and for concentration on the main points. Luke is noteworthy for care in historical research. John is noteworthy for theological depth in interpreting the significance of events.

We should also remember that all four Gospels are God's writing, not simply the product of the human authors. The differences between them in their approaches to writing history illustrate that God himself is comfortable with using distinct perspectives in revealing what happened and its significance. The significance in God's mind is infinitely deep. He enriches us by providing us four windows on his wisdom rather than merely one.

---

[9]See Blomberg, *Historical Reliability*, 233–34.

PART THREE

ATTITUDES
IN HARMONIZATION

11

CONFIDENCE AND DOUBT

Human study of the Gospels or human study of the Bible as a whole, like any other human activity, takes place within a context of ethical responsibility. Most fundamentally, as creatures made in the image of God, we have an obligation: "love the Lord your God with all your heart and with all your soul and with all your mind" (Matt. 22:37). God in his majesty is worthy of all our commitment. Our obligations toward God impinge on us in every area of life. In tune with this overarching obligation, we also have an obligation to become disciples of Christ and to follow him.[1] We are not "off-duty" when we study the Gospels.

We can appreciate moral obligations by using the three perspectives on ethics developed by John Frame: the normative, the situational, and the existential perspectives.[2] The normative perspective focuses on the norms, that is, God's commands. The situational perspective focuses on the situation in which a person acts, and it asks what will promote the glory of God within that situation. The existential perspective focuses on the person who acts, and it inquires about his or her motives. The existential perspective can also be called the personal perspective. The three perspectives interlock. Rightly

---

[1] See Vern S. Poythress, *Inerrancy and Worldview: Answering Modern Challenges to the Bible* (Wheaton, IL: Crossway, 2012), especially chap. 31.

[2] John M. Frame, *The Doctrine of the Christian Life* (Phillipsburg, NJ: P&R, 2008); Frame, *Perspectives on the Word of God: An Introduction to Christian Ethics* (Phillipsburg, NJ: Presbyterian and Reformed, 1990; repr., Eugene, OR: Wipf and Stock, 1999).

understood, each leads to the others. If we follow out their implications, each encompasses the others. But we can focus primarily on one.

In our discussion of principles for harmonization in part two, we have mostly focused on the normative perspective. Each principle for harmonization is a normative principle. It expresses a way in which we ought to seek to do justice to the claims of the Gospels. The "ought" character of the principles is closely related to the normative perspective. The principles derive from our normative obligation to listen carefully and respectfully to the Gospels because they are God's word.

What about the situational perspective? In chapter 10 and in part of chapter 5 we focused more on the situational perspective, because we looked at the genre of the Gospels and attempted to reckon with their historical environment. Luke, for example, has a prologue that shows similarities with Hellenistic history writing. The beginning of Matthew shows similarities with Old Testament genealogies. If we start with the normative perspective, it leads naturally to an affirmation of the situational perspective. God's norms tell us that we are responsible to love God and to love the human authors of the Gospels. This responsibility implies that we will attend with care to how they want their writing to be understood within a historical environment, as well as within the linguistic environment formed by the capabilities of language (e.g., chap. 8). Thus, the normative perspective affirms the importance of the situational perspective.

God's norms also speak about our responsibilities as persons. We need to pay attention to our attitudes, because attitudes and motivations as well as overt actions are evaluated by God. These attitudes come into focus in the personal or existential perspective. In this and the next few chapters, we focus on this area of attitudes. What should our attitude be in approaching the tasks and the challenges of interpreting the Gospels, especially in those areas where they differ from one another?

Accepting the Bible as the Word of God

The most fundamental attitudinal issue in studying the Bible consists in making a personal decision about what kind of book it is. What do we think? Is it God's speech in writing, or is it merely a human record, parts of which might be fallibly responding to divine activity? We have already considered this question in chapter 1.[3] We must leave to other books, and ultimately to God himself, the primary task of persuading people that the

---

[3] See also Poythress, *Inerrancy and Worldview*, chap. 32.

Gospels are divine words.[4] Persuasion comes both through the evidence of the Gospels themselves and through the presence of God. God by his Holy Spirit opens people's eyes and gives them the conviction that it is he who is speaking. The presence of God is not something that we can control. So we cannot expect just to "make up our minds" on this crucial question as if we were coming with pure and unprejudiced attitudes from the beginning.[5] We must ask God for his cleansing and power to work in our minds and our hearts.

If the Gospels are the word of God, what conclusions follow with respect to our response? We can trust what they say. It no longer makes sense to apply to them the same critical attitudes we would use with a merely human source for historical information. We listen to God with a respect that is reserved for him alone. Doubting his words represents foolishness and disloyalty, because he is completely trustworthy.

Wrestling with Doubt

But we should be honest that doubts remain real. And in a finer analysis we need to distinguish different *kinds* of doubts. First, there may be doubts as to whether what we are reading is really the word of God. Satan introduced doubts when he spoke to Eve (Gen. 3:4–5), and he uses the same strategy today.[6]

Second, a temptation to doubt can be distinguished from giving way to doubt. Satan tempted Eve and put the idea into her mind. She did not sin merely by hearing the idea; but she *did* sin by giving way to the temptation that Satan introduced.

Third, we may have doubts about whether we have understood a particular verse or part of the Bible. Some parts are difficult, and it is morally responsible to assess wisely our own degree of competence, maturity, and understanding. But of course we can also fall into the temptation of using our finiteness as an excuse never to obey. We defer obedience indefinitely. Over against this temptation, we must have a wise and robust sense of where we are in the life that God has given us. Some people are called by God to give detailed attention even to small difficulties in interpretation.

---

[4]On the issue of God's giving confidence, see John M. Frame, *The Doctrine of the Word of God* (Phillipsburg, NJ: P&R, 2010).

[5]On the corruption of the mind, see Poythress, *Inerrancy and Worldview*, chaps. 28–30.

[6]We cannot undertake here a discussion of the nature of canon and how we become convinced that the four Gospels belong to the canon, the body of writings with divine authority. See Herman Ridderbos, *Redemptive History and the New Testament Scriptures* (Phillipsburg, NJ: Presbyterian and Reformed, 1988); and Michael J. Kruger, *Canon Revisited: Establishing the Origins and Authority of the New Testament Books* (Wheaton, IL: Crossway, 2012).

They may weigh many issues over a long time before having to act. Most people, however, must act in practical ways without having a very meticulously worked-through and critically weighed interpretation. They must trust that God will guide them using the parts of the Bible that are clear, even when they may have misjudged the meaning of a more obscure text or a more obscure aspect of one text.

God took our limitations into account when he designed the Bible. What is most important in the Bible is clear and gets said in multiple texts and in a variety of ways. As the Westminster Confession of Faith says,

> All things in Scripture are not alike plain in themselves, nor alike clear unto all: yet those things which are necessary to be known, believed, and observed for salvation, are so clearly propounded, and opened in some place of Scripture or other, that not only the learned, but the unlearned, in a due use of the ordinary means, may attain unto a sufficient understanding of them.[7]

Fourth, we may rightly doubt ourselves and other human interpreters. Critical questioning of human arguments, assumptions, and limitations is appropriate for our present state as finite, fallen human beings. This critical questioning of other sources should be in sharp contrast to trusting God. We show honor to God not only by positively trusting him but also by *not* trusting other sources in the same way that we trust him.

Fifth, we must recognize that God knows our hearts, even beyond what we ourselves know. If we have doubts about God and his Word, it does no good to imagine that we can hide them from God. Some of the psalms show the boldness of psalmists in setting out their struggles before God (see, e.g., Psalm 73). Doubt and mental struggle become occasions for prayer. Doubts may arise not only from circumstances of bodily suffering, but also from mental perplexity. And such perplexity may include perplexity over apparent discrepancies in the Gospels. We should not panic when we meet perplexity, nor should we imagine that God is "shocked" to see our frailty or our wavering faith. Hebrews 4:14–16 is pertinent.

> Since then we have a great high priest who has passed through the heavens, Jesus, the Son of God, let us hold fast our confession. For we do not have a high priest who is unable to sympathize with our weaknesses, but one who in every respect has been tempted as we are, yet without sin. Let us then with confidence draw near to the throne of grace, that we may receive mercy and find grace to help in time of need.

[7]Westminster Confession of Faith 1.7.

The Temptation to "Neutrality"

Followers of Christ give their loyalty to Christ, and therefore they also should be loyal to his words. Our attitude toward the Bible and toward the Gospels differs from those whose primary loyalty is to themselves or to modern or postmodern ideas. These differences in loyalty produce differences not only in attitude but also in method when we study the Gospels. When we give our loyalty to Christ, we will grow in confidence in the Gospels, even if other people do not.

Moreover, loyalty to Christ leads us to a definite view about meaning. Some radical reader-response theories of meaning multiply meanings with little regard for the intentions of speakers and authors. But people generally know, either instinctively or by conscious reasoning, that speakers and authors deserve our attention out of respect for them. So we make an effort to understand their meanings.[8]

If God is the principal author of the Gospels, then we should attend to what he means. That implies that we should reckon with everything we know about him when we read, and we should try through the power of the Holy Spirit to interpret what we read in the light of what we know about him. An analogous approach would ordinarily take place even with a human author. But differences in reading are particularly intense when we consider Scripture. The orientation of our heart makes a difference. We begin this life as sinners, with hearts in rebellion to God. God needs to change our hearts, to renew them so that we are receptive (see Ezek. 36:25–27). Until our hearts are renewed, we try to evade the reality of God's authorship, and we have distorted ideas about God when we read. So differences in people's hearts result in many different strategies and readings of the Gospels, not just one. Many of these are ethically wrong, because they rise from hearts in rebellion against God.

We must also reckon with the fact that God is actively involved in the reception of his Word. The Father and the Son and the Spirit reveal themselves in the Bible not to all, but to the humble.[9]

At that time Jesus declared, "I thank you, Father, Lord of heaven and earth, that you have hidden these things from the wise and understanding and revealed them to little children; yes, Father, for such was your gracious will. All things have been handed over to me by my Father, and no one knows the Son except

---

[8]See Vern S. Poythress, *In the Beginning Was the Word: Language—A God-Centered Approach* (Wheaton, IL: Crossway, 2009), chaps. 20–22.
[9]On humility, see Poythress, *Inerrancy and Worldview*, chap. 33.

the Father, and no one knows the Father except the Son and anyone to whom the Son chooses to reveal him. (Matt. 11:25–27)

Since we inherit pride and self-centeredness from Adam, no one starts out humble. God changes us by his power: "For God, who said, 'Let light shine out of darkness,' has shone in our hearts to give the light of the knowledge of the glory of God in the face of Jesus Christ" (2 Cor. 4:6).

The sphere of academic biblical studies and religious studies contains a widespread attitude that we need to treat the Bible in a way that uses "common-ground" assumptions for interpretation. Some may say that we must consider matters in a "religiously neutral" way, independent of the so-called prejudices of religious commitments. But of course those who call religious commitments "prejudices" show their prejudice against religious commitments. They have a commitment to this kind of conviction about religion, and that commitment for them is more ultimate than their commitment to any particular religion. This ultimate commitment is an idol, competing with allegiances to other gods. It is innately religious. It is also in rebellion against God, since people indicate by their attitude that they are suppressing the truth they know about God (Rom. 1:18–23).

There is no neutrality about such commitments. There is no common ground to be found on which we may conduct our discussions neutrally. People have different hearts, and with the differences in the heart come differences in assumptions and commitments.[10] We ought not be disloyal to Christ by pretending that our loyalty can be put aside, or subordinated to some other standards, or declared irrelevant to the discussion. Since love for God and the lordship of Christ extend to every area of life, a Christian ought not to try to leap out of his commitment when he enters literary or historical or religious discussions.

We may nevertheless find a grain of truth in the idea of adjusting to other people's expectations. We must try to find ways to communicate our own convictions and the message of the gospel of Christ clearly to those with different commitments. For instance, depending on a person's present commitments, he may be open to considering whether the Gospels are more or less reliable historical documents. If we show him evidence of historical veracity,[11] such as correspondences between the book of Acts and extrabiblical Roman historical information, he may gain some confidence in the historical claims

---

[10]These assumptions and commitments are called presuppositions in Cornelius Van Til's tradition of presuppositional apologetics (Van Til, *The Defense of the Faith*, 2nd ed. [Philadelphia: Presbyterian and Reformed, 1963]). I am indebted to that tradition.

[11]See, e.g., F. F. Bruce, *The New Testament Documents*, 2nd ed. (London: Inter-Varsity, 1970); Craig L. Blomberg, *The Historical Reliability of the Gospels*, 2nd ed. (Downers Grove, IL: InterVarsity, 2007).

of Luke, enough to start him reading Luke with a serious interest. The Holy Spirit may use his reading to lead him to faith in Christ. But during that path of coming to faith, until he actually puts his faith in Christ, he would still be in fundamental rebellion not only against Christ but against the character of the Gospel of Luke as God's word.[12]

People come to faith in Christ through many strange paths. God has mercy on them. He uses their paths. But his use of these paths does not imply his ethical endorsement.

We should be aware of many resources available today. Books written by evangelicals to defend historical reliability contain much careful weighing of evidence from the Gospels themselves, from other parts of the New Testament, and from historical sources outside the Bible. There is much here that is good and useful. This kind of material can help skeptics to reconsider their skepticism, as well as helping Christians to gain confidence in the historical claims in the Gospels. Books of this kind in many respects complement the reasoning in this book, since I have chosen to focus only on one issue out of many, namely, the question of whether the Gospel accounts are in harmony.

But I am not always fully satisfied with the *way* in which such books approach the evidence. Books present massive evidence, and present it articulately. Good. But with what attitudes and assumptions about history and truth do we approach the evidence? If we have come to the conviction that the Bible is God's word—a conviction that God himself wants us to have—it is not right to set that conviction aside when it comes to methods, argumentation, or specific claims that we may make as we address the larger world of biblical scholarship or ordinary run-of-the-mill unbelief or doubt. Nor is it right to suggest that people who are still sifting through this evidence from a position outside of commitment to Christ are doing so neutrally. They are suppressing truths that they know, according to Romans 1:18–32.

Circular Reasoning?

Some people feel uncomfortable with a procedure in which we *start* with belief in the divine authorship of the Gospels. Not only do we start with it, but it becomes the foundation for whatever else we do. Objectors might

---

[12]It is worthwhile considering the warning of Gaussen: "This disposition which judges the Scriptures, and doubts beforehand of their universal inspiration, is one of the greatest obstacles that we can oppose to their acting with effect. 'The word spoken,' says St Paul (Heb. iv. 2), 'did not profit, not being mixed with faith in them who heart it'" (Louis Gaussen, *Theopneustia: The Plenary Inspiration of the Holy Scriptures: Deduced from Internal Evidence, and the Testimonies of Nature, History and Science*, rev. ed. [Chicago: Bible Institute Colportage, n.d. (1915)], 12).

allege that such a procedure engages in "circular reasoning." We start with a conviction of divine authorship, and then the detailed investigation not only serves various other goals, but also confirms this divine authorship by searching out how we might see harmony among the different Gospel accounts in relation to the mind of God.

We should bear in mind several points. First, no one is free from assumptions or presuppositions. If we are followers of Christ, we believe that he is true and trustworthy and that he is worthy of our allegiance. These are good presuppositions. Good presuppositions help us forward in understanding the truth. Naturally, someone who is still alienated from Christ will not agree. But what basis does he have for his disagreement? If he admits that he does not know whether Christ is the way, then he should humble himself and try to find out the truth rather than criticize people who have already found the truth. If he thinks he already knows that Christ is *not* the way, then his own religious commitments to some *other* way are clearly showing. And you will find that his own religious commitments have no solid basis.[13] Such a person is himself engaging in circular reasoning.

Second, our main goal in studying the Gospels should be to listen to God in all the ways and all the dimensions of his speaking, and to serve him faithfully in response. Understanding "what happened" is one important dimension of this response. But it is only one dimension. Any confirmation or strengthening of our conviction that the Gospels have God as their author is another dimension. But there are many other dimensions, such as growing in loving God and learning who Jesus is, what he accomplished, and what it means to follow him.

Third, our own study of the Gospels involves primarily interaction with God as a person and a speaker and one who loves us. We should not confuse such interaction with the interests of apologetics in having dialogue with those outside the faith. Those outside the faith do not understand the spiritual things of the Gospels: "The natural person does not accept the things of the Spirit of God, for they are folly to him, and he is not able to understand them because they are spiritually discerned" (1 Cor. 2:14).

Fourth, in studying the Gospels we must not worry too much about what unbelievers and skeptics think about us. If they find out what we are actually thinking and how we are going about our study, they will consider us fools. But such has always been the case with Christian belief. Trying to incorporate

---

[13]I am here summarizing in a very short compass a rich expanse of material on presuppositional apologetics in the tradition of Cornelius Van Til. See, e.g., John M. Frame, *Apologetics to the Glory of God: An Introduction* (Phillipsburg, NJ: P&R, 1994).

principles belonging to unbelief *within* our own approach leads to disloyalty, confusion, and disaster.

Fifth, Christians as well as non-Christians may struggle with doubts and unbelief. We should have compassion on anyone having such struggles rather than brushing them away. We should recognize that frank discussion of difficulties and careful weighing of evidence may often help the struggling individual. We should exercise patience.

But we may also have occasion to raise questions about larger assumptions, assumptions about the nature of history, the nature of human responsibility, and God's expectations for the use of our human rational powers in studying his Word.[14] We should be ready, as opportunity offers, to alert fellow Christians to the spiritual and ethical dimensions of how we approach the Bible. In doing so, no one of us should look down on those who struggle. In practice, *any* sin expresses unbelief, that is, a lack of trust in God who has redeemed us and whose ways are wiser than ours. So none of us is free from the underlying problem.

Sixth, in the realm of thought, the basic issue separating Christians from non-Christians is the issue of autonomy of thought. Ever since the fall of Adam, non-Christians have wanted to be autonomous judges and thinkers and decision makers. They want ultimate control of their lives. And to the extent that we Christians give way to sin, we do the same thing. To an autonomous thinker, the process of studying Scripture with a commitment to God and his Word seems circular, because it involves what he thinks is a bad commitment, a commitment to treat as ultimate something outside of himself. To someone who worships autonomy, autonomy is ultimate. Commitment to Scripture seems to be a betrayal of who he is. Before he makes any commitment, the autonomous thinker wants to be allowed autonomously to judge the wisdom of such commitment.

We were created in such a way that we were meant to live "by every word that comes from the mouth of God" (Matt. 4:4). We were not meant for autonomous independence from God. And striving for such independence does not work. It leads to darkness, confusion, disaster, and condemnation.[15] The Christian has a commitment that leads to more light and truth. The non-Christian has a destructive commitment.

Moreover, non-Christians typically do not notice the circularity of their commitment. They appeal to their sense that autonomous thinking is natural and correct when they condemn a Christian approach as circular and

---

[14]Some of these issues are addressed in *Inerrancy and Worldview*, especially chaps. 5–6 on history.
[15]See Poythress, *Inerrancy and Worldview*, chaps. 34–36.

irrational. They appeal to autonomy to establish autonomy. So who is being "circular"?

Presuppositional apologetics has discussed matters of alleged circularity at length.[16] Ultimate commitments by nature are ultimate. So the "circularity" that belongs to Christian faith actually appears in analogous ways in all human living. We need not go into it all here. The main point is that *autonomous* circularity has, in modern times in the Western world, come to seem completely normal, not only to individuals desiring to be the masters of their world, but to a whole cultural atmosphere. The "normality" of it makes it mostly unnoticed, while Christian commitments stand out. Against the background of "standard" cultural assumptions, such commitments appear as not only different or odd but perverse. The feeling of normality and the judgment that Christians are mistaken proves nothing except the depth of modern captivity to sinful delusion.

Principles concerning Confidence and Doubt

We may summarize our reflections in these principles:

1. An attitude of receptivity

Christians should read the Gospels for what they are, the word of God. We may be confident that they are truthful.

2. No neutrality

Christians in dialogue with doubters and unbelievers should not pretend to be neutral, but acknowledge what it means to follow Christ in the arena of thought and knowledge.

3. Autonomy

One principal obstacle to understanding the Gospels is the desire for autonomy.

---

[16]See the discussion of circularity in John M. Frame, *The Doctrine of the Knowledge of God* (Phillipsburg, NJ: Presbyterian and Reformed, 1987), 129–33.

12

SEEKING GOD

God cares about our attitudes. "God opposes the proud, but gives grace to the humble" (James 4:6).[1] In the previous chapter we mentioned Matthew 11:25–27, where Jesus indicates that knowledge of God comes to humble "children."

Prayer for Understanding

Since we need God to give us understanding, we should come to him not only humbly, but prayerfully. We should ask for understanding. Asking is important—God wants to be asked: "Ask, and it will be given to you; seek, and you will find; knock, and it will be opened to you. For everyone who asks receives, and the one who seeks finds, and to the one who knocks it will be opened" (Matt. 7:7–8).

And yet asking is not the whole of it. James warns that some kinds of asking remain fruitless: "You ask and do not receive, because you ask wrongly, to spend it on your passions" (James 4:3). The language "spend it on your passions" may make us think first about someone praying to obtain an expensive new car or a plush new job or the affections of a desired person, that is, a prayer for pleasure or material well-being. But ungodly passions can interfere also with the life of the mind. Do we want to understand the Gospels for the sake of the glory of God and to love Christ more, or do we want to look better and wiser in our own eyes and in the eyes of admirers? Even our good

---

[1]See Vern S. Poythress, *Inerrancy and Worldview: Answering Modern Challenges to the Bible* (Wheaton, IL: Crossway, 2012), chap. 33.

works, including our pursuit of knowledge of God, become contaminated with sinful desires that mingle with godliness. Christians still need the mercy of God. We need his forgiveness for hidden sins as well as for open sins.

So we should include a prayer for godliness. We should pray that we will seek God for the right reasons. We should pray that, being made pure in heart, we "shall see God" (Matt. 5:8). The principle in the beatitudes that we shall see God probably applies primarily to seeing God in the consummation, in the new heavens and the new earth. But, when applied in a broader way, the principle has relevance for seeing God in a metaphorical sense by understanding him and having communion with him through his Word, including his word in the Gospels.

Punishment of the Wayward

The same principle applies in reverse to people whose hearts operate in rebellion against God. Their hearts are not in tune with God, and the desires of their hearts are opposed to actually seeking God. However much they may learn about certain aspects of the Gospels, they miss the main point—communion with God through Christ. They do not understand.

The lack of understanding has more than one cause, on more than one level. On the divine level, people in rebellion do not understand because God brings a judgment of darkness on them as punishment for their rebellion and unbelief.

> The wrath of God is revealed from heaven against all ungodliness and unrighteousness of men, who by their unrighteousness suppress the truth. (Rom. 1:18)

> And since they did not see fit to acknowledge God, God gave them up to a *debased mind* to do what ought not to be done. (Rom. 1:28)

We read of a particularly intense case in 2 Thessalonians 2.

> Therefore God *sends them a strong delusion*, so that they may believe what is false, in order that all may be condemned who did not believe the truth but had pleasure in unrighteousness. (2 Thess. 2:11–12)

Next, on the human level, people do not understand because their hearts are not in tune with the things of God.

> The natural person does not accept the things of the Spirit of God, for they are folly to him, and he is not able to understand them because they are spiritually discerned. (1 Cor. 2:14)

They [Gentiles, unbelievers] are darkened in their understanding, alienated from the life of God because of the ignorance that is in them, due to *their hardness of heart*. (Eph. 4:18)

Finally, Satan and his agents act to confuse and block true understanding.

The coming of the lawless one is by the activity of Satan with all power and false signs and wonders, and with all wicked *deception for those who are perishing*, because they refused to love the truth and so be saved. (2 Thess. 2:9–10)

And even if our gospel is veiled, it is veiled to those who are perishing. In their case *the god of this world* [Satan] *has blinded the minds* of the unbelievers, to keep them from seeing the light of the gospel of the glory of Christ, who is the image of God. (2 Cor. 4:3–4)

God may perhaps grant them [opponents of the gospel] repentance leading to a knowledge of the truth, and they may come to their senses and escape from *the snare of the devil, after being captured by him* to do his will. (2 Tim. 2:25–26)

. . . and by the signs that it [the False Prophet as an agent of Satan] is allowed to work in the presence of the beast it *deceives* those who dwell on earth, telling them to make an image for the beast that was wounded by the sword and yet lived. (Rev. 13:14)

Human hardness of heart and satanic deceit become means in the hands of God by which he works judgment against unbelief.

Pertinence for Believers

The passages we have just cited from the Bible mostly deal with overt unbelief. But covert unbelief lurks even in the recesses of the minds of Christians. All the more do we need to pray, not only for deliverance from sin and for purity of heart, but for grace from God in the midst of remaining sin. Such seeking of God makes sense when we reckon with the fact that ever since the fall of Adam, our hearts and minds have been working corruptly, even when they work very cleverly. Even after our minds are renewed through union with Christ and the Spirit of God (Rom. 12:1–2; Col. 3:10), there remain subtle corruptions, and we remain abnormal in comparison with what we were created to be.

We grow in understanding the Gospels or other parts of the Bible through God's work in delivering us from sinful corruptions that interfere with our humbly receiving what God says.

13

LIMITATIONS IN HUMAN KNOWLEDGE

Even when we study the Gospels carefully, prayerfully, and attentively, we do not understand everything. And what we do understand, we still do not understand to the very bottom. We remain human and finite, and contaminated by sin. We remain limited in knowledge. These limitations operate in all our understanding of life, including our understanding of the Bible.

Limitations with Respect to Issues in Harmonization

Most of the issues in harmonization in the Gospels have to do with apparent historical discrepancies or differences between two or more accounts in the Gospels. Because the Gospels are God's words, we ought to believe that each account in each Gospel gives us truth about what happened and its significance. And by God's wisdom each account contains resources that help us to understand God and to love what we come to understand. We should confidently believe that God knows what he is saying and that he is speaking truthfully at every point when we read the Gospels.

But we sometimes still do not know how it "all fits together." How do we hold together apparently discrepant accounts? If we knew about the events in massive detail, and if we had direct access to God's mind or direct answers from God to all the questions we might ask, we could be confident that we would see the solution to many difficulties.

Things related to God's infinity—and everything relates to God's infinity—include mystery. We will never become God. We will never understand exhaustively, in the same way that God understands himself. But if we knew enough details and enough of his mind—yet still within the capacity of our finiteness—many of our difficulties would have a clear solution.

We know that God knows all the solutions. Yet we cannot demand a clear solution to all our difficulties right now. We do not have massive informative detail about each episode recorded in the Gospels. We have only what the Gospels themselves choose to tell us. And we have certain bits of extrabiblical knowledge, which are more or less reliable but not infallible. For example, we can find out about Jewish customs of the times, the geography of Palestine, the practices of government in the Roman Empire, and the views of various parties like the Pharisees, the Sadducees, and the Essenes. We try to piece it all together.

God knows all the details about what happened. It all makes sense in his mind. But we have our piecemeal knowledge. We cannot insist before God that he must always give us enough information in order to "solve" or dissolve all the difficulties that we perceive. He is God. He does as he pleases (Ps. 115:3). He acts according to the infinitude of his wisdom, a wisdom that he has revealed in a wonderful and spectacular way in the mystery of the crucifixion and resurrection of Christ. He is wise, but we cannot always see that when we want to have more information than the Gospels provide. We must patiently submit to his wisdom in such cases.

This means that we may not always be able to envision a way to explain the events so that we can *see* (rather than just believe) that the various Gospel accounts are in harmony. Even if we struggle and work hard and research well and pray ardently, we may still have to say, "I don't know" or "I can't yet see how they harmonize." That is the kind of life we are in. We are finite and do not know all there is to know. Nor do we know all we would *like* to know or all that we think in *our* wisdom we *should* know in order to live most effectively as Christians. We must be "content" (Phil. 4:11) to let God be God and not to insist that we have the privilege of looking over his shoulder in order to check out whether he has it right.

> O Lord, my heart is not lifted up;
>   my eyes are not raised too high;
> I do not occupy myself with things
>   too great and too marvelous for me.
> But I have calmed and quieted my soul,
>   like a weaned child with its mother;
>   like a weaned child is my soul within me.

O Israel, hope in the LORD
     from this time forth and forevermore. (Psalm 131)

But suppose that after careful work and prayer, we do come up with a harmonization. Usually we can only say that our proposed solution is *possible* or maybe *probable*. A harmonization fills in details taken from more than one account. And in so filling in, it adds to what the Bible directly says. But there may be other possible ways that the details from multiple accounts could fit together. We should not pretend in this situation to be more confident than we have a right to be.

The Ultimacy of the Gospels

Any one account within one Gospel is still completely true. We can trust what it says. We know something—in fact, a good deal. But we cannot confidently fill in all the details. As we have observed (chap. 6), the accounts within the Gospels, because they are God's own word, always remain more ultimate than a hypothetical reconstruction that we undertake to provide on the basis of several Gospels, because our reconstruction brings in speculative elements. God chose to present the accounts as they are in the Gospels. We do not need to go behind them to get "the real truth." We already have the real truth in each Gospel account. But we have the real truth in the context of remaining mysteries concerning details and concerning implications. That is the way it is in listening to God's Word, not only in the Gospels, but every biblical text. God invites us to come deeper into his Word and to deepen our fellowship with him. Thus we may summarize:

1. Finiteness

Not having all the answers is part of our situation as finite creatures.

2. Having enough

We do not need all the answers. Scripture is a sufficient infallible guide for faith and life.

3. Mystery

We have knowledge through the Gospels in the context of remaining mystery. We do not have all the details, nor can we always know definitively how the different accounts in the Gospels fit together.

Limitations in Apologetics

What do we do in addressing unbelievers? In apologetic dialogues with unbelievers, we must simply do the best we can. We must remain consistent with our commitment to being followers of Christ, consistent with our understanding of the folly of unbelief, and consistent with the compassion that we should have toward people who are on average no better or worse than we would be apart from the grace of God.

It is not easy. We are tempted either to become unrighteously irritated at the folly of unbelievers or to sympathize so much with their folly that we no longer consider it folly. We compromise with unbelief by sliding past its sinfulness and too easily agreeing. Or we compromise by adopting a pretended neutral approach. When we have a dialogue with people who inhabit an unbelieving context, we have to be discerning about what is folly and what is a grain of truth—perhaps even a truth that we ourselves have not yet acknowledged. Apologetics is hard, and there is much to be said.

With respect to the Gospels and their harmonization, we must avoid expecting too much or promising too much. We cannot guarantee that we can solve all harmonization problems even to our own satisfaction, much less to the satisfaction of an unbeliever. It is part of our finiteness that we have to say, "I do not know." Sometimes, of course, unbelievers have a specific problem with one or two passages. And sometimes we may be able to help by offering a possible harmonization. But we should admit that our harmonization is only a possibility. We do not know it to be the definitive explanation.

At other times an unbeliever's objections may be more far-reaching. He wants to "check out" everything and have all problems solved before he seriously considers changing his life. Does this "checking out" include the principle of autonomous thought underneath? Many times it does. Then the checking out can never lead to faith, because the underlying attitude already rebels against submitting to God's ways. As opportunity offers, we may still explain how we deal with apparent discrepancies. But we may also find an occasion to indicate gently and firmly that the deepest problem lies elsewhere. Unless an unbeliever sees the problems of his own life and his own would-be autonomy as more life-threatening than the alleged problems in the Gospels, on a human plane he is unlikely to warm up to the mystery of the gospel.

Moreover, we should readily acknowledge to unbelievers that we have placed our faith in Christ and have trusted in the Gospels and their accounts because they are God's word. We have given this trust and this commitment *before* we have "solved all the problems." That is part of what it means to reject autonomy in thought. We reject the serpent's invitation to Eve to judge for herself—independent of God's word. That is part of what it means to be a disciple of Christ. If this kind of topic comes up for discussion in apologetics—and of course it may not—it is just as well that an unbeliever know something about the cost of discipleship (Luke 14:26–33).

Dialogue with Fellow Christians Who Are Not Sure

Analogous principles apply when we are in dialogue with fellow believers who have doubts. We have already spoken about doubts. They are of many kinds. We should not deal with other people's doubts in a way that suggests that we are immune from doubts ourselves, including doubts that embody sinful attitudes. We are saved by grace. That is a good principle never to forget, but rather to apply to the whole Christian life, not just its beginning.

We may address doubts about the claims of the Gospels on several levels: by offering evidence for their being the word of God, by offering possible harmonizations that address alleged discrepancies, and by talking about general principles for addressing difficulties, more or less as we are doing in this book. Much depends on the person we are addressing. People have a variety of struggles and doubts. Some people are more troubled emotionally. Others are more troubled intellectually. Not all of the doubts are necessarily sinful. Some are trials, in which Satan and his agents assail a believer, but the believer has not yet given in.

It is never wrong to be honest before God about where we are in our struggles. It is sometimes not wise to reveal too much of our struggles to a fellow believer who has little understanding or sympathy. Or a fellow believer may be prone to weakness in this area and fall into temptation himself rather than helping us out. But we can often find help from the body of Christ, which God gave us for our edification. Especially godly pastors, scholars, and wise people from previous generations may help.

Responding to the Bible, as we have already indicated, involves ethical responsibility. We have responsibility before God. So matters of doubt need to be addressed ethically, using the normative, situational, and existential perspectives. Some people may be helped by emphasis on the norms, such as God's truthfulness and our obligation to trust him. Others may be helped by emphasis on the situation, which includes a modern cultural atmosphere of autonomy, the finiteness of our knowledge, and our vulnerability to temptation. Others may be helped by emphasis on the existential aspect. With them we may talk about attitudes of autonomy and pride, or submission and humility, or distress and comfort, or doubt and confidence. All these are open to God's inspection, even when human beings do not fully know what is going on in their hearts.

> For the word of God is living and active, sharper than any two-edged sword, piercing to the division of soul and of spirit, of joints and of marrow, and discerning the thoughts and intentions of the heart. And no creature is hidden from his sight, but all are naked and exposed to the eyes of him to whom we must give account. (Heb. 4:12–13)

This same holy God has compassion and mercy in Christ, even when he looks on the ugliness and unholiness of sinful attitudes. "Let us then with confidence draw near to the throne of grace, that we may receive mercy and find grace to help in time of need" (Heb. 4:16).

14

INTELLECTUAL SUFFERING

What happens when we do not succeed in explaining an apparent discrepancy in the Gospels or elsewhere in the Bible? We continue working, in the hope that we will find a resolution and thus advance our understanding of what God says. We may work for a long time. Often, effort of the right kind yields fruit. But suppose nothing comes. Or we find that other people before us have suggested solutions, but none of them seems attractive. None seems right.

Then maybe we should just go on to some other task. We all have limited time on this earth, and we must use that time fruitfully: "Look carefully then how you walk, not as unwise but as wise, making the best use of the time, because the days are evil" (Eph. 5:15–16). If we have to abandon our efforts without fruit, it helps if we keep in mind the ways of God we touched on in the previous chapter. God does not guarantee or promise that we as finite creatures will always find satisfying answers to all our questions, even our questions about the Bible. It is for him to decide how much information and how much insight we have. "We walk by faith, not by sight" (2 Cor. 5:7).

Struggles

Sometimes, depending on the circumstances and the people involved, we may find that we cannot just "walk away" from a difficulty. It troubles us. It eats on our mind. Or it depresses us. Perhaps it tempts us to greater doubts. The question rises in our mind (a temptation from Satan), "Maybe this is not really God's word." Or "maybe you have to reassess how God communicates to human beings; maybe he adopts erroneous channels for his purposes." Sometimes such thoughts do not trouble us. They just flit through the mind and out again. But sometimes they stay. Whether they do stay depends—but on what? We do not always know. We do not know ourselves to the very bottom. Nor do we know the purposes of God to the bottom. Nor do we know when for his own wise and sovereign purposes God may permit temptations from the voice of Satan or his demons to assail us. We do not know all the hidden sins buried in our hearts.

Intellectual Suffering

Intellectual suffering for believers does not always occur merely because of their foolishness or pride. Look at Job. He suffered in the body from his sores (Job 2:7–8). He suffered emotional grief from the loss of his children and his possessions (Job 1:13–19). He suffered intellectually because of the barbs of his "friends," Eliphaz, Bildad, and Zophar. He suffered spiritually because God did not answer—at least not immediately—and what God was doing to him made no sense to him.

Abraham did not know all the answers when he was about to sacrifice Isaac (Heb. 11:17–19). It seemed to make no sense that God would command him to sacrifice the very son who was heir to God's own promises.

The psalmist in Psalm 73 struggles over the prosperity of the wicked.

> For I was envious of the arrogant
> > when I saw the prosperity of the wicked.
>
> For they have no pangs until death;
> > their bodies are fat and sleek.
> They are not in trouble as others are;
> > they are not stricken like the rest of mankind. . . .
>
> But when I thought how to understand this,
> > it seemed to me a wearisome task,
> until I went into the sanctuary of God;
> > then I discerned their end. (Ps. 73:3–5, 16–17)

Psalm 73 is notable for its wrestling with why the wicked prosper. Quite a few other psalms wrestle with why the righteous suffer—in particular, why the psalmist himself is suffering. "My God, my God, why have you forsaken me?" (Ps. 22:1).

Suffering in Fellowship with Christ

The influences of sin and evil in the world are many. Sin and evil produce, as one indirect result, mental conflict for the believer. Believers sometimes struggle with their faith, with an apparent absence of God, with tension between God's promises and his delay in fulfilling them, with the fact that suffering comes to the righteous. This suffering includes mental suffering in circumstances where believers do not find immediate intellectual answers to their questions. All this suffering comes to a climax in the suffering of Christ on the cross. And that suffering, though it can be doctrinally explained, is also mysterious, in the sense that we as human beings never fathom the bottom of it or completely take it in. It seems foolish to the world.

In some of the psalms, as well as in Job, the mental sufferings include mental anguish over the tension between God's promises and his seeming inaction when the righteous suffer. Righteous sufferers cry out, "How long?" (Ps. 13:1–2); "Why do you hide your face? / Why do you forget our afflic-tion and oppression?" (Ps. 44:24); "Why, O LORD, do you stand far away?" (Ps. 10:1). These psalmists struggle with how all God's promises could fit together harmoniously. Maybe we should not be shocked to find that it can at times be desperately hard for *us* to fit disparate Scriptures together, and to fit them together with our own lives, particularly when we are struggling with temptation to doubt God.

So intellectual struggles provide a glimpse, offered by God himself, into the sufferings of others, like those who cry out in the Psalms. According to the New Testament, the Psalms point forward to Christ. The righteous suffering in the Psalms anticipates and foreshadows the suffering of the one uniquely righteous sufferer, Christ on the cross. In his anguish Christ cried out, "My God, my God, why have you forsaken me?" (Ps. 22:1). This cry seems to show that Christ's relation to the Psalms includes a relation to the element of intellectual suffering in the Psalms. Dare we think it? Did Christ himself suffer in *this* intellectual way also as a man, yet without sin (Heb. 4:15)? What does it mean that he cried out, "My God, my God, why have you forsaken me?" What does the "why" mean? Did Satan attack him with doubts?

Christ repulsed the attacks, whatever they were. He did not succumb when tempted. But Satan did tempt him, according to Matthew 4:1–10. Did Christ suffer even more intensely than we do when we experience intellectual struggles? Is this one aspect of our being given the privilege of sharing "his sufferings" (Phil. 3:10)? With awe and reverence, we may understand how intimately Christ sympathizes with our weaknesses (Heb. 4:15–16).

Dying and Rising with Christ

Intellectual as well as spiritual growth comes in a healthy way through union with Christ. This kind of intellectual growth means dying and rising with Christ. In a sense, the dying and rising with Christ takes place once, when we become Christians and are first united to him (Rom. 6:4, 8; Col. 2:20; 3:1). But the pattern is then repeated, in a lower key as it were, throughout this life.

> . . . always carrying in the body the death of Jesus, so that the life of Jesus may also be manifested in our bodies. For we who live are always being given over to death for Jesus' sake, so that the life of Jesus also may be manifested in our mortal flesh. So death is at work in us, but life in you. (2 Cor. 4:10–12)

God and man have been reconciled, and so there will be fruit in the progressive reconciliation taking place in our hearts. Our hearts become reconciled to God not only in the sense that God forgives our sins, but in the sense that our hearts come more and more into submission and conformity to the mind of God and of Christ, who is the Logos, expressing himself in Scripture. Christ calls us as his disciples to bear our cross daily that we may "know him [Christ] and the power of his resurrection, and may share his sufferings, becoming like him in his death" (Phil. 3:10). We may therefore expect to have our minds and our hermeneutical principles and all that is intellectually dear to us suffer and be crucified and raised, in the process of having our minds conformed to the rationality of the Logos (Rom. 12:1–2). Intellectual anguish among God's people is for our good (Heb. 12:5–11).

We may conclude that intellectual difficulties with the Bible are not, in the end, alien to the mystery of the suffering of Christ. In knowing God's Word we know truly, but not transparently, and not without being beset by mental anguish at times. All these reflections have a place within orthodox thinking about the unity of the teaching of Scripture.

Intellectual Pride

Why do people avoid the route of intellectual suffering? Part of the answer is that we are protective of our own comfort and prefer a certain kind of intellectual comfort to mental suffering. But there is another, complementary answer that also gets close to the root of the matter. Human sin always has at its root human pride and self-centeredness. "You will be like God," Satan promises (Gen. 3:5). And one form of pride in intellectual circles like those of biblical scholarship is intellectual pride. Human intellectual pride reflects a desire to be like God in the arena of knowledge. A person wants to be autonomous in knowledge, both in order to sit in judgment on alleged revelations from God and to be able to escape the claims of God (when they prove uncomfortable) through intellectual excuses.

Spiritual War

Temptations sometimes find a hold because we leave hidden sin in our lives, and this remaining sin becomes a key point of entry for more temptation. The same is true for temptations of an intellectual sort. We may have in our hearts a remnant of intellectual pride. We tell ourselves that we are smart and that we can figure out this or that apparent discrepancy in the Bible. The disappointment in not "figuring it out" opens a platform for temptation. The remnant of autonomy in our heart says, "I will decide on what terms answers will come, and in this case I insist that an answer must come." Such autonomy presumes to tell God what he must do. And then the heart may say, "If I find no answer, there is no answer." This reasoning has underneath it the attitude that the human mind is the final arbiter for answers. It says, "This piece in the Bible represents an error; it is not trustworthy."

Such thoughts may go through our minds even as our minds partly shrink back from them. A mental war rages. It is an instance of spiritual warfare.

> Finally, be strong in the Lord and in the strength of his might. Put on the whole armor of God, that you may be able to stand against the schemes of the devil. For we do not wrestle against flesh and blood, but against the rulers, against the authorities, against the cosmic powers over this present darkness, against the spiritual forces of evil in the heavenly places. Therefore take up the whole armor of God, that you may be able to withstand in the evil day, and having done all, to stand firm. Stand therefore, having fastened on the belt of truth, and having put on the breastplate of righteousness, and, as shoes for your feet, having put on the readiness given by the gospel of peace. In all circumstances take up the shield of faith, with which you can extinguish all the flaming darts of the evil one; and take the helmet of salvation, and the sword of the Spirit, which is the word of God, praying at all times in the Spirit, with all prayer and supplication. To that end keep alert with all perseverance, making supplication for all the saints. (Eph. 6:10–18)

The equipment for the war is just what the passage describes. Knowledge of the gospel and of God and his Word are vital. The battle is not easy—our whole heart is involved.

Accumulations in Situational and Personal Perspective

Sometimes doubts and temptations take hold not after one apparent difficulty, but after an accumulation of them. A student from a believing background may attend a college or a seminary where professors profess to be pious but rain down on the student an ever-larger accumulation of difficulties about the Bible. Perhaps they enlist multiple instances of discrepancies in the Gospels. They also promote an atmosphere or framework for knowledge and investigation that redefines the significance of such apparent discrepancies. The professors offer to tell us what has significance, how we assess it, and why a modernist, postmodernist, materialist, neoorthodox, or other framework makes the most sense.

A student in such a setting needs to assess the *situation* and not naively concede that it is giving him the right norms. The student needs *normatively* to ask whether God is calling him to remain in a situation when he has the freedom to walk away. He may go to some other school and learn from people whom the Bible pronounces wiser (Prov. 1:7). He needs to ask *existentially* whether his pride in his capabilities keeps him in a situation that he normatively should avoid.

Intellectual pride can expose us. When I was in a doctoral program in New Testament, I was concentrating on the writings of the apostle Paul and his theology. I remember vividly to this day one book that had played a prominent role in the history of scholarly thinking about Paul. I will not mention which one. I judged that I had to read it because it represented quite original thinking in its time. I read through it all, but found myself having to read it in small pieces because it made me almost physically sick by its blasphemous attitude.

An ordinary believer, I would say, should put such a book down after a few pages once its tendency becomes visible. There is no need to do otherwise, and no time either. We must use the time wisely (Eph. 5:16). We must be circumspect, rather than show pride by reading anything and everything and showing that we are smart enough and hardy enough to survive.[1] "Finally, brothers, whatever is true, whatever is honorable, whatever is just, whatever is pure, whatever is lovely, whatever is commendable, if there is any excellence, if there is anything worthy of praise, think about these things" (Phil. 4:8). I nevertheless read the book because I judged that the Lord was calling me to specialized work. And I believe that the Lord protected me, partly *by* the

---

[1] See Vern S. Poythress, *In the Beginning Was the Word: Language—A God-Centered Approach* (Wheaton, IL: Crossway, 2009), chap. 21.

physical revulsion that he allowed the book to produce in me. The physical revulsion helped to warn me against its spiritual poison.

I mention this case because it is better to walk away from soul-destroying attacks in college or seminary or doctoral work than to press on pridefully to prove to yourself and others your intellectual ability and spiritual stamina. I am not saying that a person should retreat into a ghetto where he no longer asks or hears challenging questions. I am saying that a person may have to step back for a while in order to have time and thought and prayer and resources from other godly people, and above all from God. Resources that the Holy Spirit provides enable a person in the long run to grow in abilities not only to resist temptation himself but also to impart skills that help in rescuing others. There is a spiritual war on, my friends, and intellectual attack is a part of it.

Pride within Orthodoxy

Mainstream critical scholarship represents only one form of intellectual pride. Intellectual pride can also contaminate theological work within the orthodox camp. But the temptations differ from one person to another. Many people are not tempted in this area. They humbly receive the Bible as God's word and do not worry about difficulties. They simply trust the Lord and are confident about what the Bible teaches. They leave to experts the consideration of puzzles and difficulties in harmonization. Their attitude is commendable.

But what about those who do enter into a consideration of difficulties? Challenges confront them. For example, a Bible student may identify his human understanding of the Bible with divine understanding. The prideful orthodox may think, "The Bible is so transparently clear to me that I can master its meaning as the meaning of God without ifs, ands, or buts." Thus he subtly twists the doctrine of the clarity of Scripture into an abolition of the Creator-creature distinction in the area of epistemology. He thinks, "When I read the Scripture in a reasonable mood, my thought is purely identical with God's thought." And so he makes himself divine, in his pride and his imagination, and then begins to lord it over others on the strength of his alleged divine understanding. Few people exercise this kind of pride in a thoroughgoing way. But the tendency can still be there in subtler forms.

When we deal with difficulties in harmonization, this kind of pride can mislead in more than one direction. In one direction lies "wooden harmonization." Overconfidence can create harmonization accounts that are forced and artificial. It can push texts in directions they do not invite out of pressure to come up with an answer. And sometimes the artificial answer is the product of artificial standards for precision or exactitude, standards that do not fully appreciate the Gospels themselves, with their ordinary language and their omission of details.

In the second direction lie temptations for people who want to deny that difficulties exist. Suppose, for example, that Tom does not want there to be any difficulties. Tom has a robust doctrine of Scripture, the doctrine summarizing the Bible's teaching about itself. That is all to the good. He is confident about his doctrine, but does not want to answer other people's questions about detailed difficulties. He would rather brush aside the difficulties because they create tensions with a comfortable world of thought he has made for himself, in which he imagines that there are no difficulties. He is impatient with the people who become troubled with the difficulties. He may impatiently dismiss other people with a simple recipe that their questions are "unspiritual."

Mirroring Pride

In fact, intellectual pride among the critics and among the orthodox can be mirror images of one another, in the sense that each can feed off the other. The orthodox in reaction to the critics' prideful refusal to submit to the plain meaning of Scripture champions the plain meaning, even when in particular cases it is not as plain as he thinks. He is angry about the critics' sin of unbelief. But his anger is not wholly righteous anger. It is contaminated by the pride in his supposed superiority to the critics, in that he has seen the fallacy and disloyalty to God that underlie critical approaches. His righteous anger moves him to destroy the opponents' heresy. But the contamination by human pride tempts him to triumph over autonomous intellectuals with the power of his own reason, and this move conceals autonomous desire on his own part.

And the converse holds: the critic, detecting the pride and woodenness and defensiveness on the part of the orthodox, reacts to the opposite side of the pendulum. Through his intellectual keenness he detects the intellectual dishonesty in the prideful orthodox. He takes pride in his "intellectual honesty" and in having seen through the proud dishonesty of his opponent. He thinks he clearly sees the proper fix for the authoritarian dogmatism of the prideful orthodox. So he tries to "fix" orthodoxy by reinterpreting—actually, misinterpreting—the transcendence of God as if it meant that God's thoughts were completely inaccessible. His view is that no one is allowed to be authoritarian because no one can know. And so the critic attacks his opponent, not with principles of biblical truth, but with his proud distortion of those principles.

Pride exists on both sides: an autonomously conceived biblical exegesis is allowed by modernist theology and neoorthodoxy; a dictatorial theological dogmatism can spring up within the bounds of orthodoxy. God gives us the Bible as a "light to my path" (Ps. 119:105). We can have genuine confidence when we receive his instruction. But this confidence can be perverted through sin into pride. The prideful orthodox thinks he has an exact mastery of every question, and he can look down on anyone who does not agree with his opinions. The prideful neoorthodox, emphasizing the wholly hidden god deriving from his conception of transcendence, intends to cut off the pride of the orthodox. But he allows for autonomous reason to feel that it has competence to expose fallibility and error in particular texts and in their alleged disharmony with one another.

We may illustrate the operation of pride by returning to our example with the centurion's servant. The orthodox person might pridefully come with a preconceived idea that the Bible must present us with a correct mental picture. Since reading Matthew alone leads to a mental picture in which the centurion talks directly to Jesus, a direct exchange *must* have taken place subsequent to the messages conveyed by the Jewish elders and the centurion's friends in Luke 7:1–10. In the earlier discussion of these passages (chap. 2), I have indicated that I think it is possible that the centurion came in person at a separate stage; but such a sequence of events should not be insisted on as if it were the only possibility. If someone *insists* that it is the only possibility, based on a mental-picture theory of truth, I believe he is offering a wooden harmonization. It presumes to expect too much and has become distorted by reliance on the flawed mental-picture theory.

In fact, I think the solution offered by Augustine and Calvin is more likely. But then in making these judgments I am not completely free from pride myself. Perhaps my pride has led me too quickly to dismiss alternatives, to which I should listen respectfully.

On the other side, we can imagine a critic overconfidently taking the reference to the centurion's servant as a "clear case" of error that allegedly undermines the "ignorant" view that the Bible is God's word. The critic is likely to be bringing in unwarranted expectations and standards about error and about what a divine communication would look like. Pride may be a factor keeping him from questioning his assumptions, as well as keeping him from admitting that he needs a supernatural remedy not only from his sins in general, but from the sinful effects on his intellectual judgments.

Summary Principles about Suffering

1. The reality of intellectual suffering

People may suffer intellectually and spiritually because of difficulties in the Bible, including apparent discrepancies for which they find no satisfying solutions.

2. God's understanding in Christ

God understands our sufferings, and Christ our high priest "sympathizes with our weaknesses" (Heb. 4:15).

3. Suffering revealing Christ

God can use intellectual suffering for making us grow in appreciation of the suffering of Christ on our behalf.

4. Pride avoiding suffering

Pride may try to avoid suffering by producing simple but heavy-handed solutions.

15

Positive Purposes
for Difficulties

Why did God write a Bible with difficulties in it? Some doctrines, like the doctrine of the Trinity, are innately mysterious. Difficulties for human understanding *necessarily* accompany such a doctrine because God is innately beyond our ability to comprehend. But why does God include in the Bible extra, seemingly "unnecessary" difficulties like the apparent discrepancies in Matthew's and Luke's accounts about the centurion's servant?

God's Transforming Us

God always speaks wisely. But he does not tell us everything about his wisdom. He does not tell us all the whys. But we may sometimes get a glimmering about some of the possibilities as to why. In the case of the centurion's servant, the differences help Matthew to highlight the centurion's Gentile status and to highlight the contrast between his faith and Jewish unbelief (Matt. 8:10–12). Luke's mention of the elders of the Jews and the contrast between "worthy" (Luke 7:4) and "not worthy" (Luke 7:6) highlights the centurion's humility and thereby underlines the importance of humility in the lives of those who would follow Jesus.

If we pay careful attention to the distinct nuances in the two accounts, we may be richer than if we just had one account (see chap. 2). The difficulty in the differences between the two accounts may be used by God to force us to pay closer attention in the hope of finding some solution. As we pay attention, God has his purposes not merely to provide information, but also to transform us.

Engendering Humility

God may use the difficulties in a less obvious way, not so much to teach things that we might otherwise overlook, but to engender humility in our attitudes. Any difficulty that does not quickly yield to our investigation testifies to the fact that God is greater than we are and that he understands what we do not. Moreover, when we confront a difficulty, it may test whether we think we are right and God is wrong. We then have an opportunity for reflection. We can take time to remember that our mental abilities and our discernment and our insights belong *under* the supremacy of God.

We may also grow in humility. We exercise humility if we resist the temptation to think ourselves superior. We acknowledge our weakness, our fallibility, our limited knowledge, and the possible interference of sin. We acknowledge God's superiority. We deepen our worship of God and grow in our desire to honor him rather than ourselves. We acknowledge these things both to ourselves and to God, and, as appropriate, to others.

Intellectual Pride

The difficulties in the Bible serve to raise the issue of pride. Pride—really, the worship of self—finds itself at the root of many sins. In some sense it may be the root of them all. Adam and Eve valued their own judgment over God's. And that was the beginning of pride in the human race. To reconcile us to God, God has to destroy that pride.

Should it be surprising that in intellectuals, pride frequently takes the form of intellectual pride, pride in one's ability to think, discern, evaluate, separate truth from error? After all, the intellectuals, if they allowed themselves to admit it, might say that they have plenty to be proud about. They might say that mental power is worth more than mere physical power, as the builder of a bomb or of a skyscraper could say about a ditch digger. Knowledge is power. And mental power is power to gain knowledge and master knowledge. Of course it is all the gift of God (1 Cor. 4:7). But whatever gifts we may have, we find it convenient in pride to forget the giver.

All people are vulnerable to being proud of what they are good at. So intellectuals take pride in intellectual ability. When God rescues us, he has to crucify this pride.

Crucifixion with Christ

Crucifixion means painful death. Christ underwent death for our sake. He bore the punishment of sin as our substitute. If we trust in him, we are free (Rom. 8:1). But Christ's crucifixion and death apply to us in another way. We are joined with him, united with him, in such a way that his crucifixion and death have effects in transforming us. "We know that our old self was *crucified with him* in order that the body of sin might be brought to nothing, so that we would no longer be enslaved to sin" (Rom. 6:6). *We* have to die to pride and to our old life. Intellectuals have to die to intellectual pride. They have to undergo *mental crucifixion*. It is agonizing. It is possible only because Christ is with them. He underwent it first—not that he had any sinful pride, but in his crucifixion he underwent the agony in order to deliver *us* from our pride. And this deliverance includes deliverance from intellectual pride.

That is one reason why suffering is necessary. And for intellectuals, intellectual suffering is necessary. Do not be surprised. Do not seek to avoid the Lord's discipline in this area (Heb. 12:3–14).

Encouraging Faith in God

Intellectual suffering may have other benefits. God may be glorified and honored in the midst of suffering. Glory may come to God in ways of which we are not aware. But in addition, we ourselves may benefit. We grow in faith when we learn to trust God for what we do not yet understand, as well as to trust him in what we do understand from his Word. Difficult cases challenge us more radically because they confront us with the challenge to trust God when it looks as though he cannot be trusted. This experience is not new or unique to the present time. What did Abraham think when God called on him to sacrifice Isaac? Did it seem to Abraham that God was not trustworthy in this one instance? What did David think when he was pursued by Saul? What did Job think? Supremely, what did Jesus think when he confronted the cross?

The scoffers at the cross said, "He trusts in God; let God deliver him now, if he desires him. For he said, 'I am the Son of God.'" (Matt. 27:43). "He trusts in God." Yes, he did. He did so in spite of the fact that superficially all the supposed "evidence" appeared to show that God had abandoned him and was letting him die in a situation of horrid injustice. Superficially, there was an intellectual and spiritual discrepancy between his being left to die and God's explicit commitment to deliver the righteous. He trusted in God. We should too.

In a fundamental way, trust in the matter of intellectual questions or historical difficulties or apparent discrepancies or biblical paradoxes remains part of the general obligation to trust God in every area of life. We have good grounds for trust, because of God's character and the faithfulness of his Word. He is infinitely good. We have grounds also in the demonstration of his goodness and faithfulness throughout history. Supremely, we have grounds in the crucifixion and resurrection of Christ. God shows there his supreme commitment to righteousness: Christ was vindicated and sin received its due payment in Christ as substitute. God showed there his supreme commitment to truth: his promises of redemption proved true, at supreme cost to himself. He showed his supreme commitment to *us* in the love that he manifested in the cross. He displayed the glory of his character and of his love.

> God shows his love for us in that while we were still sinners, Christ died for us. (Rom. 5:8)

> If God is for us, who can be against us? He who did not spare his own Son but gave him up for us all, how will he not also with him graciously give us all things? Who shall bring any charge against God's elect? It is God who justifies. Who is to condemn? (Rom. 8:31–34)

In Paul's expression of confidence in Romans 8, he includes reflections about suffering.

> Who shall separate us from the love of Christ? Shall tribulation, or distress, or persecution, or famine, or nakedness, or danger, or sword? As it is written, "For your sake we are being killed all the day long; we are regarded as sheep to be slaughtered." No, in all these things we are more than conquerors through him who loved us. (Rom. 8:35–37)

We should trust God when we suffer. It gives us an occasion to remember God's promises and to reflect on the wonder involved in the suffering of Christ for us. In particular, intellectual suffering gives us opportunity to exercise faith in difficult circumstances. "Suffering produces endurance" (Rom. 5:3) and other graces.

God also sends trials to test people. He tested the Israelites in the wilderness. Testing can confirm and strengthen faith or reveal lack of faith. What is true for testing in general is true for intellectual testing in particular. The difficulties in the Bible have purposes, even when we may not be aware of those purposes.

Simple Relief

Some modern people who would like to "help out" the Christian faith attempt to give us an easy way out of intellectual suffering. The most common outlet consists in just going along with the crowd. The voices offering relief may say: "People nowadays just can't believe that old stuff. Christianity must jettison all its ancient unnecessary baggage and get down to the essence of the matter, which consists in loving God and loving neighbor"—as if that alleged essence were easy, or as if practicing love by itself were an answer to the threat of punishment for sins already committed.

Other detractors offer more detail in their notions of help. Here are some proposals:

- "The Bible is a mix of good and bad. Accept the fact."
- "The Bible has errors in it. Just accept it. You can still hold to the main points."
- "The Bible is merely a human report of divine action or divine revelation. The difficulties are merely the product of the human channel."
- "God is okay with errors in his book as a witness to the humanity of the channel he uses."
- "The Bible becomes the word of God when God uses it. There are errors in it, but these too can become a channel for God's coming to you. Do not confuse the channel with God."

People have put out these and still other recipes. We may expect to see more in the future. And we have certainly seen similar formulas in the past. Satan's original temptation consisted in throwing doubt on the reliability of God's word (Gen. 3:4–5). He will not give up on this kind of attack.

People who put out such recipes are searching for some way to live with two sides: (1) They want in some sense to affirm a religious presence in the Bible, perhaps even a voice from God. (2) They want to assure us that once we have their solution, the discrepancies or our intellectual struggles over the discrepancies may quickly dissolve. These people appear to mean well. Many of them look compassionately at the Christian college students laboring to hold up under the loads delivered by skeptical professors.

Despite the apparently good intentions, all such recipes appear to boil down to one conclusion: intellectual crucifixion is not necessary. This conclusion is cheap religion. It is a lie. A comfortable lie, but a lie none the less.

People who have come up with these proposed solutions may do so for a great variety of reasons. Some of them may have suffered intellectual agonies themselves at an earlier point in their lives, when they held to the view that the Bible was infallible. I do not depreciate their sufferings. But the renunciation of suffering short-circuits the truth about Christian living.

And, at the end of the day, it fails at the center: the cross of Christ. Christ suffered. Are you willing to suffer with him? Abraham suffered when he went to offer up Isaac.

I said that I do not depreciate the agonies of intellectual suffering that some people may have gone through. Only God knows the story of each of us. But for the sake of balance I should also note that sometimes we give in to temptation under less violent circumstances. Most of us have not come to the point of being screaming martyrs stretched on the rack or whipped until unconscious (Heb. 12:4). Instead, we give in for fear of snickers! We swallow the propaganda that the Bible is outmoded for fear of being thought foolish or ignorant or uncool. Or maybe we yield when we face the threat of losing a grade or a job or a diploma.

Or maybe, without admitting it to ourselves, we toy with disloyalty to the Word of God because that is convenient for our pleasures. We create for ourselves space for some independence of judgment in one area (history or science). But it leads to something else. It offers the opportunity, by a subtle transition, to loosen up elsewhere concerning the demands of God's holiness. We makes space for ourselves to participate in our hedonistic environment, but retain a good conscience by refraining from the grossest excesses. We are lured by "Babylon the great, mother of prostitutes and of earth's abominations" (Rev. 17:5). We excuse ourselves by telling ourselves that we are only adapting to the world for the sake of winning souls who are in the world. The temptation is more insidious because less violent and less direct. How much will we sell for the sake of pride or pleasure?

Judgmental Purposes in the Difficulties

God's purposes, we have said, are mysterious. But we can see some purposes. And one further purpose that God's Word serves is to bring judgment on those who resist it.

> For we [proclaimers of the gospel] are the aroma of Christ to God among those who are begin saved and among those who are perishing, to one a fragrance from death to death, to the other a fragrance from life to life. (2 Cor. 2:15–16)

> And he [God] said, "Go, and say to this people:
>
>> "'Keep on hearing, but do not understand;
>> keep on seeing, but do not perceive.'
>> Make the heart of this people dull,
>>   and their ears heavy,

> and blind their eyes;
> lest they see with their eyes,
> and hear with their ears,
> and understand with their hearts,
> and turn and be healed." (Isa. 6:9–10)

First Corinthians 3:19 says, "For the wisdom of this world is folly with God. For it is written, 'He catches the wise in their craftiness.'" Difficulties in the Bible can catch "the wise." They catch those who are proud in their vaunted "wisdom." The proud know, they think, when they see an error. But God uses his Word to bring darkness on them, the darkness of having misunderstood and mistakenly evaluated.

God is wise. An intellectual will not win in a duel against him.

Principles concerning Purposes in Difficulties

1. Mystery in difficulties

We do not know all the reasons why God has seen fit to put difficulties in the Bible.

2. Positive divine purposes in the difficulties

God has purposes in the difficulties. He encourages care, attention, human transformation, humility, faith, endurance. He receives glory and honor, perhaps in ways of which we are not aware.

3. Intellectual suffering

Intellectual suffering is to be expected as one aspect of Christian calling to follow Christ. Intellectual suffering, properly received, gives us fellowship with the suffering of Christ (Phil. 3:10). We honor God by suffering for his sake.

4. Crucifixion of pride

Intellectual suffering, properly received, is used by God to destroy pride, particularly intellectual pride. We learn to honor God as God.

5. Recipes for relief

Simplistic formulas for relieving intellectual suffering over the difficulties in the Bible evade the necessity of the cross. They open the door to making man autonomous.

6. Trapping "the wise"

God uses the difficulties in the Bible to bring darkness to the proud—in particular, those who fancy themselves able to sit in judgment over what is true and false in the Bible.

It is wise, then—for negative as well as positive reasons—that we come to God and diligently ask him to give us open ears and humble hearts. May he free us, through the cleansing blood of Christ and the power of his resurrection, from the haunting curse of pride. May he lead us as the good shepherd into a life of freedom in serving him and loving him. May we honor him as God and display his glory by our obedience, especially when that obedience is hard. Such service and love should play a central role in our study of the Gospels, as well as in the study of the rest of God's Word. They have a role in all of life.

PART FOUR

SPECIAL ISSUES
IN HARMONIZATION

16

The Synoptic Problem

We have now considered the normative, situational, and personal perspectives on the ethics of studying the Gospels. We are almost ready to plunge into a study of particular passages and their difficulties. But two more specialized issues remain in the wings. We will consider them briefly in this and the next chapter. Our first topic is the synoptic problem. What is it, and how does it affect our interpretation of the Gospels in their details?

The Nature of the Synoptic Problem

Briefly, the "synoptic problem" is the name scholars have given to discussions about the *literary relationship* between the three Synoptic Gospels, namely Matthew, Mark, and Luke.[1] In comparison with the Gospel of John, Matthew, Mark, and Luke show many commonalities, not only in the episodes that they include, but also in the manner in which they present the events. These three Gospels have been called synoptic because they share a common view. As we have seen, each of the three Synoptic Gospels at a finer level of analysis has its own distinctiveness. But they have many similarities.

The similarities include considerable commonality in the order of episodes—though there are variations as well. And the similarities extend to the

---

[1] See, e.g., D. A. Carson and Douglas J. Moo, *An Introduction to the New Testament*, 2nd ed. (Grand Rapids: Zondervan, 2005), 85–103; Donald Guthrie, *New Testament Introduction*, rev. ed. (Downers Grove, IL: InterVarsity, 1990), 136–208, 1029–45; Richard T. France, *Matthew: Evangelist and Teacher* (Downers Grove, IL: InterVarsity, 1989), 24–49; David Alan Black and David R. Beck, eds., *Rethinking the Synoptic Problem* (Grand Rapids: Baker, 2001).

words describing the events, not merely the events themselves. The similarities are so extensive that many scholars have suspected that the Synoptic Gospels have a direct or indirect literary relationship to one another. The most common theory is that Matthew and Luke both used Mark. Matthew and Luke also share material that is not found in Mark, composed mostly of sayings of Jesus. Some scholars have hypothesized that in addition to Mark there once existed another source, "Q," which contained these sayings.

Two Ways of Using a Source

Let us begin by concentrating on two pieces of this puzzle. Did Luke use Mark? And if he did, what difference does it make in how we read Luke?

First, did Luke use Mark? Would such use be consistent with God's inspiring Luke and making the Gospel of Luke God's writing as well as Luke's? Inspiration affirms the divine authority of the product, the text of Luke. By itself, it does not specify the means that God may have used in the processes leading up to the product. Some books, like the book of Revelation, came about as a product of special visions that God gave to the human author. Luke 1:3 indicates that Luke engaged in historical research: "It seemed good to me also, having *followed all things closely for some time past*, to write an orderly account for you." God superintended this research. At the end of this period of research, God through his Holy Spirit empowered Luke in his writing in such a way that the Gospel of Luke, the product, was God's speech in written form: "For no prophecy was ever produced by the will of man, but men spoke *from God* as they were carried along *by the Holy Spirit*" (2 Pet. 1:21). We can have confidence in the product without knowing all the means that God used in Luke and in his research to bring about the product.

Luke 1:2 mentions "eyewitnesses and ministers of the word." It is likely that Luke interviewed some of them. He also mentions written sources: "many have undertaken to compile a narrative" (1:1). Nothing forbade Luke from using Mark if Mark was one of these written sources available to him. In addition, nothing forbade him from using ordinary, noninspired sources as well, as long as we understand that the Holy Spirit supervised his use of all his sources and that the resulting product really is God's writing through Luke.

How Do We Weigh the Use of a Source?

So Luke could have used Mark. Suppose he did. What difference does it make in how we read Luke? It depends on *how* Luke used Mark. What does Luke indicate about his use? We can consider a variety of ways in which one author uses another. Consider an ordinary human situation. Suppose Sue uses a writing by Donna. Sue could state explicitly that she is using Donna's material. She could do so without directly evaluating Donna's material, or she could express approval or disapproval of this or that piece of it. If Sue chooses to make Donna's material an explicit subject for discussion, we obviously have to consider the interaction between what Donna says and what Sue says about it, because Sue herself constrains us to do so. But Luke does not do that. He does not explicitly quote Mark or explicitly indicate that he is approving or disapproving of some source.

What if Sue uses some of Donna's material, but makes no explicit mention of what she is doing and gives no special indication of her source or sources? In our day we have expectations and social conventions about so-called intellectual property. Intellectual property is actually a debatable label and involves many issues.[2] Prior to the last few centuries, in ordinary communication people like Sue freely used other people's ideas and words without always explicitly acknowledging it. If Sue quoted from a culturally well-known source, her recipients could be expected to recognize what she was doing. If the source was regarded as authoritative, that might make a difference in reinforcing or grounding what Sue claimed. For example, the Jews regarded the Old Testament as authoritative—but many Gentiles in the Roman Empire did not. But whether or not Sue used authoritative sources as further support, she would have to take responsibility for what she said.

What happens if we assume that Luke used Mark? Luke's use of Mark is not quite like Luke's explicitly citing the Old Testament. An explicit citation makes visible the source, and the source in the Old Testament would have been well known at the time when Luke wrote. In contrast to the Old Testament, Mark would have been a recent writing. Luke could not be sure that all his readers would be so familiar with it that they would immediately recognize what he was doing. Even if they did recognize it, Luke, by not making Mark visible to readers, made a commitment to take responsibility himself for what he was writing. He took responsibility for what he added to Mark, and for what he altered from Mark, and for what he left the same.

So-called "redaction criticism," when it was first used, paid special attention to changes that an editor made to his sources. It asked how Luke *differs* from Mark. Highlighting the differences can sensitize us to subtleties and nuances that we might otherwise overlook. This sensitization can in fact be valuable, whether or not Luke used Mark. Even if we assume that the two Gospels just appeared side by side, with no literary dependence, their differences highlight some of the distinctive concerns both of Luke and of Mark.

---

[2]See Vern S. Poythress, "Copyrights and Copying: Why the Laws Should Be Changed," 2005, accessed June 7, 2010, http://www.frame-poythress.org/poythress_articles/2005Copyrights.htm.

Integrity of a Single Discourse

But there is a danger that in proceeding this way we may in fact exaggerate the differences. In fact, in the use of redaction criticism, some scholars fell into the pattern of thinking that what Luke added or changed was his, whereas what was the same as in Mark could be ignored. That is not fair to Luke. If he included a passage from Mark completely unchanged, it was because he wanted to include it unchanged. By including it he made it his own. It is what Luke says, just as much as are the things that he says that do not happen to appear in Mark. It is all his. More significant, it is all God's: God speaks all of it. We should read it all and pay attention to all of it.

We can make a similar point by considering the procedure of a redaction critic: he reads Luke line by line, or even word by word, with Mark constantly at his side, doing line-by-line and even word-by-word comparisons. He tries to second-guess why certain changes were made. He asks himself, "What was the motivation here?" But this kind of reading is artificial. It is not really the way Luke invites us to read his writing. He wants us not to read what he wrote in a comparative way, line by line, but to read it "originally"—we are supposed to treat his book as a full-blooded writing in its own right. When Luke says the same thing that Mark says, God wants us to read it just as seriously as when he puts in something that Mark did not say. Both kinds of pieces are God's communication through Luke.

In other words, God invites us to read Luke as a whole piece. Yes, God wrote other discourses, including the Gospel of Mark. But he wrote each as a distinct whole. We need to pay attention to what God says in all of Luke, taking the whole book together. And we pay attention to what he says in all of Mark, taken together. This attentiveness includes both what is distinctive and what is common to both. Because both books are part of a larger collection—the biblical canon—God also invites us to read the two together. But when we do so, we do it in a way that also respects what each says as a whole book. That means that whether Luke used Mark or Mark used Luke or both used a common source or both wrote independently has little effect. Each writing is to be taken as having full communicative power, both according to God's design and according to the design of the human author working under God's power. R. T. France makes a similar point.

> To approach Matthew without a firm conviction either of the priority of Mark or of that of Matthew does not prevent one from listening to his gospel as a whole, allowing it to make its own distinctive impact through its structure, its selection of themes, and its recurrent emphases. Nor does a suspension of judgement on the question of literary relationships prevent one from compar-

ing Matthew fruitfully with each of the other gospels, not in terms of one of them "using," "following" or "changing" another, but in order to see where the differences lie. To be unwilling to say that at this point Matthew has altered Mark's text (or vice versa) in a particular way does not disqualify one from noticing that they present the same story or the same teaching in different ways, and from drawing the appropriate conclusions as to their distinctive theological interests.[3]

We can put it another way. The meaning of a discourse, that is, of a verbal communication, consists in what it says, not in the history of its origin. This principle in fact holds even when a discourse explicitly cites from and discusses an earlier source. Even in this kind of special case of citation, the author calls on us to attend to what he says. What he says invokes an earlier source, and his *saying* so invites us to reflect on that source as part of what he wants to communicate. The earlier source in this case becomes explicitly part of the subject matter in the communication taking place at the later time. How the author came to know about the earlier source, or how he gradually developed the views that he has finally come to articulate—such issues are part of the history of the origin. But they are not part of the meaning, unless, of course, the author makes his sources an explicit topic and begins to discuss with us how he received his information. Then the history of his investigations becomes part of the subject matter within the contemporary discourse in its own proper moment of communication.

The upshot of all this is that whether Luke used Mark has little or no direct bearing on his meanings. Nor does it affect the fact that Luke is an inspired writing with full divine authority. We find the meanings of the Gospel of Luke by reading Luke. We do not have to solve the synoptic problem first.

The Gospels in Context

We are undertaking to interpret the Gospels. God wrote them. When God speaks or writes, he takes account of contexts. These include the context of his own character and plan, the context of the human beings whom he has chosen to convey his communication, the context of the identity of the recipients, and the context of their social and historical situation. The meanings of what he says cohere with these contexts. There is much to consider. We cannot do it all in detail. Many good commentaries undertake the task.

Among these contexts are the contexts of Luke or Mark as an author. It is possible that knowing more about Luke, including whether he used Mark,

---

[3]France, *Matthew: Evangelist and Teacher,* 48.

can fill in a more detailed picture of who he was. And ancient readers were being invited to read the Gospel of Luke against the background of what they could be expected to know about both the human and the divine authors. But we should not get confused. Authors do not demand or expect that we know *everything* that could possibly be known about them. They have to make allowances when writing for a large audience, such as Luke was doing. The meaning of a text does not include the biography of its author. We still have to attend to what the text says, though we do so against the background of whatever basic knowledge of the author that we have.

In dealing with apparent difficulties in the differences between the Gospels, we will therefore focus on what the Gospels themselves say and the claims that they imply. We need to recognize that the Gospels are writings inspired by God. But we do not need to know in addition to this basic fact a detailed history of their origins.

Addressing the Synoptic Problem

We may nevertheless briefly consider the most likely directions for addressing the synoptic problem. We have already mentioned that it is possible that Luke used Mark, or that Matthew used Mark, or that Mark used Matthew—there are various combinations. Is any one of these more likely than the others? Or do we need to consider still further options, such as the possibility that all the Evangelists used oral teaching by the apostles? Did Matthew use his memory of the events?

I have found help from two sources especially. First, consider the prologue in Luke 1:1–4. Luke says that "many have undertaken to compile a narrative." It has been claimed that the word "many" is conventional. But even if there are other instances of such rhetoric in Hellenistic history writing, Luke makes a positive claim by choosing to put in the word when he had other alternatives. Therefore, we can infer that there were many. Mark may have been one of the "many," but we may infer that there were others—"many" others. Most of these have evidently been lost (by God's providential design).

Next, consider an article by E. Earle Ellis, "New Directions in Form Criticism."[4] In brief, Ellis observes that Jesus was an itinerant preacher, and that from fairly early in his ministry he had some following. People were interested. At the same time, many people were able to see and hear him only when he came to their town or to a town nearby. So they would have a natural desire for further information. Within this context, Ellis wonders

---

[4] E. Earle Ellis, "New Directions in Form Criticism," *Jesus Christus in Historie und Theologie*, ed. Georg Strecker (Tübingen: Mohr, 1975), 299–315.

whether the apostles or their hearers produced some written material for these followers. We can also ask whether some people would naturally have asked relatives to tell them what Jesus said and did when he was in towns in which their relatives lived. Ellis indicates that there was considerable use of Greek in Palestine, so some of these written pieces would have been in Greek as well as Aramaic.[5]

We may therefore suspect that not one or two but hundreds of written materials would have been in some circulation even while Jesus was still carrying out his ministry on earth. Some of these written materials would have been small in scope. Some, perhaps partly compiled using earlier pieces, might have been more extensive.

In addition to these written materials, we would of course have oral materials. In the early church the apostles had a prominent role. Their teaching and preaching would have been attended to. Others would have spoken about Jesus's earthly ministry as they were able.

Over this entire situation God sovereignly ruled, by his providential control of history. He ruled over each piece of communication, whether written or oral. Each piece came about in accordance with his comprehensive plan.

As a result of the joint presence of many factors, we confront the possibility of many sources, both written and oral. We have a situation where Matthew and Luke may have used not one source (Mark) or two (Mark and "Q"), but possibly many, most of which have now perished. This situation is a nightmare for anyone trying to construct a definitive modern "solution" to the origins of the Gospels. The presence of many possible sources produces a situation far too complex for us to draw firm conclusions. Luke clearly knew about many sources and probably used some, maybe many. We do not know what they were. We never will within this life. The same may have been the case for Matthew or Mark. As a result, I think that the synoptic problem is unsolvable.

So we have another reason to concentrate on the Gospels as we have them.

---

[5]Ibid., 307–8.

17

TEMPORAL ORDER OF EVENTS

The Gospels do not always present the events in the same *literary* order, that is, the *written* order on the page. For example, Matthew includes the narrative about the healing of the paralytic following his narration about the Gadarene demoniacs (Matt. 8:28–9:7). In Mark the healing of the paralytic occurs between the healing of the leper and the call of Levi (Mark 1:40–2:17), as it does in Luke (5:12–32). The episode with the Gadarene demoniac appears later on in Mark and Luke (Mark 5:1–20; Luke 8:26–39). How do we treat differences in order like this one?

The basic principle here is to distinguish between *written* order and *chronological* order. The written order or literary order is the order on the page. The chronological order is the order of events within Jesus's earthly ministry as it actually unfolded in time. At many points the Gospel writers do not offer explicit information about chronological order. The mere fact that two events occur in a particular written order does not by itself necessitate that they are arranged in chronological order. On the other hand, if one or more Gospel writers provide explicit information about chronological order, that information is true and reliable. Such information allows us in some particular cases to reconstruct a chronological order. In other cases, where the Gospels do not provide the information, the exact chronological order of events may have to remain uncertain.[1]

---

[1]Augustine has a discussion of chronology in the Gospels in *Harmony of the Gospels*, in vol. 6 of *NPNF1*, 2.21.51–52, where he advocates the same basic stance: "When the order of times [chronological order] is not apparent [the text does not specify an order], we ought not to feel it a matter of any consequence

Dealing with Evidence

Let us consider the events involving the Gadarene[2] demoniacs. We must first ask, as usual, whether we are dealing with the same events in all three Gospels. The details in the narratives correspond well, so it seems reasonable to assume that we are dealing with the same events.

Next, what information do the Gospels actually provide about chronological sequence? Mark 4:35–41 records the stilling of the storm. At that point the disciples were in a boat. In Mark 5:2 Jesus has "stepped out of the boat." The expression "the boat" refers back to the boat in which the disciples were traveling when the storm came. Mark 5:2 says, "When Jesus had stepped out of the boat, immediately there met him out of the tombs a man with an unclean spirit." In this sentence Mark does seem to give us a chronological sequence: he places the incident with the Gadarene demoniac chronologically after the stilling of the storm. Going backward in the text, we come to Mark 4:35, the opening verse telling about the stilling of the storm. It says, "on that day." What day? It seems to refer to a time when Jesus told parables, beginning with Mark 4:1: "Again he began to teach beside the sea." The text does not give further information about when Jesus gave the teachings in parables. Thus, the fact that in Mark this time of teaching occurs in *written order* after the narration of the healing of the paralytic (Mark 2:1–12) does not imply any *chronological* claim. The event of the Gadarene demoniac may have preceded the healing of the paralytic. Luke also is not specific; he says, "One day," to introduce the episode of the stilling of the storm.

Matthew at first glance may appear to be more specific. The episode with the paralytic is introduced by the expression, "And getting into a boat he crossed over and came to his own city" (Matt. 9:1). Presumably he crossed over from some other part of the Sea of Galilee, and the region of the Gadarenes, mentioned in Matthew 8:28, is the obvious candidate. Yet Matthew does not actually say that the crossing was from that region. Nor does he say that the crossing took place immediately after the episode with the demons. The information is sparse. I do not think we can draw definite conclusions about the chronology from Matthew. It seems likely that the healing of the paralytic took place right after the incident with the Gadarene demoniacs. But can we be certain? I am not certain.

---

what order [written order] any of them may have adopted in relating the events. But whenever the order is apparent, if the evangelist then presents anything which seems to be inconsistent with his own statements, or with those of another, we must certainly take the passage into consideration, and endeavour to clear up the difficulty" (2.21.52).

[2]Some manuscripts have Gergesene or Gerasene. See Gleason L. Archer, *Encyclopedia of Bible Difficulties* (Grand Rapids: Zondervan, 1982), 324–25. All the Synoptics have an expression "country of the Gadarenes/Gerasenes/Gergesenes," designating the "country" rather than a more exact location.

Likewise, Mark and Luke do not supply exact chronological information about the paralytic. They place the healing of the paralytic at an early point *literarily*. But neither of them provides detailed chronological information. Luke indicates that Jesus's call to Levi came *after* the healing of the paralytic ("*After this* he went out," Luke 5:27). But that is all. We do not know *how long* afterward. The Gospel of Luke does not offer further information that would enable us to construct a detailed chronology.

Flexibility in Ordering

We may consider broader principles for chronological order. Each Gospel has a great deal of flexibility with regard to order. The Gospels commit themselves to writing what happened. But they have flexibility as to the order in which they *tell* about the events—the written order. In some cases they may choose to write things up in chronological order. But they may also group the events in terms of common themes. To some extent we must treat each particular case on its own terms. In some instances the Gospels *do* offer chronological information; in other instances they do not. The details will differ depending on which passages we consider.

For example, all three Synoptic Gospels appear to have grouped together Jesus's parables to some extent. They may have done so partly because Jesus told parables in groups ("And he was teaching them many things in parables," Mark 4:2). But as he traveled around, he may also have repeated parables, sometimes with variations. The Gospels have doubtless been selective. As John says, "Now there are also many other things that Jesus did. Were every one of them to be written, I suppose that the world itself could not contain the books that would be written" (John 21:25).

It helps for us to see parables grouped together, in order to confront their similarities more directly. Gospels may also group material together in broader, looser ways: miracles can be grouped with other miracles; tensions with Jewish leadership may be displayed in several different episodes; and we may see grouped together intersecting issues like the relationship between parables, miracles, fellowship with sinners, and opposition. Such groupings are illuminating and helpful, since the coming of the kingdom of God is the coming of a unified work of salvation, all of whose aspects are related to one another in complex ways.

Thus, we may expect flexibility in ordering. Whenever a Gospel tells event B after telling event A, a typical reader may tend to develop a "mental picture" in which event B not only follows event A in the text, that is, in the written sequence of words on the page, but also follows event A in *actual time.* The easiest mental picture contains events in a temporal order exactly matching the written order. But if we have such a mental picture, we ought not to deduce that our mental picture *must* represent the correct chronological order. Mental pictures fill in details. They put in more detail than verbal communication warrants. If we want to know what the text actually promises, we must go to the text and not to the mental picture.

In those cases where the Gospels do not provide explicit chronological claims, the Evangelists had flexibility in their decisions about the order in which material is structured on the page.[3] But we must also take into account contrastive claims about temporal order. *Sometimes,* but not always, the Gospels make explicit claims about temporal order. These claims are usually not the main point. But they may nevertheless be a minor point. Whenever the Gospels do make claims about chronology, we should believe these claims because of their divine authority.

When do the Gospels make explicit claims about temporal order? Jesus's resurrection appearances followed his resurrection. His resurrection followed his death. His death followed his crucifixion. His crucifixion followed his trial. His trial followed his arrest. His arrest followed his journey to Jerusalem. These connections are fairly obvious and belong to the nature of the events.

Consider another example. Mark 4:35–41 tells about the stilling of the storm while Jesus and his disciples were in a boat. In Mark 5:2 Jesus is said to have "stepped out of the boat," which seems to imply a continuation from the earlier episode. Mark 5:21 begins another episode with the expression, "And when Jesus had crossed again in the boat to the other side, a great crowd gathered about him, and he was beside the sea."[4] The gathering of the crowd beside the sea comes chronologically *after* the healing of the demon-possessed man in Mark 5:1–20. Here Mark at least implicitly makes some claims about a temporal order. We can then reconstruct the actual order of events.

On the other hand, in other passages Mark presents us with many loose or flexible connections between events. "One Sabbath . . ." (Mark 2:23). "Again he entered the synagogue . . ." (Mark 3:1). "Jesus withdrew . . ." (Mark 3:7).

---

[3] "If one applies the principle of assuming a chronological connection between two portions of the Synoptics only when the text explicitly presents one, then the apparent contradictions of sequence vanish" (Craig L. Blomberg, *The Historical Reliability of the Gospels,* 2nd ed. [Downers Grove, IL: InterVarsity, 2007], 169).
[4] The wording about crossing the sea in Mark 5:21 is similar to the wording in Matt. 9:1. Yet I have earlier expressed uncertainty as to whether Matthew is claiming an explicit chronological order. Matthew says, "getting into a boat." There is no explicit connection with earlier events. Mark 5:21 says, "crossed *again* in *the* boat." (There are some text-critical variations in the Greek of both verses, but the stronger textual alternative leads to what the ESV gives us in English.) In Mark 5:21 "again" and "the"—little words by themselves—build a stronger connection with the events in Mark 5:1–20. These connections intimate the presence of a chronological sequence much more than does Matthew's generic wording.

"And he went up on the mountain . . . " (Mark 3:13). "And the scribes who came down from Jerusalem were saying . . . " (Mark 3:22). In my judgment, all of these expressions, which introduce new episodes, show flexibility. They do not specify any explicit temporal order. Maybe the events are put together on the page in the same order as their original temporal order. But maybe not. Mark does not say one way or the other.[5] There is therefore no reason for people to allege inconsistency if later we should find that the events on the page are in a different *written* order than their order in time.

We should also admit that it may not be clear in some individual cases whether the text implies a claim about temporal order. Commentators may disagree. In some cases a claim about order may be explicit. Then we should have confidence. In other cases a definite claim is made even if the claim is indirect or implied (as with Mark 5:2). In still other cases we may have a hint. But how definite is this hint? We must understand that the Gospels may possibly invite us to see two events as closely related not only because one event immediately succeeded the other in time, but also because the two are related thematically in various ways. We must be willing to follow the lead of the Gospels even when this lead takes the form of an intimation rather than an explicit statement. On the other hand, we must assess carefully what *kind* of intimation we have. We must be satisfied sometimes with tentative knowledge.

I should also underline the fact that in these questions my own personal judgments are fallible, as are those of any commentator. In expressing some judgments, my desire is not to give an overconfident judgment in any one case, but to talk about what kinds of processes lead to making judgments that respect the character of the Gospels as the word of God.

Calvin's View

John Calvin understands the flexibility with regard to chronology in the Gospels. In connection with the episode of the cursing of the fig tree he states more general principles.

> . . . for though they appear to indicate an uninterrupted succession of events, yet as they do not name a particular day, there would be no impropriety in dividing what we find to be connected in their writings. . . . any one who will consider how little care the Evangelists bestowed on pointing out dates [i.e.,

---

[5]Eusebius, *Ecclesiastical History*, trans. Kirsopp Lake (London: Heinemann; Cambridge: Harvard University Press, 1965), 3.39.14–16, quotes Papias, who says that Mark's Gospel does not preserve chronological order: "Mark became Peter's interpreter and wrote accurately all that he remembered, *not, indeed, in order*, of the things said or done by the Lord" (italics mine).

they usually omitted this information] will not stumble at this diversity in the narrative.[6]

The Word for "Then" in Matthew

Finally, we may note one detail about Matthew that is useful when dealing with questions about chronological order. It concerns the Greek word *tote*, which is often rendered as "then" in the ESV and other essentially literal translations. This word sometimes stands at the beginning of a new episode in Matthew.[7]

> *Then* Herod, when he saw that he had been tricked by the wise men . . . (Matt. 2:16)

> *Then* Jesus came from Galilee to the Jordan to John . . . . (Matt. 3:13)

The English translation "then" may make it sound as if there is an immediate chronological succession: the one episode chronologically follows the other. But a look at the range of meaning of the Greek word *tote* shows that it has a broader variation of usage. The standard New Testament Greek lexicon offers two senses: (1) *"at that time"*; and (2) "to introduce that which follows in time . . . *then, thereupon."*[8] The second sense indicates chronological succession. But what about the first sense? It is used to indicate that one event happens within a certain time framework, but not necessarily in immediate chronological succession to another specific event. For example, 2 Peter 3:6 speaks of "the world that *then* [Greek *tote*] existed," meaning the world *at the time* before Noah's flood.

When Matthew introduces an episode using the Greek word *tote*, "then," it often means that the episode so introduced took place within the same general time frame as the preceding. In effect, he is saying that "at that time" such and such happened. The episode may have immediately followed in chronological order ("then this happened, right after that"). But it might also be the case that it happened during the same broader time period.[9] Matthew, by using the connecting word *tote*, indicates that we should see

---

[6]John Calvin, *Commentary on a Harmony of the Evangelists, Matthew, Mark, and Luke*, 3 vols., trans. William Pringle (Grand Rapids: Eerdmans, n.d.), 3:9–10.

[7]By my count, the word *tote* ("then") occurs 90 times in Matthew, 6 times in Mark, 15 times in Luke, and 10 times in John. By comparison with the other Gospels, it is a favorite word for Matthew.

[8]Frederick William Danker, ed., *A Greek-English Lexicon of the New Testament and Other Early Christian Literature*, 3rd ed. (Chicago: University of Chicago Press, 2000).

[9]Augustine also notes the possibility of the meaning "at that time" (*Harmony of the Gospels*, in vol. 6 of *NPNF*1, 2.34.81).

the episode in relationship to what precedes. But the *kind* of relationship remains chronologically flexible. A range of possibilities remains open.

Summary of Principles for Chronology

We may summarize the principles for chronological ordering.

1. Flexible chronological order

If two episodes lie literarily side by side within a Gospel, but the Gospel does not give an indication about their chronological relation, they may or may not be in chronological order.

2. Specified chronological order

If two episodes lie side by side within a Gospel, and the Gospel gives indication that one chronologically follows another, we may be confident that this is so.

3. More than one event

If we find a difficulty over the chronological order of events, we should explore the possibility that distinct accounts in different Gospels refer to distinct events.

Over the course of Jesus's public ministry, he may from time to time have encountered similar circumstances and may then have responded in similar ways. People in various locations needed to receive similar teaching about the kingdom of God; people needed to be healed; demons needed to be cast out; the temple may have needed cleansing more than once (see the next chapter).

4. Uncertainties

Sometimes one Gospel may link two episodes in such a way that the Gospel may be *indirectly* providing a suggestion that they are in chronological order. Because of the indirectness, we may not always be sure. It may sometimes not be easy to decide if the Gospel is providing information about chronology, because such information is not in focus.

5. Limited human knowledge of chronology

We may sometimes not have enough information from the Gospels to determine with confidence details in the chronological order of events.

PART FIVE

INDIVIDUAL CASES

18

CLEANSING THE TEMPLE

Let us now consider some other cases, beginning with those where temporal order is one of the issues. Jesus's cleansing of the temple occurs in John near the beginning, in John 2:13–22. Matthew, Mark, and Luke all include the cleansing of the temple toward the end, in association with the events of the final days leading to Jesus's crucifixion (Matt. 21:12–13; Mark 11:15–19; Luke 19:45–46). What do we do with the difference in order?

As usual, we should ask whether we are dealing with one event or two or more. There is little difficulty in deciding that Matthew, Mark, and Luke are describing the same event, because all three locate it at about the same time in Jesus's ministry, in close connection with Jesus's final entry into Jerusalem. Commentators disagree about the event in John 2. Is it the same event as the one described in the Synoptics?[1]

For convenience we may view the text of the four accounts side by side.

Matthew 21:12–17	Mark 11:15–19	Luke 19:45–46	John 2:13–22
			[13] The Passover of the Jews was at hand, and Jesus went up to Jerusalem.
[12] And Jesus entered the temple	[15] And they came to Jerusalem. And he entered the temple	[45] And he entered the temple	
			[14] In the temple he found those who

---

[1] See discussion in Andreas J. Köstenberger, *John* (Grand Rapids: Baker, 2004), 111; D. A. Carson, *The Gospel according to John* (Grand Rapids: Eerdmans, 1991), 177–78.

Matthew 21:12–17	Mark 11:15–19	Luke 19:45–46	John 2:13–22
			were selling oxen and sheep and pigeons, and the money-changers sitting there. 15 And making a whip of cords,
and drove out all who sold and	and began to drive out those who sold and those	and began to drive out those who sold,	he drove them all out
bought in the temple,	who bought in the temple,		of the temple, with the sheep and oxen. And he poured out the coins of the money-changers
and he overturned the tables of the money-changers and the seats	and he overturned the tables of the money-changers and the seats		and overturned their tables.
of those who sold pigeons.	of those who sold pigeons.		16 And he told those who sold the pigeons, "Take these things away;
	16 And he would not allow anyone to carry anything through the temple. 17 And he was teaching them and		
13 He said to them, "It is written, 'My house shall be called a house of prayer,'	saying to them, "Is it not written, 'My house shall be called a house of prayer for all the nations'?	46 saying to them, "It is written, 'My house shall be a house of prayer,'	do not make my Father's house a house of trade."
but you make it	But you have made it	but you have made it	
a den of robbers."	a den of robbers."	a den of robbers."	17 His disciples remembered that it was written, "Zeal for your house will consume me."
14 And the blind and the lame came to him in the temple, and he healed them. 15 But when the chief priests and the scribes saw the wonderful things that he did, and the children crying out in the temple, "Hosanna to the Son of David!" they were indignant, 16 and they said to	18 And the chief priests and the scribes heard it		

Matthew 21:12–17	Mark 11:15–19	Luke 19:45–46	John 2:13–22
him, "Do you hear what these are saying?" And Jesus said to them, "Yes; have you never read, "'Out of the mouth of infants and nursing babies you have prepared praise'?"			
			[18] So the Jews said to him, "What sign do you show us for doing these things?" [19] Jesus answered them, "Destroy this temple, and in three days I will raise it up." [20] The Jews then said, "It has taken forty-six years to build this temple, and will you raise it up in three days?" [21] But he was speaking about the temple of his body. [22] When therefore he was raised from the dead, his disciples remembered that he had said this, and they believed the Scripture and the word that Jesus had spoken.
	and were seeking a way to destroy him, for they feared him, because all the crowd was astonished at his teaching.		
[17] And leaving them, he went out of the city to Bethany and lodged there.	[19] And when evening came they went out of the city.		

The accounts share some significant common features. In John, Jesus drove out the sellers, with the oxen and sheep, and "poured out the coins of the money-changers and overturned their tables." Luke is not specific about the details, but Matthew says that Jesus drove out "all who sold and bought, and he overturned the tables of the money-changers." Mark 11 has similar wording.

What the passages have in common is fairly general. He drove out the people engaging in commercial activity. The whip of cords is mentioned only in John, as is the pouring out of the coins. John indicates that he drove out the oxen and sheep along with their sellers. That is not mentioned in the Synoptics, though it is presumably implied.

There is enough commonality that we can appreciate the tendency of commentators to see one event. On the other hand, is it necessarily only one event? Let us consider the two alternatives.

Two Cleansings?

What if, early in his public ministry, Jesus had gone to the temple and did what John describes in John 2? Did the commercial vendors or the priestly officers who gave permission to these vendors take to heart what Jesus did? Did they repent and realize that they were profaning God's house (John 2:16)?

Given the spiritual condition among the powerful, it seems likely that many of them did not repent. If they did not, they probably decided to lie low while Jesus was swaying the crowds. But when he went back to Galilee, would they not go back to "business as usual"? If some years later, Jesus came to Jerusalem for the last time, is it probable that he would have found a situation similar to what he had found earlier? If he did, would a similar reaction have been appropriate? That would explain all of the commonalities between John and the Synoptics. The commonalities arise from the similarity of the two situations and the similarity in the appropriate righteous reaction to the situation. All of these reasonings, in my opinion, open the real possibility that there were in fact two different cleansings of the temple, at two different times during Jesus's ministry.[2]

Augustine reasons "that this act was performed by the Lord not on a single occasion, but twice over; but that only the first instance is put on record by John, and the last by the other three."[3]

One Cleansing?

We should also explore the opposite side. Do the texts *require* us to say that there were two cleansings? We have to be careful. Once again, we must avoid

---

[2]See also Craig L. Blomberg, *The Historical Reliability of the Gospels*, 2nd ed. (Downers Grove, IL: InterVarsity, 2007), 216–19.
[3]Augustine, *Harmony of the Gospels*, in vol. 6 of *NPNF*1, 2.67.129.

committing ourselves to a mental-picture theory of meaning. Perhaps we read John and picture the cleansing described in John 2:14–15 in immediate connection with the preceding and following parts of John's narrative. We picture it as occurring near in time to the "first of his signs" narrated in 2:11. We picture it near the beginning. But this is a mental picture, not necessarily reality.

We have to ask whether John or any of the synoptic accounts make contrastive claims about temporal location. John 2:13 says, "The Passover of the Jews was at hand, and Jesus went up to Jerusalem." Which Passover? We are not told. It is natural for readers to see this going up to Jerusalem as proceeding from the location last mentioned, namely Capernaum, where Jesus stayed a few days (John 2:12). But John does not explicitly tell us about a direct temporal succession here. The "hint," if there is one, is simply the juxtaposition of two episodes in the written neighborhood of one another. But might John have had other reasons for a juxtaposition like this one?

Do we get any help from what follows the cleansing of the temple? What follows is John 3:1ff., the passage about Nicodemus. Thematically, it is connected with the general statement in John 2:25 that Jesus "knew what was in a man." But there is no explicit temporal connection. We do not get information about the chronology of events. The placement of the episode in the text is, in my opinion, chronologically flexible. So would it be possible that John told the narrative about the same cleansing of the temple that is there in the Synoptics, but that he placed it here to introduce a theme of which he wants us to be aware as we read further? I think it is possible. God could have so designed it.

If so, we do not know for sure whether there was only one cleansing of the temple or two. But even with this lack of exhaustive knowledge, we know a good deal. We know that Jesus cleansed the temple. And we know about his zeal and his reasons for doing it, whether it happened once or twice. We need to pay attention to John's special emphasis on Jesus's zeal (John 2:17), which fulfilled the Scriptures, and on the symbolism about Jesus's body being the more ultimate and satisfactory temple (John 2:22). We also need to pay attention to the emphasis in Matthew and Mark about the misuse of the temple. They point out that the practice of buying and selling undermined God's purpose, that the temple would be a place of prayer for the nations. Instead, the temple was perverted to serve commercialism and profiteering ("robbers"). Note also the connection with using the temple for teaching and for compassion on the weak (the blind, the lame, children). We can profit from these points made in the Gospels without knowing everything. "The secret things belong to the LORD our God, but the things that are revealed belong to us and to our children forever, that we may do all the words of this law" (Deut. 29:29).

19

THE REJECTION OF JESUS AT NAZARETH

Next we consider the narratives about the rejection of Jesus at Nazareth. There are accounts in each of the three Synoptic Gospels, which we may view side by side.

Matthew 13:54–58	Mark 6:1–5	Luke 4:16–30
	¹ He went away from there and came to his hometown,	¹⁶ And he came to Nazareth, where he had been brought up.
⁵⁴ and coming to his hometown	and his disciples followed him.	
		And as was his custom,
he taught them in their synagogue,	² And on the Sabbath he began to teach in the synagogue,	he went to the synagogue on the Sabbath day, and he stood up to read. ¹⁷ And the scroll of the prophet Isaiah was given to him. He unrolled the scroll and found the place where it was written, ¹⁸ "The Spirit of the Lord is upon me, because he has anointed me to proclaim good news to the poor.

Matthew 13:54–58	Mark 6:1–5	Luke 4:16–30
		He has sent me to proclaim liberty to the captives and recovering of sight to the blind, to set at liberty those who are oppressed, ¹⁹ to proclaim the year of the Lord's favor." ²⁰ And he rolled up the scroll and gave it back to the attendant and sat down. And the eyes of all in the synagogue were fixed on him. ²¹ And he began to say to them, "Today this Scripture has been fulfilled in your hearing." ²² And all spoke well of him and marveled at the gracious words that were coming from his mouth.
so that they were astonished,	and many who heard him were astonished, saying,	
and said, "Where did this man get this wisdom and these mighty works?	"Where did this man get these things? What is the wisdom given to him? How are such mighty works done by his hands?	
⁵⁵ Is not this the carpenter's son? Is not his mother called Mary? And are not his brothers James and Joseph and Simon and Judas? ⁵⁶ And are not all his sisters with us? Where then did this man get all these things?" ⁵⁷ And they took offense at him.	³ Is not this the carpenter, the son of Mary and brother of James and Joses and Judas and Simon? And are not his sisters here with us?" And they took offense at him.	And they said, "Is not this Joseph's son?"
		²³ And he said to them, "Doubtless you will quote to me this proverb, 'Physician, heal yourself.' What we have heard you did at Capernaum, do here in your hometown as well."
But Jesus said to them, "A prophet is not without honor except in his hometown and in his own household."	⁴ And Jesus said to them, "A prophet is not without honor, except in his hometown and among his relatives and in his own household."	²⁴ And he said, "Truly, I say to you, no prophet is acceptable in his hometown.
		²⁵ But in truth, I tell you, there were many widows in Israel in the days of Elijah, when the heavens were shut up three years and six months,

Matthew 13:54–58	Mark 6:1–5	Luke 4:16–30
		and a great famine came over all the land, ²⁶ and Elijah was sent to none of them but only to Zarephath, in the land of Sidon, to a woman who was a widow. ²⁷ And there were many lepers in Israel in the time of the prophet Elisha, and none of them was cleansed, but only Naaman the Syrian." ²⁸ When they heard these things, all in the synagogue were filled with wrath. ²⁹ And they rose up and drove him out of the town and brought him to the brow of the hill on which their town was built, so that they could throw him down the cliff. ³⁰ But passing through their midst, he went away.
⁵⁸ And he did not do many mighty works there,	⁵ And he could do no mighty work there, except that he laid his hands on a few sick people and healed them.	
because of their unbelief.		

Two Events?

We should first ask whether we are dealing with more than one event. The Gospel of Luke places its account near the beginning of the account of Jesus's public ministry, while Matthew and Mark place it somewhere in the middle, close to the death of John the Baptist (Matt. 14:1–12; Mark 6:14–29) and the feeding of the five thousand (Matt. 14:13–21; Mark 6:30–44). It certainly looks as though Matthew and Mark are telling about the same episode. The dissimilarities between them are minor differences as to what details they include and what exact wording they give. But what about Luke? Is Luke talking about another episode at another time? Were there two rejections?

It is possible that there were two. Some people may be struck by the similarities between Luke and the other two accounts. But these similarities could have been produced by similarities in the events themselves.

Suppose that the episode in Luke took place early in Jesus's public ministry. When the people of Nazareth rejected Jesus, he may have decided never to return. But then again he may have decided out of compassion to give them one more chance. If and when he went back, their reaction was still the same. It is quite possible that, because they remained in opposition, they produced the same basic reasons for opposition that they had used before. They asked,

"Is not this Joseph's son?" and so on. Jesus in response might fittingly have reminded them a second time of the rejection of Old Testament prophets: "A prophet is not without honor except in his hometown" (Matt. 13:57; Mark 6:4). There is nothing unreasonable about similar circumstances leading to a similar interaction.

One Event?

We must also ask whether the accounts could all refer to the same episode. One of the issues concerns the chronology. Does the Gospel of Luke give us a different chronological placement for the event that it narrates?

Luke places the account at 4:16–30, shortly after the material describing Jesus's temptation in the wilderness (Luke 4:1–13). But before Luke comes to the episode at Nazareth, it gives us a summary statement: "And Jesus returned in the power of the Spirit to Galilee, and a report about him went out through all the surrounding country. And he taught in their synagogues, being glorified by all" (4:14–15). Then Luke introduces the time at Nazareth: "And he came to Nazareth" (4:16). *When* Jesus came is not indicated. This transition gives chronological flexibility. It does not specify when. The preceding summary in 4:14–15 indicates that much was going on. Luke simply does not indicate when, in the midst of all Jesus's activity, the visit to Nazareth took place. Moreover, Jesus's mention of Capernaum (4:23) indicates that he had done miracles in other places, and that enough time had passed for the people of Nazareth to hear about such things.

Do we get specific chronological information from the transition at the end of the time at Nazareth, in Luke 4:30? We do not. Luke 4:31 continues with another episode, "And he went down to Capernaum, a city of Galilee." It gives no explicit chronology. Therefore, Luke provides no indication of when Jesus visited Nazareth, other than the fact that it was after he had done miracles at Capernaum.

Other Difficulties in Relation to Matthew and Mark

The main remaining question concerns how the episodes end. Luke 4:30 ends with Jesus escaping from a murderous mob. Matthew 13:58 and Mark 6:5 end quietly. If we assume that all three accounts are referring to the same visit to Nazareth, can we account for these differences?

There are several possibilities. It is easy to assume that Luke 4:30 marked the termination of Jesus's activity in Nazareth. He went away from the town because of its murderous intent. Maybe so, but I do not think that is certain. The text does not tell us. It is, at that point, silent. It is easy to fill in our mental picture, but the mental picture then fills in what the text does not claim. It is possible that Jesus "went away" *back to* Nazareth from the brow of the hill, rather than leaving the city completely. His escape from the mob seems to have been miraculous. Somehow, the people in the mob found that they could not do what they were intent on doing. So he could safely go back to the town, where they *still* would not be able to murder him. Or maybe Jesus went away from the town until later in the evening, and then returned when the people in the mob had cooled down. Maybe he ministered quietly for a few more days. The text does not say. Silence is not an error or a contradiction.

It might also be that Jesus's reading in the synagogue as described by Luke 4 took place after he had already been in Nazareth quietly for some days. Maybe he had healed a few sick already, but not in a public context. The people at Nazareth expected more (Luke 4:23).

I conclude that the synoptic accounts, taken together, do not provide enough detailed, positive chronological information to enable us to know the precise relationship between the healing mentioned in Mark 6:5 and the synagogue episode in Luke 4:16–30. It is possible that both could have taken place during one visit to Nazareth. It is also possible that they represent two separate visits, one earlier in Jesus's ministry and the other later. We can be confident that events took place as the Gospels describe them. But with our limitations in human knowledge, we remain with some uncertainties about the chronological relations of the details. It was not God's purpose to provide us with all the details, but to provide us with meaningful "sparse" accounts that give us a grasp of Jesus and his ministry. These accounts are historically reliable and expound to us the meaning of Jesus's life. He has accomplished salvation.

Paying Attention to Luke's Placement

If we decide that there was only one visit to Nazareth, described in all three Gospels, it might be tempting to juggle the events around in our mind. We mentally transpose Luke 4:16–30 to its "proper" chronological place in Jesus's ministry, namely, the place before the death of John the Baptist, as given in Matthew and Mark.

Having a chronological outline in mind is of some value. The Gospels all provide us with at least a basic outline: (1) a time before Jesus's public ministry; (2) his public ministry; (3) his final days at Jerusalem. Beyond these basic facts, it is important to underline that the events of Jesus's life were real events in time and space. Since they were events in time, they did have a definite chronological order. But God has not been pleased to give us all the information about this chronological order, and we must sometimes be satisfied with guesses and probabilities when we try to speculate about the details.

But we should also reckon with the fact that God through Luke has a purpose in placing the account about Nazareth where he did. It is programmatic. In Luke 4:18–19 Jesus quotes from Isaiah 61:1–2, which announces the final year of jubilee, "the year of the Lord's favor" (Luke 4:19). This announcement gives us an indication of some of the meaning of Jesus's *entire* public ministry. His entire ministry is about announcing and bringing the year of jubilee promised in the Old Testament.

The Year of Jubilee in Leviticus 25 was the fiftieth year in a cycle of years for Israel. In that year debts were canceled, slaves released, and rented land returned to the original owner. These practices pointed forward to a final spiritual jubilee (as indicated in Isa. 61:1–2), when we would be freed from sin and spiritual slavery through the work of Christ.

So Luke 4 gives us a *theological* statement with theological significance. Jesus's reading from Isaiah 61 is also significant because of the murderous reaction to it. The near murder in Luke 4:16–30 anticipates the antagonism that Jesus would receive throughout his public ministry. And this antagonism culminated in actual murder—the crucifixion. By placing Luke 4:16–30 near the beginning, Luke highlights the ominous theme of opposition. It turned out to be the case in a principial way that Jesus as a prophet had no honor among his own people, the Jews.

Luke—and God writing through Luke—tells us to take this significance into account as a fundamental truth when we read all the way through the rest of Luke. If we suppose that Jesus spoke about Isaiah 61 somewhere in the chronological middle of his ministry, it is still the case that chronology is not everything. Every part of Jesus's ministry helps us to interpret every other part, because it all belongs together as a ministry of the coming of the kingdom of God, when God delivers his people. We need to interpret the whole of Jesus's ministry in the light of what he says about Isaiah 61:1–2 at this one point in time. The Gospel of Luke, by placing the rejection of Nazareth at a key point, gives us something that we would not notice so easily if in our minds we transposed it to another place in the narrative. We can be grateful when the Gospels arrange material thematically instead of merely chronologically, because this kind of arrangement can help us to take the account to heart, understand it more deeply, and love our Savior more fervently. God thereby reveals more of who he is and what he wants us to know.

20

CURSING THE FIG TREE

We may continue by considering another case with a chronological difficulty, namely, the account of the cursing of the fig tree. Here are the texts:

Matthew 21:17–22	Mark 11:11–15, 19–25
[in vv. 12–16, Jesus cleanses the temple.] [17] And leaving them, he went out of the city to Bethany and lodged there. [18] In the morning, as he was returning to the city, he became hungry. [19] And seeing a fig tree by the wayside, he went to it and found nothing on it but only leaves. And he said to it, "May no fruit ever come from you again!" [see vv. 12–16] [see v. 17.] [see v. 18] And the fig tree withered at once. [20] When the disciples saw it, they marveled, saying, "How did the fig tree wither at once?"	[see Mark 11:15–18] [11] . . . as it was already late, he went out to Bethany with the twelve. [12] On the following day, when they came from Bethany, he was hungry. [13] And seeing in the distance a fig tree in leaf, he went to see if he could find anything on it. When he came to it, he found nothing but leaves, for it was not the season for figs. [14] And he said to it, "May no one ever eat fruit from you again." And his disciples heard it. [15] And they came to Jerusalem. And he entered the temple and began to drive out those who sold . . . . [vv. 15–18 describe the cleansing of the temple.] [19] And when evening came they went out of the city. [20] As they passed by in the morning, they saw the fig tree withered away to its roots. [21] And Peter remembered and said to him, "Rabbi, look! The fig tree that you cursed has withered."

Matthew 21:17–22	Mark 11:11–15, 19–25
[21] And Jesus answered them, "Truly, I say to you, if you have faith and do not doubt, you will not only do what has been done to the fig tree, but even if you say to this mountain, 'Be taken up and thrown into the sea,' it will happen. [22] And whatever you ask in prayer, you will receive, if you have faith."	[22] And Jesus answered them, "Have faith in God. [23] Truly, I say to you, whoever says to this mountain, 'Be taken up and thrown into the sea,' and does not doubt in his heart, but believes that what he says will come to pass, it will be done for him. [24] Therefore I tell you, whatever you ask in prayer, believe that you have received it, and it will be yours. [25] And whenever you stand praying, forgive, if you have anything against anyone, so that your Father also who is in heaven may forgive you your trespasses."

Analysis

Many of the differences are minor, but two are prominent. First, in Matthew the narration of the cleansing of the temple comes in written order before the episode with the fig tree. In Mark, the interactions with the fig tree occur over a period of two days. The cleansing of the temple takes place in between, namely, on the first of these days, after Jesus has already pronounced a curse on the fig tree. On the second day, as they are going toward Jerusalem, the disciples notice that the tree has withered.

Second, in Matthew the withering appears to take place "at once" (Matt. 21:19). In Mark it appears to takes place over a period of a whole day.

Commentators

Among the explanations offered by commentators, Calvin says: "Only Mark states what Matthew had omitted, that the occurrence [the fig tree withered] was observed by the disciples on the following day. So then, though Mark has stated more distinctly the order of time, he makes no contradiction."[1]

Samuel Andrews says:

Greswell, who supposes that the malediction instantly took effect, and that the tree began at once to wither, would make Matthew and Mark refer to two distinct conversations between the Lord and the disciples,—one that day, and

[1] John Calvin, *Commentary on a Harmony of the Evangelists, Matthew, Mark, and Luke,* 3 vols., trans. William Pringle (Grand Rapids: Eerdmans, n.d.), 3:9.

the other upon the next. More probably, Matthew brings together all that occurred upon both days, in order to complete his narrative.[2]

Augustine similarly says that Matthew records together Jesus's curse of the fig tree on one day and the disciples' reaction on the next day.[3]

Proposed Solution with Compression

I believe it is likely that we have here another case where Matthew has employed compression. Matthew has given us a minimal account, taking up two verses (21:19–20) for the heart of the action. Mark takes four verses for the same actions (Mark 11:13–14, 20–21). Moreover, Mark has made the whole account more complex by separating the two stages of the action into two distinct days, with the cleansing of the temple in between. Matthew, by comparison, gives the whole history of the interaction with the fig tree "in one blow," so to speak, and lets us quickly grasp the curse and its consequence. There is clearly something to be gained by this compressed approach.

If Matthew takes a compressed approach, it eliminates some contrastive possibilities. With a more extended narrative, such as Mark undertakes, the narrator can choose to make the point that the action took place in two stages over a period of two days. And this extended explanation of the action contrasts in various ways with directly asserting that all the action took place on one day, or depicting the distinct pieces of action with other kinds of extended wording. Matthew, by choosing to compress, loses some of this contrast.

We can draw up a table illustrating the possibilities. If we choose an expanded narrative, we have a contrast between statements that construe the action in one stage or in two. If we choose a compressed narrative, we lose this contrast in practice. We retain only the ability to describe in more generic terms the gist of the action. That is what Matthew has elected. There is no error, because in Matthew there is no contrastive statement that there was *only* one stage rather than two (see fig. 9).

[2]Samuel J. Andrews, *The Life of Our Lord upon the Earth: Considered in Its Historical, Chronological, and Geographical Relations* (Grand Rapids: Zondervan, 1954), 437.
[3]Augustine, *Harmony of the Gospels*, in vol. 6 of *NPNF* 1, 2.68.131. Augustine also discusses other chronological details, as does Calvin (*Harmony of the Evangelists*, 3:9–10). One may note also Ned B. Stonehouse, *The Witness of the Synoptic Gospels to Christ: One Volume Combining The Witness of Matthew and Mark to Christ and The Witness of Luke to Christ*, 2nd ed. (Grand Rapids: Baker, 1979), 160–64.

Figure 9. Effect of compression

	Compressed	Expanded
Two stages	0	✓
Only one stage narrated	✓	✓

variational range; no contrast

contrast

Immediate Withering

Matthew says that the withering took place "at once" (Matt. 21:20; NKJV has "so soon"; NIV has "so quickly"). Again it helps to realize that words have variation in meaning. They are not infinitely precise. This principle of variation holds for the expression "at once" (Greek *parachrēma*).[4] The rapid withering of the fig tree contrasts with many common withering processes, which would typically take several days or several weeks. The fig tree withered with unusual rapidity. Matthew is not precise about just how long it took.

Maybe the withering took place over a period of about twenty-four hours, between the time when Jesus pronounced the course in the morning before cleansing the temple (Mark 11:14) and the time when the disciples noticed the withering on the morning of the following day (11:20). Or maybe the withering took place within a period of a few seconds or a few minutes, right after the disciples went on from the location of the tree to the temple (11:15). The disciples would then have *noticed* the withering only on the following day (11:20). Neither Matthew nor Mark supplies minute details about the process of withering.

Here again the mental-picture theory of truth can get in our way. Matthew does not fill in the details about whether the action was spread over a period of two days. If we start from his sparse narrative and try to make a mental picture, our picture will have all the action taking place within one day—in fact, within a period of minutes. We might even picture the fig tree as withering within seconds. Poof!

No doubt Jesus had power to accomplish an instantaneous withering. And maybe that is the way it happened. But Matthew's narrative does not supply

---

[4]Stonehouse, *Witness of the Synoptic Gospels*, 162, discusses the Greek word *parachrēma* and notes that Moulton and Milligan give an example of the use of *parachrēma* in a case involving a delay of a month (James Hope Moulton and George Milligan, eds., *The Vocabulary of the Greek Testament: Illustrated from the Papyri and Other Non-literary Sources* [Grand Rapids: Eerdmans, 1930], 491).

the details that we might like to fill in with a mental picture. The mental picture does not correspond to the events, and then we are disappointed. But as usual the problem with mental pictures is ours. Narratives are sparse in comparison with mental pictures.

Both Matthew and Mark achieve distinctive emphases through the ways they present the events. Matthew, by putting the whole interaction with the fig tree together in one place on the page, emphasizes the power of Jesus, the power of faith, and the quickness of the result.[5] Mark, by dividing up the fig tree incident into its distinctive parts, invites us to notice the relation between the fig tree and the temple. The cleansing of the temple stands between the two halves of the fig tree incident. The cleansing of the temple has something to say about the failure of Israel to follow the Lord with the appropriate purity—purity of heart and of behavior. The fig tree incident is in a sense addressing the same issue, because the fig tree is intended figuratively to represent the fruitlessness of Israel.

---

[5]"So here Matthew apparently subordinates strict chronological order to the homiletic aim of stressing the lesson of the fig-tree episode in terms of the dramatic effect of faith" (R. T. France, "Inerrancy and New Testament Exegesis," *Themelios* 1 [1975]: 15).

21

COMMISSIONING THE TWELVE

Jesus's instructions in commissioning the Twelve for their mission occur in all three Synoptic Gospels. Below are the texts for comparison:

Matthew 10:1–15	Mark 6:7–13	Luke 9:1–6
[1] And he called to him his twelve disciples	[7] And he called the twelve and began to send them out two by two,	[1] And he called the twelve together
and gave them authority	and gave them authority	and gave them power and authority
over unclean spirits, to cast them out, and to heal every disease and every affliction. [2] The names of the twelve apostles are these: first, Simon, who is called Peter, and Andrew his brother; James the son of Zebedee, and John his brother; [3] Philip and Bartholomew; Thomas and Matthew the tax collector; James the son of Alphaeus, and Thaddaeus; [4] Simon the Zealot, and Judas Iscariot, who betrayed him. [5] These twelve Jesus sent out, instructing them, "Go nowhere among the Gentiles and enter no town of the Samaritans, [6] but go rather	over the unclean spirits.	over all demons and to cure diseases, [2] and he sent them out

Matthew 10:1–15	Mark 6:7–13	Luke 9:1–6
to the lost sheep of the house of Israel. 7 And proclaim as you go, saying, 'The kingdom of heaven is at hand.' 8 Heal the sick, raise the dead, cleanse lepers, cast out demons. You received without paying; give without pay. 9 Acquire		to proclaim the kingdom of God and to heal.
no gold or silver or copper for your belts,	8 He charged them to take nothing for their journey except a staff— no bread, no bag, no money in their belts—	3 And he said to them, "Take nothing for your journey, no staff, nor bag, nor bread, nor money;
10 no bag for your journey, or two tunics or sandals or a staff, for the laborer deserves his food.	9 but to wear sandals and not put on two tunics.	and do not have two tunics.
11 And whatever town or village you enter, find out who is worthy in it and stay there until you depart.	10 And he said to them, "Whenever you enter a house, stay there until you depart from there.	4 And whatever house you enter, stay there, and from there depart. [Luke 10:5–6]
12 As you enter the house, greet it. 13 And if the house is worthy, let your peace come upon it, but if it is not worthy, let your peace return to you. 14 And if anyone will not receive you or listen to your words, shake off the dust from your feet when you leave that house or town.	11 And if any place will not receive you and they will not listen to you, when you leave, shake off the dust that is on your feet as a testimony against them."	5 And wherever they do not receive you, when you leave that town shake off the dust from your feet as a testimony against them."
15 Truly, I say to you, it will be more bearable on the day of judgment for the land of Sodom and Gomorrah than for that town. [vv. 16–42 contain further instructions]	12 So they went out and proclaimed that people should repent. 13 And they cast out many demons and anointed with oil many who were sick and healed them.	6 And they departed and went through the villages, preaching the gospel and healing everywhere.

In addition, Luke 10:1–12 contains directions that Jesus gives to the seventy or seventy-two (there is textual variation in the manuscripts over the exact number). This commissioning involves a distinct group and a distinct time, so it need not receive detailed attention.

We can see two main apparent discrepancies. Matthew says no staff or sandals, while Mark permits both. Luke says, "no staff," but says nothing about sandals.

A Proposed Solution

The sharp, direct differences among the three accounts might seem at first to permit no solution. But Henry Alford has offered a reasonable explanation.[1] Some of the keys lie in the particular wording in the three accounts, and comparisons with Luke 10:1–12. Luke 10:4 says, "*Carry . . . no sandals.*" The disciples were not to have a second pair. But they could wear the ones they already had. It would be completely unrealistic to go barefoot. Jesus was addressing the fact that on a long journey sandals could wear out. The disciples might have thought that they had to make provision beforehand by buying ("acquiring") a second pair.

In Matthew 10:9–10 the operative verb is "acquire" (Greek *ktēsēsthe*), that is, "purchase." The corresponding verb in Mark is "take" (Greek *airōsin*), which, Alford observes, "has not quite the precision of the other [verb]. They were not to procure *expressly for this journey* even a staff: they were to take with them their usual staff only."[2]

Bengel offers a similar solution: "He who had no staff, was not to care about procuring one, for our Lord says 'do not procure'; he however who possessed a staff, might take it with him, for convenience, not defence."[3]

The difficulty arises partly because of the range of meaning in the verb for "take" within its sentence. It may or may not include purchasing, depending on the context. This difficulty is particularly instructive when we compare Mark and Luke. Mark 6:8 and Luke 9:3 contain the same verb "take" (Greek *airō*). They also contain the same word for "staff" (Greek *rhabdon*). Mark says you may "take." Luke says you may not. It looks like a flat contradiction. But Matthew introduces the word "acquire," which shows that there are more dimensions to the process of preparing for the journey. If we did not have Matthew, we might never realize that there was a possible solution to the

---

[1] Henry Alford, *The Greek Testament . . .* , vol. 1, 7th ed. (London: Longmans, Green, 1898), 103.
[2] Ibid.
[3] Johann A. Bengel, *Gnomon of the New Testament*, 2 vols. (Philadelphia: Perkinpine and Higgins, 1860), 1:239. See also Gleason L. Archer, *Encyclopedia of Bible Difficulties* (Grand Rapids: Zondervan, 1982), 326.

difficulty, consisting in the difference between acquiring a staff expressly for
the journey and merely taking the one they already had.

Alternative Explanations

Since this particular case presents a challenging difficulty, we may expect
that other solutions have been proposed. Calvin offers the following:

> But there is an ambiguity in the use of the Hebrew word שבט, (*shebet;*) [for
> "staff"] and the Evangelists, though they wrote in Greek, used the word ῥάβδος
> in various senses. Matthew and Luke mean by it a *rod* which would be burden-
> some to the person who carries it: while Mark means by it a *walking-stick* to
> support and relieve a traveller. It is evident, that in making a journey it was
> customary to carry a *staff.*[4]

John McClellan's solution is similar.[5] It appeals to variation in the meaning
of "staff." Such variation, as we have observed, is characteristic of language
(chap. 8). I prefer Alford's solution (above) because it relies more directly
on positive evidence in the text.

Augustine says that Mark is talking about a spiritual staff, namely, the
power that the Lord had given them.[6] The immediate context in Mark does
indeed mention that the apostles are empowered through Jesus's commission
(Mark 6:7). But when "staff" is ranged alongside other articles such as bread,
bag, and money, the context indicates that we should take it as signifying a
physical staff. Augustine's interpretation is therefore not doing full justice
to the text. In a case like this, we are better off admitting that this is not an
adequate solution, even if we have no better solution. We would then be
acknowledging the limitations in our knowledge.

Next, M.-J. Lagrange quotes with approval Maldonat (on Matt. 10:10):
"Both [Matthew and Mark] express elegantly the same sense with contrary
words. For both, giving not the words of Christ but the sense, wished to
signify that Christ ordered the Apostles that they should not have anything
but what was necessary for the present."[7] Lagrange adds that "Jesus wanted
them to entrust themselves to Providence. The tradition has preserved this

---

[4]John Calvin, *Commentary on a Harmony of the Evangelists, Matthew, Mark, and Luke*, 3 vols., trans.
William Pringle (Grand Rapids: Eerdmans, n.d.), 1:444.
[5]John Brown McClellan, *The New Testament of Our Lord and Saviour Jesus Christ, a New Translation . . .*,
vol. 1 (London: Macmillan, 1875), 1:652.
[6]Augustine, *Harmony of the Gospels*, in vol. 6 of *NPNF*1, 2.30.74.
[7]Marie-Joseph Lagrange, *Évangile selon Saint Marc*, corrected and augmented (Paris: Gabalda, 1947),
151n8. The words are my translation from Maldonat's Latin.

counsel in two forms . . . ."[8] Lagrange is right to counsel us to focus on the main point, which all three accounts serve. And he is right to focus on the sense of the words, rather than merely on the words themselves. But details in the wording still contain elements of contrast. It is not enough to absorb the main point. We also want to take in the details. And in this respect other commentators are right to devote some energy to trying to understand the significance of the staff and the sandals.

Distinctive Emphases

Can we appreciate some distinctive emphasis in each account? By leaving out qualifications, Luke emphasizes the main point, which is that the disciples are to depend on God for their provision, and subordinately to depend on the hospitality of those who receive them. By putting in details about the staff and the sandals, Mark provides a realistic picture of what the disciples would actually have had with them.

Supplying this kind of detail could run the danger of distracting some people from the main point. But there is a reverse danger: people might get distracted wondering about the details if they just had Luke's account (as indeed we are likely to get distracted from the main point if we only pursue the details when we compare the three accounts).

With the word "acquire," Matthew helps us to realize that one of the aspects at issue would be preparations for the journey, including possible purchases.

We can see the selectiveness of the accounts by focusing on the difference between "acquiring" a staff and "taking" a staff. The two verbs focus on two distinct stages in the complex of actions involved in the journey. If a narrator wants to be pedantically precise, he may of course enter into an extended discussion and make an explicit distinction between the stage of acquiring a staff and the stage of actually taking it on the journey. But suppose the narrator has decided to write a simpler, more focused account. Having made that decision, he does not have the liberty to distinguish explicitly the two stages and their nuances. He must be content with a summary. We can therefore summarize the communicative situation using two dimensions (fig. 10). In one dimension we have the choice between an elaborate narrative and a simpler narrative. In the other dimension we have the distinction between one stage and two stages.

When a narrator decides for a compressed narrative (the left-hand column of fig. 10), he is no longer making a contrastive claim about distinctions

---

[8]"Jésus a voulu qu'on se confiât à la Providence. La tradition a pu conserver cet avis sous deux formes . . ." (ibid., 151–52n8).

Figure 10. Effect of compressed narration

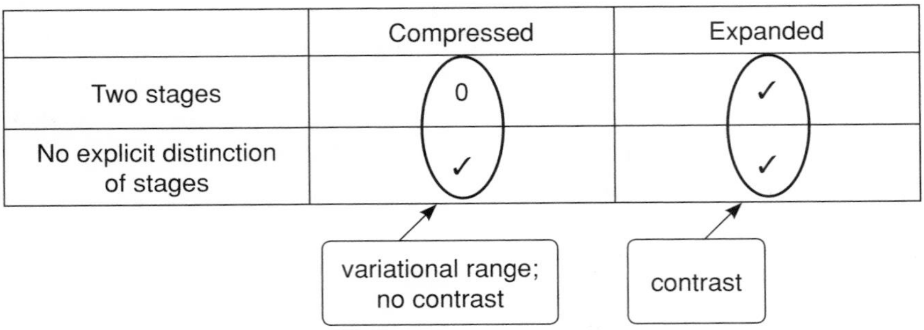

	Compressed	Expanded
Two stages	0	✓
No explicit distinction of stages	✓	✓

variational range; no contrast

contrast

between "acquiring" and "taking." He is vaguer in that respect, but he has gained in simplicity and focus on the main point.

In sum, all three accounts agree on the central points. In addition, the details are harmonizable. But even in the process of seeking a possible harmonization, we need to realize that (1) we do not need to know everything in order to know the main points; (2) our particular harmonization, though possible, does involve some guesswork on our part; (3) each detail in each Gospel is supplied for a purpose and is not to be brushed aside or dismissed by vague arguments that its purpose is *merely* theological and not historical; and (4) efforts for harmonization in this case involve details and do run the danger of tempting us to lose focus on the main points. In addition, we need to recognize that God has purposes in giving us difficulties (part three). He humbles us, increases our dependence on him, and makes us realize the limitations of our knowledge and our assumptions.

PART SIX
REPORTING SPEECHES

22

STILLING THE STORM

We now consider a case involving reported speech.

Comparing the Passages

All three Synoptic Gospels—Matthew, Mark, and Luke—describe a situation in which the disciples and Jesus were in a boat on the sea of Galilee, and he calmed a storm.[1] Here are the three passages, arranged side by side:

Matthew 8:23–27	Mark 4:35–41	Luke 8:22–25
[23] And when he got into the boat, his disciples followed him.	[35] On that day, when evening had come,	[22] One day
	he said to them, "Let us go across to the other side."	he got into a boat with his disciples, and he said to them, "Let us go across to the other side of the lake."
	[36] And leaving the crowd, they took him with them in the boat, just as he was. And other boats were with him.	So they set out,
		[23] and as they sailed he fell asleep.
[24] And behold, there arose a great storm on the sea, so that the boat was being	[37] And a great windstorm arose, and the waves were	And a windstorm came down on the lake, and they

---

[1]This set of passages was drawn to my attention by Robert H. Gundry, *Matthew: A Commentary on His Handbook for a Mixed Church under Persecution*, 2nd ed. (Grand Rapids: Eerdmans, 1994), 625. I do not, however, agree with the conclusions that Gundry draws from this and other passages.

Matthew 8:23–27	Mark 4:35–41	Luke 8:22–25
swamped by the waves;	breaking into the boat, so that the boat was already filling. 38 But he was in the stern,	were filling with water and were in danger.
but he was asleep. 25 And they went and woke him, saying, "Save us, Lord; we are perishing." [see v. 26b]	asleep on the cushion. And they woke him and said to him, "Teacher, do you not care that we are perishing?" 39 And he awoke and rebuked the wind and said to the sea, "Peace! Be still!" And the wind ceased, and there was a great calm.	[see v. 23a] 24 And they went and woke him, saying, "Master, Master, we are perishing!" And he awoke and rebuked the wind and the raging waves, and they ceased, and there was a calm.
26 And he said to them, "Why are you afraid, O you of little faith?" Then he rose and rebuked the winds and the sea, and there was a great calm.	40 He said to them, "Why are you so afraid? Have you still no faith?" [see v. 39]	25 He said to them, "Where is your faith?" [see v. 24]
27 And the men marveled, saying, "What sort of man is this, that	41 And they were filled with great fear and said to one another, "Who then is this, that	And they were afraid, and they marveled, saying to one another, "Who then is this, that he commands
even winds and sea obey him?"	even wind and sea obey him?"	even winds and water, and they obey him?"

We will focus particularly on Jesus's statement about the disciples' lack of faith.

Matthew 8:26	Mark 4:40	Luke 8:25
"Why are you afraid, O you of little faith?"	"Why are you so afraid? Have you still no faith?"	"Where is your faith?"

How do we deal with the differences between the three accounts?

The Same Incident?

First, we should ask whether the accounts in Matthew, Mark, and Luke are recording the same incident. The three have many similarities, and all three accounts are followed by accounts about a Gadarene demoniac. We have good reason to think that all three are talking about the same incident.

Different Wordings

We must consider whether Jesus could have said all of the things recorded in the three Gospels, one after the other, more or less like this: "Why are you so afraid, O you of little faith? What is the matter with you? Where is your faith? You have been with me for some time. You have seen the things that God has done. Have you still no faith?" In fact, he could have said much more even than this. The Gospels may have given us only a small portion of the total of what he said. This kind of situation is not much different from what we have seen in other cases. The Gospels report truly, but they are selective. They do not include every possible detail. The same principle applies to speeches.

Some people may be tempted to make fun of the idea that Jesus might have said things several different ways on one and the same occasion. But actually we do not know. We were not there. We need to be cautious. We should not overestimate our knowledge or our intuitions as to what is psychologically likely. At first it may seem absurd for someone to repeat himself. We think that saying it once is all a person needs. But when mothers are disappointed with their children, they sometimes give out a whole stream of rebukes. They may repeat themselves, with slightly different wording: "Why did you do that? What is the matter with you? What were you thinking? Didn't you realize it would be unkind to your sister? Where is your common sense? Don't you ever do it again. What makes you think you are the center of the world? What do you say for yourself? Why did you do it? What got into you? You were selfish, weren't you?" The stream and repetition may issue from mere petulance, or they may be a product of love—love that hopes that reinforcement and multiple questions may break through the obtuseness of a foolish heart and foolish behavior.

Assumptions about Logic and Contradiction

Jesus's words to his disciples may still appear difficult in this case because some people might claim that there is an actual contradiction. A objector may reason as follows: "According to Matthew 8:26 the disciples have little faith. Mark and Luke indicate that they have no faith. 'No faith' is not the same as 'little faith.' This discrepancy is an out-and-out contradiction that cannot be bridged."

But such reasoning is flawed. We cannot enter here into all the details. But we can make a beginning. What about the expressions "no faith" and "little faith"? True, these two are not identical, nor do they have exactly the same meaning. But their meanings do not function within the Gospels in isolation from the full sentences in which they occur, and the sentences do not function in isolation from the whole Gospels in which they occur. Meaning in robust natural language is colored by context, whereas Aristotelian logic has an artificiality to it: it requires sentences that function in pure isolation and—in principle—with infinite precision. When used uncritically it can push us toward a wooden conception of how logic and language function.[2]

Appreciating the Meanings in Detail

So we need to consider how words function within their contexts. When we do that, nuances become evident. Matthew 8:26 does not assert directly that the disciples have "little faith." It puts the Greek expression for "little faith" in the Greek vocative case, so that it is a label for the addressees. It is not the main point. But it is indeed a minor point, attached subordinately to the main point, which is a rhetorical question about the disciples' fear. Clearly we can infer that their fearful reaction stems from having little faith.

This remark about faith fits into a larger theme developing in Matthew about "little faith" (Matt. 6:30; 14:31; 16:8; 17:20). Using a worldview with "bare events" (see chap. 4), people could claim that this theme is a Matthean addition. It is indeed a contribution coming from Matthew as a human author. It is also a *divine* contribution, because God is the divine author of the Gospel of Matthew. In addition, the theme of little faith is a reality in the world that God governs. It is a reality not only for the world of the disciples during Jesus's lifetime, but also for the world of present-day struggles of present-day disciples with their tendencies to unbelief. Jesus had this reality in mind.

The passage is pastorally relevant. A critic, seeing the pastoral relevance, might claim that it must be an invention or an addition. But that is incorrect. The pastoral implications that we can see are making explicit the meaning already inherent in the events—a meaning that involves relationships not only to the mind of God but also to struggles throughout history. History hangs together according to the comprehensive plan of God. Different instances of unbelief or struggling belief have an organic relation to one another. Only with a defective view of history do we generate difficulties for ourselves.

When Mark 4:40 says, "Have you still no faith?" that is a question, not a direct assertion. It might seem to imply that the disciples have no faith. But the question does not immediately answer itself. We can imagine a mother saying to her child, "Do you have no brains?" Obviously the child does have brains, in the literal sense. But the mother may be effectively making the rhetorical point that he is not acting as if he did. Her question is a rhetorical question and does not call for a straightforward, simple "no" answer. Moreover, even if we convert Jesus's question into an assertion, it might be hyperbolic. If we

---

[2]On logic, see Vern S. Poythress, "Reforming Ontology and Logic in the Light of the Trinity: An Application of Van Til's Idea of Analogy," *Westminster Theological Journal* 57, no. 1 (1995):187–219. See also Vern S. Poythress, *Inerrancy and Worldview: Answering Modern Challenges to the Bible* (Wheaton, IL: Crossway, 2012), chap. 11.

were to say that someone has "no faith," we could be speaking hyperbolically to assert in a striking way that he has little faith.[3]

We should also take note of the word "still."[4] Mark 4:40 has an integral relation to other verses in Mark that show the disciples struggling with faith. Mark 4:40 occurs fairly early in the Gospel, so it is not clear what sort of progress in time is in view when Jesus says "still." The disciples were Jews. Many of them had a "faith" of some kind in God even before they became disciples of Jesus. They had no faith specifically with respect to Jesus until they became his disciples. Mark later paints an unflattering picture of the disciples, indicating that "their hearts were hardened" (6:52); likewise Jesus said, "Do you not yet perceive or understand? Are your hearts hardened?" (8:17).

Part of the problem that people perceive may be with the word "faith." It is a single word, but it can have a range of usages (chap. 8). What counts as faith? It depends on the context. Is it faith in God, or faith in the Messiah who is to come, or faith in the promises of God, or faith in a specific promise, or faith in Jesus now that he has come? And what quality of faith is it? James points out that "the demons believe—and shudder!" (James 2:19). That sort of faith is not sufficient for salvation.

If we travel beyond the Gospel of Mark and use the whole Bible as our anchor, we begin to obtain some insights into these matters. Faith, in fact, is a complex reality. We need a robust view of faith that leaves room for many kinds of variation. Faith appears in many forms, with many degrees of strength, weakness, and failing. This variation occurs in the examples found in Scripture. And, if we are at all observant, we see that it occurs today as well.

Finally, we need to include the Gospel of Luke. Luke says, "Where is your faith?" A simplistic reader might conclude that Luke is asserting that the disciples have no faith. But that it not precisely what he says. He gives us a question. And it is not a question that necessarily has a clear-cut answer. Jesus is challenging the disciples. Their actions have not been exhibiting faith. But that is part of the whole challenge that he is presenting to them.

---

[3] "The Chicago Statement on Biblical Inerrancy" helpfully reminds us: "We further deny that inerrancy is negated by Biblical phenomena such as a lack of modern technical precision, irregularities of grammar or spelling, observational descriptions of nature, the reporting of falsehoods, *the use of hyperbole* and round numbers, the topical arrangement of material, variant selections of material in parallel accounts, or the use of free citations" (italics mine; from article 13, accessed July 12, 2011, http://www.bible-researcher .com/chicago1.html).

[4] Among the Greek manuscripts there are several variant readings. One notable variant, characterizing the Byzantine text type, can be translated "Why are you so afraid *in this way? How is it that* you *do not* have faith?" Text-critical criteria favor the reading represented in the ESV translation, "Have you still no faith?" or, more literally, "Do you not yet [Greek *oupō*] have faith?" I proceed with the assumption that this variant represents the original text; but the discussion would be similar if one of the textual alternatives is original.

The challenge can help the disciples to evaluate themselves realistically, to repent, and to turn more heartily to Jesus—thereby growing in faith! Jesus's question is somehow not the kind of question that most suits a context where would-be disciples have no faith whatsoever in any sense. In fact, Luke 8:25, when taken in context, supplements what we find in the other Gospels.

Theological Emphases

The differences between the Gospels include differences in thematic patterns. Matthew, we noticed, includes a theme of "little faith" that occurs not only in 8:26 but also in 6:30; 14:31; and 16:8. Luke 12:28 contains a statement parallel to Matthew 6:30, but the other occurrences of "little faith" in Matthew have no exact parallels in the other Gospels. It appears that God gave Matthew a distinctive emphasis on this theme. This distinctiveness agrees with what we have earlier observed about different emphases in the Gospels (chap. 4). It is not a problem when understood in the light of God's purposes for the diversity as well as the unity of the four Gospels.

23

VARIATIONS IN CITATIONS

In the previous chapter, we considered the possibility that Jesus said things in more than one way. His rebuke to the disciples may have been a whole string of rebukes that included the precise wording found in all three of the Synoptic Gospels. But is that the only possibility compatible with the full divine authority and inerrancy of the Gospels? We must consider the question carefully.

Jesus is God. So Jesus's speeches are divine speech. The four Gospel writers are human beings, but they were inspired by the Holy Spirit so that what they wrote is also divine speech. Whenever the Gospel writers report things from Jesus's speeches, we are seeing God's report of what God himself said.

Citations from the Old Testament

Rather than looking only at the Gospels, we may first consider other cases where God gives words that cite an earlier divine speech. Specifically, we may consider New Testament citations from the Old Testament. Consider first Matthew 21:13: "He [Jesus] said to them, 'It is written, "My house shall be called a house of prayer," but you make it a den of robbers.'" The key citation, "My house shall be called a house of prayer," comes from Isaiah 56:7, which says,

> . . . my house shall be called a house of prayer
>   for all peoples.

Matthew cites what Jesus said, and Jesus cites what Isaiah said, so there are actually three distinct levels, all inspired by God: Matthew's writing, Jesus's oral speech, and Isaiah's writing. Matthew cites only part of the verse in Isaiah, but what he does cite has identical wording to Isaiah.

There are still differences, because in this case the three levels use two or three different languages. Isaiah was written originally in Hebrew. The Palestinian Jews of Jesus's day spoke primarily Aramaic as their mother tongue. But Greek and Hebrew were also known in Palestine. Jesus probably used Aramaic most of the time in his preaching, but he could also have used Greek or Hebrew on occasion. Finally, the Gospel of Matthew was written in Greek. When the Gospel of Matthew cites Jesus or the Old Testament, it does not reproduce the Hebrew of Isaiah or an Aramaic saying from Jesus syllable by syllable. But Matthew does represent the *meaning* of Isaiah. And in this case, the representation in Matthew 21:13 matches Isaiah 56:7 word for word. In the ESV, the wording in English is the same in the two verses, thereby exhibiting in English the close match between the Hebrew of Isaiah and the Greek of Matthew.

But there are technical details when we leave English and directly inspect the Hebrew of Isaiah and the Greek of Matthew. We may begin with the phrase "my house." The Greek in Matthew for "my house" consists in three words, which can be rendered woodenly as "the house my." The Hebrew in Isaiah has only one word, a noun with a suffix, which represents "my house." Next, the expression "shall be called" translates one word in Greek and one word in Hebrew. "A house of prayer" translates two words in Greek and two in Hebrew. The word order for the verse also differs. The Greek and Hebrew both have the order "house my house prayer shall-be-called." Translators rearrange the order in English in order to have a grammatical sentence.

In addition, other English translations show slight variations. The KJV has "Mine house" in Isaiah 56:7 and "My house" in Matthew 21:13. The NASB has "will be called" in Isaiah 56:7 and "shall be called" in Matthew 21:13. The NKJV has wording identical to the ESV.

A Difference in Wording

The text in Matthew and the one in Isaiah are very close, as close as is feasible when moving between two languages. But other instances in the New Testament show differences. For example, consider the descriptions of Jesus's mention of the greatest commandment. We compare Matthew 22:37 and Mark 12:30, both of which cite from Deuteronomy 6:5.

Deuteronomy 6:4–5	Matthew 22:37	Mark 12:29–30
	And he said to him,	[29] Jesus answered, "The most important is,
[4] "Hear, O Israel: The LORD our God, the LORD is one.		'Hear, O Israel: The Lord our God, the Lord is one.
[5] You shall love the LORD your God with all your heart and with all your soul and	"You shall love the Lord your God with all your heart and with all your soul and with all your mind. "	[30] And you shall love the Lord your God with all your heart and with all your soul and with all your mind and
with all your might."		with all your strength.'"

The original language of Deuteronomy 6:5 is Hebrew, while Matthew and Mark are in Greek. So the variation between the word "might" in Deuteronomy and the word "strength" in Mark is the sort of variation that can easily arise in translation. The meaning is essentially the same. More noteworthy is the occurrence of the extra phrase "with all your mind" in Matthew and Mark. "Mind" in Mark cannot be merely a substitute for "might" in Deuteronomy, since Mark includes a total of four phrases, instead of the three in Deuteronomy. Deuteronomy has "heart," "soul," and "might." Mark has "heart," "soul," and "strength," corresponding to the three words in Deuteronomy, *plus* "mind."

We first need to ask whether Matthew and Mark are recounting the same episode from the life of Jesus. In both Gospels the episode appears in the text right after the episode in which the Sadducees ask about the resurrection (Matt. 22:23–33; Mark 12:18–27). The inquirer to whom Jesus replies is identified in Matthew as a "lawyer," while in Mark he is "one of the scribes." These can easily be two descriptions of the same person. It certainly appears that we are dealing with the same episode in both texts.

The main question is what we make of the citation from Deuteronomy. The easiest explanation for the variation between Matthew and Mark is that Mark included a fuller account of what Jesus said, while Matthew left out the phrase "with all your strength." What Matthew included was indeed what Jesus said. He simply did not include all of it. This kind of selectivity is in accord with what we have already observed. The Gospel writers are selective in their description of the events. They may also be selective in their description of speeches. They report what various people said, but they do not promise us that they will always include *everything* that people said. We may recall the principle that the Gospel of John states explicitly: "Now there are also many other things that Jesus did. Were every one of them to be written, I suppose that the world itself could not contain the books that would be written" (John 21:25).

What do we say about the relationship of Jesus's words to Deuteronomy? The phrase "with all your mind" does not occur explicitly in Deuteronomy 6:5. But the verse includes this idea implicitly as an aspect of its *meaning*. In Deuteronomy 6:5 the expressions "all your heart" and "all your soul" overlap in their coverage, and together they cover the same kind of meaning that occurs in the expression "all your mind." So the meaning "all your mind" is implied by Deuteronomy 6:5. "Heart" in Hebrew is not merely the source of *emotions*, as we tend to think of it in English. It is the center of one's being. We find in the Old Testament that people *think* with their heart (Gen. 6:5; Isa. 10:7, ESV; Est. 6:6, KJV; Prov. 23:7, KJV). So Jesus's citation from Deuteronomy brings out an implication of the verse that is actually there.

Is this change of wording compatible with inerrancy? Of course it is. We can understand what is going on. Jesus refers to Deuteronomy 6:5 in a way that helps to make plain the fullness of its implications. Since Jesus is God, he has the authority to indicate the real divine meaning of the earlier words in Deuteronomy. He can repeat them exactly if he wishes. Such repetition occurs in Mark 12:29b, "Hear, O Israel: the Lord our God, the Lord is one." He can also draw out the meaning, as he does in Mark 12:30 when he includes the expression "with all your mind."

The Nature of Referring to Earlier Words

A difficulty may arise for some people because modern English translations use quotation marks. In the ESV of Mark 12:29–30 there are actually two sets of quotation marks, an outer one (double quotation marks) and an inner one (single quotation marks). The outer quotation marks indicate that Mark is providing us what Jesus said, while the inner quotation marks indicate the part within Jesus's speech where he is citing Deuteronomy 6:4–5. But these quotation marks are part of the English and are not present in the original languages. The Bible in the original languages has no special graphical symbol like a quotation mark to indicate the beginning and the end of any quotation. As far as we know, such marks were not part of the written form of ancient Hebrew and Greek. The ancient texts simply did not have any such graphical convention.

That is God's choice for how he is communicating. He does not make everything explicit. What he says, he always says truly. But he does not provide marks for the beginnings and ends of passages that refer to earlier words. When we turn to the King James Version, we find essentially the same thing. The KJV does not have quotation marks. There are just words.

So the Bible in the original languages and in the KJV leaves it up to the reader to figure out whether something is a reference to an earlier text or an earlier speech. And, significantly, we also have to ask what *kind* of a reference it is. Is it a *verbatim* citation, or does it rephrase some earlier speech to reexpress its meaning? Our earlier example, Matthew 21:13, gives something more like a verbatim citation (within the constraints of grammatical differences between languages). Matthew 22:37 and Mark 12:30 give us a more interpretive rendering or interpretive citation.

In modern formal academic writing, quotation marks are used to indicate an exact, verbatim quotation. The rules are very strict. Any omissions have to be marked with ellipsis points (. . .), and anything added for clarification must be clearly marked—usually enclosed in brackets or else placed completely outside the quotation in the form of a commentary or explanation. These procedures are modern conventions. They are quite convenient in their own way when people want to specify unambiguously what is the exact wording from an original.

But in modern life we meet other situations in which people report a speech by giving the meaning but not claiming to give the exact wording. In ordinary life, particularly when no quotation marks appear, one person's report of another's speech may give the gist of it, but use different words to express the gist. A newspaper report may summarize in a single page a half-hour or hour-long political speech.

This kind of thing happens even in court testimony, where issues of truthfulness become weighty. For example, a witness on the stand may testify that he heard the accused person make a promise: "John told Donna that he would pay it all back in a week." The defense attorney says, "Were those his exact words?" The witness can truthfully answer, "No, but that is what he said." In other words, the witness is not claiming to give the exact wording, but he *is* claiming to give the meaning.

Now the Bible is divine testimony, not merely human testimony. So it is not completely parallel to any of these modern cases. We need to take the Bible on its own terms. We ought not to force the Bible into our modern mold, in which academic literature has precise conventions for exact quotations. The Bible in the original does not have quotation marks. It does not make explicit the modern distinction between an exact quotation and an interpretive citation.

This lack of explicitness allows flexibility. *Sometimes* the Bible gives an exact quotation; *sometimes* it gives an interpretive citation. We know that *both* kinds of citation are faithful to the original that is being cited because God is always consistent with himself. He is free to repeat his earlier words exactly at a later time. He is also free to cite an earlier speech in a way that brings out implications. God knows the end from the beginning (Isa. 46:10). He intends from the beginning the implications that he may make explicit by a later interpretation.

Citations with Application

In addition, sometimes God indicates the significance that an earlier passage has when taken in the light of later fulfillment. Consider, for example, 2 Corinthians 6:17, "Touch no unclean thing." This wording comes from Isaiah 52:11. In the immediate context of Isaiah 52:11, God is giving instruction about not touching the unclean to "you who bear the vessels of the LORD." The instruction has in mind the fact that only the Levites were supposed to carry the holy objects used in the service of the house of God (see Num. 4:1–33; 18:4–7). They had to be ceremonially "clean" when they did this special service. These regulations for ceremonial holiness came to an end when Christ accomplished his work as the final high priest (Heb. 10:9). Speaking through the apostle Paul in 2 Corinthians 6:17, God takes account of these changes and applies the principle of "touch no unclean thing" to the sanctification of believers and their separation from sinful practices. God is applying the meaning of the passage to a new epoch in the history of redemption.

The Bible always has depths to it because it is the word of God. But it is also accessible. We can understand it as God opens our hearts and overcomes our resistance to its message through the work of the Holy Spirit. We can understand that God can from time to time cite earlier speeches in more than one way.[1]

The Principle of Truthfulness

But we must introduce an important qualification, which depends on God's truthfulness. God's own character as the faithful and true God means that we can always rely on him to speak the truth. If God *were* to indicate in his speech that he is providing an exact, verbatim record of an earlier speech, we could rely on him and confidently believe that what we have is indeed an exact, verbatim record. Even when God does not explicitly indicate that he is providing a verbatim record, we see from cases like Matthew 21:13 that

---

[1]We could add still more kinds of uses of the Old Testament to those discussed so far. See G. K. Beale and D. A. Carson, eds., *Commentary on the New Testament Use of the Old Testament* (Grand Rapids: Baker, 2007); G. K. Beale, *Handbook on the New Testament Use of the Old Testament: Exegesis and Interpretation* (Grand Rapids: Baker, 2012).

he can do so if he wishes. But he can also provide an interpretive citation, as he does in Mark 12:30. It is up to him. Remember, *there are no quotation marks in the original.*

The Chicago Statement on Biblical Inerrancy, drawn up by the International Council on Biblical Inerrancy in 1978, acknowledges in its formulations this principle about references to earlier Scripture.

> We further deny that inerrancy is negated by Biblical phenomena such as a lack of modern technical precision, irregularities of grammar or spelling, observational descriptions of nature, the reporting of falsehoods, the use of hyperbole and round numbers, the topical arrangement of material, variant selections of material in parallel accounts, or the use of *free citations*.[2]

What the statement calls "free citations" are uses of earlier Scripture such as we have just seen.

Another Example: Matthew 15:7–9

Consider another example. We may compare Isaiah 29:13; Matthew 15:7–9; and Mark 7:6–7.

Isaiah 29:13	Matthew 15:7–9	Mark 7:6–7
And the Lord said: "Because this people draw near with their mouth and honor me with their lips, while their hearts are far from me, and their fear of me is a commandment taught by men . . ."	"7 You hypocrites! Well did Isaiah prophesy of you, when he said: 8 "This people honors me with their lips, but their heart is far from me; 9 in vain do they worship me, teaching as doctrines the commandments of men."	6 And he said to them, "Well did Isaiah prophesy of you hypocrites, as it is written, "'This people honors me with their lips, but their heart is far from me; 7 in vain do they worship me, teaching as doctrines the commandments of men.'"

Matthew picks up in the middle of the verse 29:13 in Isaiah, with "honor me," but supplies "this people" from the beginning to the verse. "Their fear of me" in Isaiah corresponds to the expression "in vain do they worship me"

---

[2] "The Chicago Statement on Biblical Inerrancy," article 13 (italics mine), accessed July 12, 2011, http://www .bible-researcher.com/chicago1.html. See also Archibald A. Hodge and Benjamin B. Warfield, *Inspiration*, with introduction by Roger R. Nicole (repr., Grand Rapids: Baker, 1979), 44.

in Matthew. "A commandment taught by men" in Isaiah becomes "teaching as doctrines the commandments of men" in Matthew.

The exact wording is different in these expressions, but we can see that the substance is still there. Isaiah 29:13 refers to Israelite worship in the early part of the verse, in the expression "draw near with their mouth." The expression "draw near" evokes the Old Testament custom of drawing near to the presence of God in the tabernacle and the temple. The expression "with their mouth" indicates that the Israelites engage in prayer and praise. They are worshiping God. But their worship is hypocritical. The citation in Matthew and Mark explicitly uses the word "worship," which superficially does not match the corresponding expression in Isaiah, namely, "their fear of me." But substantively it does match. The fear of God can be expressed either in formal worship or in daily behavior. In Isaiah the context is at least partly one of formal worship. So Matthew and Mark in their wording "they worship me" do correspond to the substance of what Isaiah is talking about. God is saying that the behavior of religious leaders in Jesus's time is like the hypocritical worship that Israelites offered in Isaiah's time.

Isaiah implies that their fear is "in vain," though Isaiah does not use those precise words. By including the expression "in vain," Matthew and Mark bring out the implication of the text in Isaiah. The point fits the circumstances in Jesus's earthly life. Jesus was objecting to the Pharisaic and scribal traditions that obscured and even contradicted the law of Moses. The situation he addressed was somewhat different in its details from the rote worship that Isaiah faced during his lifetime. But the principle is the same: both confronted instances where people practiced rote worship and followed tradition rather than God. The citation of Isaiah is appropriate, but the new wording helps to bring out the implications of Isaiah for the time in which Jesus lived.[3]

Is this change of wording compatible with inerrancy? It is. The citation from Isaiah helps to make plain how the Pharisees and scribes were violating the word of God for the sake of their tradition. God uses interpretive wording that helps to bring out the implications.

Other Cases

We can look at other cases in the Bible. These confirm the inferences that we have already made. For example, compare Deuteronomy 29:4 and Isaiah 29:10 to Romans 11:8.

---

[3]The situation is more complicated because the wording in the Gospels is quite similar to the wording in the Septuagint, the ancient Greek translation of the Old Testament. The main point still holds: the wording does bring out the implications of the Hebrew original of Isaiah.

Deuteronomy 29:4	Isaiah 29:10	Romans 11:8
But to this day the LORD has not given you a heart to understand or eyes to see or ears to hear [see Deut. 29:4a]	For the LORD has poured out upon you a spirit of deep sleep, and has closed your eyes (the prophets), and covered your heads (the seers)	. . . as it is written, "God gave them a spirit of stupor, eyes that would not see and ears that would not hear, down to this very day."

The book of Romans reads "God gave *them*" where Deuteronomy 29:4 and Isaiah 29:10 both have "you."[4] The adjustment in wording is appropriate, since Deuteronomy 29:4 and Isaiah 29:10 are both directly addressing people who are spiritually blind. The book of Romans, by contrast, is directly addressing the Christians at Rome, who are no longer blind, and is instructing them about the meaning of the blindness that remains among unbelieving Jews. God is showing how his earlier word in Isaiah applies in the circumstances of the New Testament.

Instances of so-called "free citations" could be multiplied. Here is one more:

Isaiah 42:1–4	Matthew 12:17–21
¹ Behold my servant, whom I uphold, my chosen, in whom my soul delights; I have put my Spirit upon him; he will bring forth justice. to the nations ² He will not cry aloud or lift up his voice, or make it heard in the street; ³ a bruised reed he will not break, and a faintly burning wick he will not quench; he will faithfully bring forth justice. ⁴ He will not grow faint or be discouraged till he has established justice in the earth; and the coastlands wait for his law.	¹⁷ This was to fulfill what was spoken by the prophet Isaiah: ¹⁸ "Behold, my servant whom I have chosen, my beloved with whom my soul is well pleased. I will put my Spirit upon him, and he will proclaim justice to the Gentiles. ¹⁹ He will not quarrel or cry aloud, nor will anyone hear his voice in the streets; ²⁰ a bruised reed he will not break, and a smoldering wick he will not quench, until he brings justice to victory; ²¹ and in his name the Gentiles will hope."

In addition to other small differences, it might be noted that the Gospel of Matthew does not have an equivalent to the expression "I uphold" in Isaiah

---

[4]In addition, Rom. 11:8 and Isa. 29:10 have some similarity with Isa. 6:9–10, which in v. 10 does use "their."

42:1. Instead of "whom I uphold, my chosen . . ." Matthew has "whom I have chosen, my beloved." The expression "my beloved" in Matthew 12:18 has no direct equivalent in Isaiah 42:1. But Israel, for whom the servant (Jesus) is a representative head, is addressed in the next chapter of Isaiah as "precious in my eyes, and honored, and I love you" (43:4). God through Matthew is bringing to expression meanings that are already implied in Isaiah 42 and are made more explicit in Isaiah 43:4.

In another example Romans 9:32–33 uses Isaiah 28:16 and Isaiah 8:14.

Isaiah 8:14	Isaiah 28:16	Romans 9:32–33
		[32] They have stumbled over the stumbling stone,
And he [the Lord] will become		[33] as it is written,
	Therefore thus says the Lord GOD, "Behold, I am the one who has laid as a foundation in Zion,	"Behold, I am laying in Zion
a sanctuary and	a stone, a tested stone, a precious cornerstone, of a sure foundation:	
a stone of offense and		a stone of stumbling, and a rock of offense;
a rock of stumbling	'Whoever believes	and whoever believes in him
	will not be in haste.'"	will not be put to shame."
to both houses of Israel, a trap and a snare to the inhabitants of Jerusalem.		

Romans 9:33 introduces the verse with the expression "as it is written," indicating that what follows is in the Old Testament. The rest of the verse apparently combines elements from Isaiah 8:14 and 28:16. This combination makes sense, since both passages in Isaiah use the language of "stone" to describe a future climactic work of the Lord that will bring saving security to some ("a sanctuary," "a sure foundation") and destruction to others ("a rock of stumbling"; "refuge of lies" in Isa. 28:17; compare 28:15).[5]

As usual, most English translations of Romans 9:33 use quotation marks. The quotation marks are a useful convention in English to help readers tell which part is coming from the Old Testament. But the quotation marks can also be misleading because, if they are interpreted strictly, they seem to promise us that we have an exact quotation from a single place

---

[5]For further discussion of Rom. 9:33 and the other New Testament uses of the Old Testament, see Beale and Carson, *Commentary on the New Testament Use of the Old Testament*.

in the Old Testament. There is no such indication in the original Greek of Romans 9:33.

In all these cases God is free to use wording that brings out implications of his earlier words.

24

MEANING AND INTENTION

How do we understand instances where the New Testament use of the Old Testament involves a rewording or a combination of passages? The New Testament is unlike other human writings because it is inspired by God. Since it is God's speech, and God always speaks truly, it is without error. In addition, it *does* show similarities to human writings, because God is speaking in human languages. He ordained language itself in all its variations. So at points we may be able to make helpful comparisons between the Bible and noninspired human communication.

To begin with, we know that modern preachers, who are not inspired, will sometimes express the meaning of the Bible by combining passages or rewording them. This worries no one. Such a reexpression is fair, provided (1) the modern use does not *claim to be an exact, verbatim quote*, and (2) it derives meaning from the original rather than distorting the original meaning into something else.[1]

We may then conclude that something similar can go on when the New Testament uses the Old Testament. The New Testament passage gives the meaning of one or more passages of the Old Testament. At times, it draws

---

[1] Speakers may also sometimes reuse biblical phraseology for new purposes without any close tie to the meaning in the Bible. For example, a person may say, "I escaped by the skin of my teeth." He is reusing phraseology found in Job 19:20. But the expression "the skin of my teeth" has become a stock expression in English, so that the person using the expression may or may not be aware that he is reusing something found in Job. Even if he is aware of the source, he is typically making a comment not about the meaning of Job, but only about the meaning of his own experience. We need not consider these additional complexities here.

out implications that are not completely *explicit* in the original wording in the Old Testament, but are nevertheless intended by God.

A. A. Hodge and B. B. Warfield in their book on inspiration concur: "Quotation, being essentially different from translation, any amount of deviation from the original, *in form*, is thoroughly allowable, so long as the sense of the original is adhered to; provided only that the quoter is not professing to give the exact form."[2] What Hodge and Warfield have called "quotation," I have preferred to call citation, in order further to clarify that we are not talking about exact quotation.

Perspectives on Meaning

We can confirm the importance of meaning by considering meaning and communication in a general context. Consider human communication. Human communication involves a speaker, a discourse, and an audience. For example, John the Baptist announced, "Repent, for the kingdom of heaven is at hand" (Matt. 3:2). John was the speaker, the announcement was the discourse, and the audience consisted in those who came to hear him. In John's case God himself was the divine speaker, in addition to John the human speaker, because John was a prophet. But John the Baptist can still illustrate for us the character of human speech.

In addition to oral communication, we should consider written communication. For written communication, we have an author, a text, and readers. For convenience, we will temporarily use the labels for oral communication—speaker, discourse, and audience—to cover both oral and written forms.

A human speaker intends to express meanings. Those meanings come to expression in discourse, and the audience receives meanings by attending to the discourse and its speaker. If communication is successful, the meanings agree.

A deeper analysis of communication, within the context of biblical teaching, shows that God is the foundation for all communication whatsoever. God the Father speaks his Word from all eternity (John 1:1). He also speaks particular utterances in bringing about the creation of the world. "And God said, 'Let there be light,' and there was light" (Gen. 1:3). After God created human beings, he spoke to them (Gen. 1:28–30).

God's communication is the original, while human communication is derivative. Except for special cases where God speaks through human beings

---

[2]Archibald A. Hodge and Benjamin B. Warfield, *Inspiration*, with introduction by Roger R. Nicole (repr., Grand Rapids: Baker, 1979), 63 (italics are original); similarly Louis Gaussen, *Theopneustia: The Plenary Inspiration of the Holy Scriptures: Deduced from Internal Evidence, and the Testimonies of Nature, History and Science*, rev. ed. (Chicago: Bible Institute Colportage, n.d. [1915]), 162–64.

in inspiration, human speech is not inspired. But it still shows analogies to divine communication because we are made in the image of God.

So let us consider divine communication. The most foundational communication of all is the communication in the Trinity, expressed in the statement, "In the beginning was the Word, and the Word was with God, and the Word was God" (John 1:1). In God, intention and expression go together. God the Father's mind is expressed in a discourse, namely the Word, the second person of the Trinity. Between the Father and the Son there is fellowship and coinherence. This fellowship is unique to God. But it is reflected on a created level when a human being speaks his mind.

In such human speech we can see coherence between the mind of the speaker and the expression of his mind in discourse. If the speaker has a receptive audience, there is a coherence between intention, expression, and what the audience receives. Thus, a focus on intention is implied when we try to understand a discourse. It is natural for the New Testament to focus on the meaning and intention of the Old Testament when it uses the Old Testament.

Reexpression of Meaning

In ordinary communication, we may also reexpress what a speaker says using different words. This ability to reexpress meaning also derives from God. As human beings made in the image of God, we can know God. We can "image" in our mind the truths in God's mind. Of course we are creatures, not the Creator. God's mind is original, ours is derivative. But there is still a sense in which, when we know truth, we are reexpressing in our mind what God has in his mind.

This pattern of reexpression has an origin in God himself. The Son is the "exact imprint" of God's nature (Heb. 1:3). He is "the image of the invisible God" (Col. 1:15). This imaging on the part of the Son is the original instance of a kind of reexpression. The Son reexpresses the character of the Father. The Son's reexpression is completely faithful to the original: "Whoever has seen me has seen the Father" (John 14:9). The Son is the perfect image of the Father. God's speeches to us express meanings that can be found first of all in the Father, in the Son, and in the Spirit, in their communion with one another.

When he speaks to us, God can reexpress what he has said earlier. When he does so, he may express himself in different words from an earlier speech. Or, when he wishes, he may repeat exactly the same words. The New Testament uses of the Old Testament are instances of such reexpression. In all such cases, the most important thing to recognize is that God speaks *both* addresses, the earlier one and the later one.

In the case of the Gospels, where we may have more than one parallel account, God speaks *each* of the accounts, not just what is common to them all. The same is true for parallel passages within the Old Testament. First and Second Chronicles have many parallels in 1–2 Samuel and 1–2 Kings. Some parallels have nearly identical wording; but at some places there are small differences. Psalm 18 is parallel to 2 Samuel 22, with mostly the same wording, but some small differences. In some cases, a later speech from God may bring out more clearly implications that were less immediately visible in an earlier wording.

Hebrews 1:1–2 indicates that God's speech to his people has a *progressive* character. What God says later on, in the time of the New Testament, builds on what God said before. Sometimes God reiterates what he said earlier, as in the case of word-for-word quotes from the Old Testament. Sometimes God supplements what he said earlier. Sometimes he also draws out implications. God indicates that promises are being fulfilled in Christ, and what he accomplished in Christ brings to a climax what he intimated in the Old Testament: "In these last days he has spoken to us by his Son" (Heb. 1:2), in contrast to the preliminary character of the communication when "God spoke to our fathers by the prophets" (1:1). When Christ made "purification for sins" (1:3), he brought to fulfillment the Old Testament ceremonial rites of purification (Heb. 10:11–14). God says more when he draws out the symbolic meaning of the Old Testament by explaining its fulfillment in Christ.[3]

In all these cases, God's new expression images the original. This pattern of reexpression imitates the eternal reexpression of God the Father in God the Son. It is thoroughly compatible with who God is and with his truthfulness. The Son, let us remember, is the true image of the Father, and at the same time the Son is distinct from the Father. He is not the Father a second time, as if there were no differentiation. By analogy, God can reexpress himself using different words if he so chooses.

We as creatures are not on that divine level. But we are images of the Creator. If we as human beings receive a message from someone, and then reexpress it in different words that have the same meaning, the result may be faithful to the meaning of our source.[4] Of course, because we are fallible,

---

[3] On the progressive character of God's speech and his work of redemption, see Geerhardus Vos, *Biblical Theology: Old and New Testaments* (Carlisle, PA: Banner of Truth, 1975).

[4] On truth, see Vern S. Poythress, *In the Beginning Was the Word: Language—A God-Centered Approach* (Wheaton, IL: Crossway, 2009), chaps. 30, 35–36.

there may be other times when our human reexpression is *not* faithful to the source. Our fallibility means that our speech differs from the speech of God.

It follows, then, that *in principle* reexpression using different words may legitimately convey meaning. Some, but not all, human speech legitimately reexpresses meaning. With God's speech, the reexpression is always faithful because God is always faithful to himself.

The same principle becomes even clearer when we consider translation from one language to another. If we are dealing with translation from Aramaic to Greek or Greek to English, we necessarily use different words in the different languages. God has given us language with rich resources, so that we can accomplish such reexpression.[5] When human translators or interpreters render meanings from one language to another, they are of course fallible. On the other hand, when God does it, he is infallible. God provides just such renderings whenever the Bible gives us speeches in Greek that Jesus originally spoke in Aramaic, and whenever it gives in Greek meanings from the Old Testament that were originally in Hebrew.

Distorted Meanings

We have already observed that human beings, unlike God, may distort meanings as well as reexpress them faithfully. A distortion may creep in either deliberately or accidentally. Distortion easily ensues when a person gives only a vague paraphrase. But it can also happen even when someone reports words with comparative exactitude. In modern times, people sometimes complain that they have been "quoted out of context." Their words may be accurately reported, and yet not their meaning.

In fact, the Devil can quote Scripture for his own purposes.

Then the devil took him to the holy city and set him on the pinnacle of the temple and said to him, "If you are the Son of God, throw yourself down, for it is written,

"'He will command his angels concerning you,'

and

"'On their hands they will bear you up,
       lest you strike your foot against a stone.'"

---

[5] The possibility of reexpression belongs to language, because language itself shows coherence as well as distinctions between meanings, on the one hand, and their expressions in particular grammatical forms and sounds, on the other. See ibid., chap. 32.

Jesus said to him, "Again it is written, 'You shall not put the Lord your God to the test.'" (Matt. 4:5–7)

The Devil employs two citations from Scripture: Psalm 91:11 and 91:12. The citations in Matthew match the Old Testament original: The ESV translation has exactly the same wording in Psalm 91 and in Matthew 4:5–7; if we go to the original languages, the Hebrew of Psalm 91 and the Greek of Matthew 4:5–7 are very close. The words are right, but the Devil's meaning is wrong. The Devil twists the meaning by urging Jesus to treat the verses as if they were a kind of magic formula from God. He implies that they could be used to manipulate God to get him to do what you want rather than submitting to his will. The Devil's interpretation radically misses the point because it detaches the verses from the context of Psalm 91, where the person designated by "you"—ultimately the Messiah—is trusting in God and not trying to invent his own way. The Devil's interpretation also detaches the verses from the character of God. God is not a God who can be manipulated to perform our bidding.

And so the words of Psalm 91:11–12, which God speaks as promises, cannot mean what the Devil says. They cannot mean something that contradicts the character of God. In addition, their meaning should be interpreted in the light of what the whole Old Testament teaches, both about the character of God himself and about the appropriate godly response to his words. Jesus masterfully refutes the Devil's interpretation by citing another verse (Deut. 6:16), which indicates the nature of a godly response to God, and which is reinforced by the whole rest of the Old Testament.

Words taken out of context, even the very words of Scripture, have been perverted by the Devil to have a meaning at odds with their actual meaning as words spoken by God. The true meaning becomes clear as we listen to what Jesus says about them, and as we consider the words in their context in the Old Testament.

So we have found two complementary principles. First, mere mechanical repetition of earlier words does not in itself guarantee that a speaker is doing justice to the meaning. The Devil can pervert the meaning. Second, reexpression of meaning, using either the same or different words, can at times faithfully represent meaning. But it depends on whether the speaker is reliable. The perfect reliability of God should give us confidence that his speech is always reliable in its meanings. The unreliability of the Devil should make us watch out. Human beings, of course, are in the middle. Sometimes they are reliable, and sometimes not. This middle kind of reliability can include cases of faithful reexpression of meaning and other cases of distortion, either major or minor.

25

Speech When Jesus Stills the Storm

We return to the parallel passages that describe Jesus's stilling the storm: Matthew 8:23–27; Mark 4:35–41; and Luke 8:22–25 (see chap. 22). What do we do with the harmonization questions?

Our primary principle is that God is reliable. So all three accounts faithfully represent the events, including what Jesus and his disciples said. All three accounts are selective, so that they do not necessarily include every detail, nor do they necessarily include everything that Jesus or his disciples said. We already saw in chapter 22 that the accounts are harmonizable. Despite alleged tensions between expressions like "little faith" (Matt. 8:26) and "no faith" (Mark 4:40), the expressions are substantively in harmony. The disciples are not showing faith.

What about the wording of Jesus's speech and the disciples' speech? People may ask what exact words they said. It seems likely that the speeches were originally in Aramaic, though it is possible that they were in Greek. People are curious and might want speculatively to reconstruct the Aramaic word for word (even though in fact God has not supplied us enough information to do so).

Comparison with Citations from the Old Testament

Can we learn from the patterns that we observed in citations from the Old Testament (chap. 23)? There are some similarities between citations from the

Old Testament and reports of speech in the Gospels. In each case the report itself (the New Testament passage as we have it) is God's word. The earlier speech (the Old Testament citation) being reported is also God's word. In some cases in the Gospels, namely, when they refer to a speech of Jesus, the earlier speech being reported is God's word. In other cases, however, the Gospels give inspired reports of earlier noninspired speeches, speeches from either the disciples or Jesus's opponents, or still others. For example, Matthew 22:16 says that the Pharisees "sent their disciples to him [Jesus], along with the Herodians, saying, 'Teacher, we know that you are true and teach the way of God truthfully.'" This verse in the Gospel of Matthew provides an inspired report of an earlier speech and faithfully indicates what this group of people said to Jesus. But the inspiration of Matthew's report does not imply that the group of people were themselves inspired. In fact, they were deceitful, and Jesus detected it: he was "aware of their malice" (Matt. 22:18).

When we consider the New Testament citations from the Old Testament, there is a change of language from Hebrew or Aramaic (the original languages of the Old Testament) to Greek. In some of the cases in the Gospels, we have reports that refer to speeches originally in Aramaic, but we do not know which speeches were originally in Aramaic and which were in Greek or perhaps even in Hebrew.[1]

The citations from the Old Testament have no quotation marks when we look at the Greek of the New Testament. Some give us word-for-word representations of the meaning, while others draw out implications. May we expect the same thing to happen when the Gospels report what various people said?

The Gospels in the Greek original do not include quotation marks. So the parallel with the New Testament citations from the Old Testament suggests that they may sometimes have word-for-word representation and may sometimes reexpress the meaning in other ways. The point to be underlined is that, because God is faithful and reliable, every case gives us a faithful representation of the meaning. Every case gives us the truth in the exact words that God decided to use when he wrote each Gospel through the human author.

But there is at least one significant difference between the Gospels and the New Testament citations from the Old Testament. In the case of citations from the Old Testament, the Bible as a whole gives us both (1) the earlier Old Testament passage, that is, the passage or passages being cited, and (2) the later New Testament passage, the passage that does the citing. The New

---

[1]An exception occurs when a Gospel directly transliterates an Aramaic expression: e.g., Mark 5:41; 14:36; 15:34.

Testament writers, and God himself speaking through them, knew that their readers could access the original passage. The task of the New Testament writing, as designed by God, was not *merely* to report the meaning of the Old Testament in such a way that the reader could know for the first time what it is. Rather, the task was to comment on the meaning. The comments often occur in the larger paragraph around the citation. There God points out some of its implications for understanding the work of Christ or for bringing home some application for the readers.

Now sometimes this process of drawing out the implications can begin with the wording of the citation itself. A particular choice of wording in reporting the passage begins to indicate what the Old Testament passage says when we take into account that God intended it to function in pointing forward to Christ and in instructing us "on whom the end of the ages has come" (1 Cor. 10:11; see Rom. 15:4).

By contrast, in the case of the Gospels, we do not have any additional, earlier canonical document (outside the Gospels themselves) that reports the very same speech we have in the Gospels. God and the human writer inspired by him take into account this situation. As a result, we can expect that the Gospels are extra-sensitive in the way in which they report the meaning of the speeches. They accurately give us the meaning. But they may not always give us a verbatim report. They do not explicitly claim to give a verbatim report, so in any one case, we do not know whether they are giving an exact quote or a summary or a reexpression.

Hodge and Warfield on Inspiration

Archibald A. Hodge and Benjamin B. Warfield in their book on inspiration confirm this principle. They start with attention to the purpose of a particular biblical passage.

> We do not suppose that inspiration made a writer false to his professed purpose, but rather that it kept him infallibly true to it. No objection [to inerrancy] is valid, therefore, which overlooks the prime question: What was the professed or implied purpose of the writer in making this statement?[2]

They then apply this principle to the issue of free citations and reports of speeches.

---

[2]Archibald A. Hodge and Benjamin B. Warfield, *Inspiration*, with introduction by Roger R. Nicole (repr., Grand Rapids: Baker, 1979), 42.

[The principle of paying attention to purpose] destroys the force of every objection [to inspiration] which is tacitly founded on the idea that partial and incomplete statements cannot be inspired, no documents can be quoted except *verbatim*, no conversations reported unless at length, etc., and which thus denies the right of another to speak to the present purpose only, appeal to the sense, not wording of a document, give abstracts of discourses, and apply, by a true exegesis, the words of a previous writer to the present need. The sum of the whole matter is simply this: No phenomenon can be validly urged against verbal inspiration which, found out of Scripture [in some other, merely human document], would not be a valid argument against the truth of the writing. Inspiration securing no more than this—*truth*, simple truth—no phenomenon can be urged against verbal inspiration which cannot be proved to involve *an indisputable error*.[3]

In this paragraph from Hodge and Warfield, two expressions are especially pertinent: (1) "appeal to the sense, not wording of a document," and (2) "give abstracts of discourses." These two expressions have links respectively to two earlier expressions, "no documents can be quoted except *verbatim*," and "no conversations reported unless at length." In the context, Hodge and Warfield are discussing the fact that critics have accused the Bible of being deficient and therefore not inspired. These critics insist, among other things, that "no documents can be quoted except *verbatim*." Over against this artificial standard, Hodge and Warfield place the practice in which a writer can "appeal to the sense, not wording of a document." This practice has also been called "free citation," which we have seen in chapter 23. In addition, in the case of oral discourses, that is, "conversations," the critics have insisted that "no conversations [can be] reported unless at length." Opposing this insistence, Hodge and Warfield observe that a writer can "give abstracts of discourses." A biblical writer can provide an abstract, that is, a summary or condensation. That form of reporting may take place both in the Gospels and elsewhere in the Bible.

We can further clarify Hodge and Warfield's statements by observing that in the quotation above they are focusing on the issue of verbatim quotation, not verbal inspiration. They make it clear elsewhere in their book that they believe that the inspiration of the Bible extends to the words, not merely the thoughts.[4] They rightly maintain that the Bible gives us, word for word, exactly what God says. That is a different point from the observation that, in the Bible's word-for-word inspired text, it may give us "the sense" or "abstract" of earlier speeches or documents.

---

3 Ibid., 43–44.
4 Ibid., 22.

Hodge and Warfield's statements first appeared in 1881 as an article in *The Presbyterian Review* (2:225–60), and then were published the same year in the book, *Inspiration*. Earlier, in 1879, Warfield had already expressed the same ideas in his inaugural lecture at Western Theological Seminary.

> Inspiration, securing absolute truth, secures that the writer shall do what he professes to do; not what he does not profess. If the author does not profess to be quoting the Old Testament *verbatim,*—unless it can be proved that he professes to give the *ipsissima verba,*—then no objection arises against his verbal inspiration from the fact that he does not give the exact words. If an author does not profess to report the exact words of a discourse or a document—if he professes to give, or it is enough for his purposes to give, an abstract or general account of the sense or the wording, as the case may be,—then it is not opposed to his claim to inspiration that he does not give the exact words. This remark sets aside a vast number of objections brought against verbal inspiration. . . . It sets aside, for instance, all objection against the verbal inspiration of the Gospels, drawn from the diversity of their accounts of words spoken by Christ or others, written over the cross, etc.[5]

In defending the inerrancy of the Bible, Warfield indicates explicitly that "the verbal inspiration of the Gospels" is fully consistent with "the diversity of their accounts of words spoken by Christ or others." He sees that an author can give a "general account of the sense."

We can rely on God's faithfulness in reporting. But we cannot really go much beyond this general principle. We must be content with what God has been pleased to provide us in the Gospels themselves. We can use with confidence all the information they provide. But when we try to go beyond what they provide, we confront uncertainty. We can easily involve ourselves in unfruitful speculation.

The Idea of Reconstructing Exact Wording of Speeches

In particular, attempts to reconstruct exact, verbatim wording for speeches involve uncertainties. We are uncertain in most cases of what language was used. In addition, the original speech may have involved more words besides those recorded in written form. Consider, for example, the disciples' speeches in the incident of the stilling of the storm. Here are the three passages, side by side:

---

[5] Ibid., ix.

Matthew 8:25, 27	Mark 4:38, 41	Luke 8:24–25
[25] And they went and woke him, saying, "Save us, Lord; we are perishing." . . .	[38] And they woke him and said to him, "Teacher, do you not care that we are perishing?" . . . [41] And they were filled with great fear and	[24] And they went and woke him, saying, "Master, Master, we are perishing!" . . . [25] . . . And they were afraid,
[27] And the men marveled, saying, "What sort of man is this, that even winds and sea obey him?"	said to one another, "Who then is this, that even wind and sea obey him?"	and they marveled, saying to one another, "Who then is this, that he commands even winds and water, and they obey him?"

We can see good substantive agreement among all three passages. But there are small differences. And the differences could lead to attempts to reconstruct an original. For example, "Teacher" in Mark 4:38 and "Master" in Luke 8:24 might both go back to the Aramaic word "Rabbi," whose meaning combines aspects of "teacher" (John 1:38) and "master." In addition, a reconstruction might speculate that the disciples said, "Rabbi, rabbi," repeating the word "rabbi," and that Luke has included this double address in the form "Master, master," while Mark has omitted the repetition for brevity. The reconstruction might also say that the disciples said, "Do you not care . . . ?" but that extra part has been omitted by Matthew and Luke. And so on. But such attempts at detailed reconstruction easily get into speculation. We have the speeches only as the Gospels give them to us.

The task is made more difficult in that several disciples were involved. It is possible that when the disciples were in distress in the storm, only one spoke up; the others saw that they had no need to speak because their spokesman had already expressed their thoughts. But surely it is also possible that a number of them spoke with excited ejaculations and pleas of various kinds. In the excitement the various speeches may have overlapped. We cannot possibly reconstruct a chronological sequence of several such speeches. All three Gospels may be summarizing a rather complicated set of pleas. Each summary is trustworthy and gives us what we need to know about the situation. The Gospels do not overwhelm us with detail about each individual speech out of three or five or even more utterances by the disciples.

Similar observations hold for the disciples' response after Jesus stilled the storm. They talked to one another about it (Matt. 8:27; Mark 4:41; Luke 8:25). It seems likely that several of them spoke, and they may have said quite a bit. If so, the Gospels give us only a short summary. Is that all right? Yes. The summary reliably condenses what they said and thought. God is telling us truthfully what he wants us to know.

Desire for Exact Wording

The main point here is that the Gospels give us information about speeches, but not exhaustive information. Human curiosity is natural. We are curious to know more. It would be interesting to hear a full verbatim transcript of everything the disciples said to Jesus and to one another. But we do not have it, nor do we really need it. If we try to imagine it, we are simply speculating.

Though curiosity is natural, other motives may drive some of the attempts at reconstruction. Why do people want more?

First, in cases of ordinary human communication, having exact wording allows us to check out fallible human claims. Suppose two people listen to the same political speech on TV. One person may report one impression, while the second reports quite a different impression. Sometimes the two impressions may be compatible, but sometimes they may be in deep tension. We may find ourselves desiring to check out the two claims by listening to the same speech ourselves, or at least obtaining a written transcript (but the written transcript lacks intonation, gestures, and facial expressions, so it is still possible to miss something quite significant).

Likewise, in the case of the Gospels, people who have doubts about the veracity of the Gospels or about their interpretations of the significance of events might like to have an exact wording, a full verbatim transcript. The Gospels, however, are different from fallible reports of merely human origin, because they are the word of God. God has not been pleased to give us a full verbatim transcript, but what he has given us is fully trustworthy. We do not need to worry.[6]

Second, in ordinary human communication we may want exact wording because we fear that we will lose something with any report that involves rewording. There are some grounds for this concern. A good human attempt to reexpress meaning conveys *basically* the same meaning. But a reexpression often changes nuances and shades of meaning in subtle ways. Even a slight rewording can result in some change.

The changes become even more visible when, say, a reporter condenses an hour-long political speech into a five-minute summary. The summary necessarily omits many details. But does that mean that it is unfair or inaccurate? No. As long as the summary does not pretend to be more than a summary, it can accurately represent the main points of the speech, and be quite useful in highlighting the main points. After all, there is always the danger of missing the forest for the trees, of being so taken up with the details that we fail to see the main points.

---

[6]For use of the Gospels in apologetic context, see chap. 11.

In the case of the Gospels, we confront the fact that the Gospels are quite selective in what they report. Again, the Gospel of John says it well: "Now there are also many other things that Jesus did. Were every one of them to be written, I suppose that the world itself could not contain the books that would be written" (John 21:25). The Gospels themselves are "summaries," in a sense, when we compare them to what it would be like to have records of everything that Jesus said and did. They are sparse. God planned it that way. We have to trust God's wisdom. He knew what would be best for us to have. He gave it to us in the four Gospels. An insistence on having more can easily represent a lack of trust and a lack of contentment with God's choice.

Critical Reconstruction

Scholarly study of the Gospels sometimes attempts reconstruction of original wording. What should we think of this? There are at least two opposite motives. First, some modern critics do not trust the divine authority of the Gospels. So they want to find out what Jesus or the disciples "really said." The critics come to the Gospels with the suspicion that what the characters "really said" contrasts with what the Gospels report them to be saying. They want to check out the Gospels according to their own independent judgment. The result, of course, involves speculation and ends in uncertainty. If they will not accept the testimony in the Gospels, they have no firm way of extricating themselves from a host of uncertainties.

In fact, the situation is still worse. Suppose, for the sake of argument, that a modern critic succeeds by chance in constructing an exact wording at some point. He still has no stable context for his wording. And, as we have seen from the Devil's use of Scripture, the *meaning* of such a wording can easily be perverted. In practice it frequently is, because a critic can attribute to Jesus meanings that are at odds with the rest of Scripture but that are pleasing to the critic.

In the case of Jesus's meanings, the difficulties are compounded. Jesus, who is God, inspired the Gospel writers to write what they did. Not only the citations from his speeches in his earthly life but everything in the Gospels is his speech. So the attempt to "get behind" the Gospels to find allegedly "the real Jesus" only succeeds in rejecting the real Jesus who is speaking today in what the Gospels themselves say. This route is really a recipe for frustration or delusion, or both. And—need we say it?—it is disobedient to God.

In fact, Jesus knew that his work on earth would have long-range effects. According to Old Testament prophecy, the effects of final salvation include "the ends of the earth" (Isa. 45:22; 52:10). When Jesus spoke during his earthly life, he intended not only that his words should be understood in the immediate context by his disciples who were present at the time, but also that they should be understood afterward in the light of further revelation.

> What I am doing you do not understand now, but afterward you will understand. (John 13:7)

> I have said these things to you in figures of speech. The hour is coming when I will no longer speak to you in figures of speech but will tell you plainly about the Father. (John 16:25)

> Go therefore and make disciples of *all nations*, . . . *teaching them* to observe *all that I have commanded you.* (Matt. 28:19–20)

It is legitimate for the Gospel writers to draw out this kind of intention, which Jesus had from the beginning. Jesus as risen and ascended Lord poured out the Holy Spirit at Pentecost (Acts 2). He also provided the Holy Spirit to the Gospel writers, who wrote according to the empowerment of the Spirit (2 Tim. 3:16; 2 Pet. 1:21). So the Gospel writers wrote in harmony with Jesus's intentions.

Answering Critics

We may also consider an opposite motive for attempting to reconstruct speeches: we may want a reconstruction so that we can answer the critics. But there are limitations. We should be honest with ourselves and with the critics. Reconstructions always have a probabilistic character and easily involve speculation.

We have already addressed similar concerns in discussing the general principle of historical reliability of the Gospels. The same principle applies for reconstructing speeches. There is some value in addressing critics on their own terms. We may provide evidence for the general reliability of the Gospels, evidence that many unbelievers may find difficult to evade. This evidence may help to persuade some people to read the Gospels, and to read their testimony seriously and soberly. God may use it as a stepping-stone to faith.

But such evidence, when taken by itself and within the presuppositions of unbelief, can never rise higher than some kind of relative credibility. We should still hope that if people come to genuine faith in Christ, they may also come to see the full divine authority of the Bible, and they may then have grounds for full confidence in everything in the Bible, rather than merely an ill-defined sense that much of it may be credible. Once we have full confidence, we do not depend on reconstruction. We have what we need when we read the Gospels themselves. The Gospels *do* give us what Jesus and other biblical figures actually said.

26

AUGUSTINE ON REPORTING SPEECHES

The idea that Scripture gives us the meaning of earlier speeches is found in Saint Augustine. He counsels us "to ascertain what is the mind and intention of the person who speaks."[1] It is worthwhile listening to his views.

Speeches of John the Baptist

At an early point in his key work *Harmony of the Gospels*, Augustine discusses reported speech for the first time when he considers the speeches of John the Baptist.[2] He discusses the issues at some length because the speeches from John provide very early cases of specific harmonistic difficulties involving speeches.

Augustine considers it foundational to accept the authority of the Gospels.

> Since the truth of the Gospel, conveyed in that word of God which abides eternal and unchangeable above all that is created, but which at the same time has been disseminated throughout the world by the instrumentality of temporal symbols, and by the tongues of men, has possessed itself of the most exalted height of authority, we ought not to suppose that any one of the writers is giving an unreliable account, if, when several persons are recalling some

---

[1] Augustine, *Harmony of the Gospels*, in vol. 6 of *NPNF*1, 2.12.29.
[2] Ibid., 2.12.25–29. Augustine's discussion could easily receive even more extended reflection than I devote to it here.

matter either heard or seen by them, they fail to follow the very same plan, or
to use the very same words, while describing, nevertheless, the self-same fact.

Augustine also makes it plain that no lapse through ordinary human forgetfulness occurs in the Gospels: "It is only seemly, however, that no charge
of absolute unveracity should be laid against the evangelists, and that, too,
not only with regard to that kind of unveracity which comes by the positive
telling of what is false, but also with regard to that which arises through
forgetfulness."[3]

Consistent with this truthfulness, Augustine thinks that the Gospel writers have flexibility with regard to exact wording.

> Neither should we indulge such a supposition [of unreliability], although the
> order of the words may be varied; or although some words may be substituted
> in place of others, which nevertheless have the same meaning; or although
> something may be left unsaid, either because it has not occurred to the mind
> of the recorder, or because it becomes readily intelligible from the other state-
> ments which are given.[4]

> . . . any one who wisely understands that the real requisite in order to get at
> the knowledge of the truth is just to make sure of the things really meant,
> whatever may be the precise words in which they happen to be expressed.
> For although one writer may retain a certain order in the words, and another
> present a different one, there is surely no real contradiction in that. Nor, again,
> need there be any antagonism between the two, although one may state what
> another omits. For it is evident that the evangelists have set forth these mat-
> ters just in accordance with the recollection each retained of them, and just
> according as their several predilections prompted them to employ greater
> brevity or richer detail on certain points, while giving, nevertheless, the same
> account of the subjects themselves.[5]

Augustine, speaks of the "recollection" and "predilections" of the human
authors of the Gospels. But we should remember that he also vigorously
affirms divine authorship of the details. The differing dispositions of the
Evangelists come under the control of God and issue in that which is fully
the word of God.[6]

---

[3]Ibid., 2.12.29.
[4]Ibid., 2.12.28.
[5]Ibid., 2.12.27.
[6]See also Archibald A. Hodge and Benjamin B. Warfield, *Inspiration*, with introduction by Roger R. Nicole
(repr., Grand Rapids: Baker, 1979), 11–17.

In our present context, some additional clarifications are in order. Augustine is pointedly not saying that the words of the Bible are dispensable. Only through words do we access meanings. As A. A. Hodge and B. B. Warfield point out, "The slightest consideration will show that words are as essential to intellectual processes as they are to mutual intercourse. . . . Thoughts are wedded to words as necessarily as soul to body."[7] Nor is Augustine adopting the modern idea that inspiration belongs only to thoughts and not to words.[8] The Gospel "has possessed itself of the most exalted height of authority" and is the very word of God. Rather, Augustine is saying that God has the authority to reexpress himself, to say the same thing in different words. Since it is God who speaks, *each* reexpression in each Gospel is fully reliable and faithfully represents the meaning of speeches that it reports.

Augustine continues: " . . . with the view of illustrating his meaning, and making it thoroughly clear, the person to whom authority is given to compose the narrative makes some additions of his own, not indeed in the subject-matter itself, but in the words by which it is expressed."[9] Augustine speaks about "the person to whom authority is given." The "authority" in question comes from God. God gave divine authority to the human writers of the Gospels. Under inspiration of the Spirit, the writer could use an alternate wording that indicated more clearly the sense or implications of what someone said.[10] In all such cases, the Gospels do not distort the meaning of what the person has said.

Augustine also anticipates an objection from a person who wants perfect precision.

Moreover, if any one affirms that the evangelists ought certainly to have had that kind of capacity imparted to them by the power of the Holy Spirit, which would secure them against all variation the one from the other, either in the kind of words, or in their order, or in their number, that person fails to perceive, that just in proportion as the authority of the evangelists [under their

---

[7]Ibid., 22, quoted from Brooke Foss Westcott, *Introduction to the Study of the Gospels, with Historical and Explanatory Notes*, 5th ed., 14–15. I do not have access to the fifth edition, but the same quote is found in the sixth edition (Cambridge/London: Macmillan, 1881), 14, and the American edition of 1902 (New York: Macmillan, 1902), 40. See also Louis Gaussen, *Theopneustia: The Plenary Inspiration of the Holy Scriptures: Deduced from Internal Evidence, and the Testimonies of Nature, History and Science*, rev. ed. (Chicago: Bible Institute Colportage, n.d. [1915]), 275–79.

[8]See the refutation of this idea in Hodge and Warfield, *Inspiration*, 18–23.

[9]Augustine, *Harmony of the Gospels*, 2.12.28.

[10]Augustine is tacitly assuming the principle that we have already discussed concerning the absence of quotation marks. There are no quotation marks either in Augustine's Latin writings or in the Latin version of the Bible that he used. There are no quotation marks in the original Greek manuscripts either, but Augustine works primarily from the Latin version of the Bible. Augustine knows that the Bible is not giving explicit indications about which wordings represent verbatim quotations and which wordings represent summaries or reexpressions.

existing conditions] is made pre-eminent, the credit of all other men who offer true statements of events ought to have been established on a stronger basis by their instrumentality: so that when several parties happen to narrate the same circumstance, none of them can by any means be rightly charged with untruthfulness if he differs from the other only in such a way as can be defended on the ground of the antecedent example of the evangelists themselves. For as we are not at liberty either to suppose or to say that any one of the evangelists has stated what is false, so it will be apparent that any other writer is as little chargeable with untruth, with whom, in the process of recalling anything for narration, it has fared only in a way similar to that in which it is shown to have fared with those evangelists.[11]

We should note an all-important difference here. The Evangelists were inspired, while other narrators, operating merely as ordinary human beings, are not. The two are not on the same level. Augustine is making a complementary point, namely, that in spite of the difference, we can learn something about standards for human testimony. Augustine sees in the variations among the Evangelists a positive benefit, namely, that they establish by their absolute authority a guideline for assessing truth in the case of ordinary human testimony.

He might have adduced other benefits as well. Saying things in more than one way can make the substance clearer to us, help us focus on the main points, make us more confident that we have grasped what was said, and enable us through differing emphases to notice additional richness in the meaning of the whole. All of these benefits operate when we consider Jesus's words during the stilling of the storm.

---

[11] Augustine, *Harmony of the Gospels*, 2.12.28.

27

THE RICH YOUNG RULER

We now consider the three accounts of Jesus's dialogue with the rich young ruler. Here are the texts side by side:

Matthew 19:16–22	Mark 10:17–23	Luke 18:18–24
[16] And behold, a man came up to him, saying, "Teacher, what good deed must I do to have eternal life?" [17] And he said to him, "Why do you ask me about what is good? There is only one who is good. If you would enter life, keep the commandments." [18] He said to him, "Which ones?" And Jesus said,	[17] And as he was setting out on his journey, a man ran up and knelt before him and asked him, "Good Teacher, what must I do to inherit eternal life?" [18] And Jesus said to him, "Why do you call me good? No one is good except God alone.	[18] And a ruler asked him, "Good Teacher, what must I do to inherit eternal life?" [19] And Jesus said to him, "Why do you call me good? No one is good except God alone.
"You shall not murder, You shall not commit adultery, You shall not steal, You shall not bear false witness, [19] Honor your father and mother, and, You shall love your neighbor as yourself."	[19] You know the commandments: 'Do not murder, Do not commit adultery, Do not steal, Do not bear false witness, Do not defraud, Honor your father and mother.'"	[20] You know the commandments: 'Do not commit adultery, Do not murder, Do not steal, Do not bear false witness, Honor your father and mother.'"

Matthew 19:16–22	Mark 10:17–23	Luke 18:18–24
[20] The young man said to him, "All these I have kept. What do I still lack?" [21] Jesus said to him, "If you would be perfect, go, sell what you possess and give to the poor, and you will have treasure in heaven; and come, follow me." [22] When the young man heard this he went away sorrowful, for he had great possessions. [23] And Jesus said to his disciples, "Truly, I say to you, only with difficulty will a rich person enter the kingdom of heaven."	[20] And he said to him, "Teacher, all these I have kept from my youth." [21] And Jesus, looking at him, loved him, and said to him, "You lack one thing: go, sell all that you have and give to the poor, and you will have treasure in heaven; and come, follow me." [22] Disheartened by the saying, he went away sorrowful, for he had great possessions. [23] And Jesus looked around and said to his disciples, "How difficult it will be for those who have wealth to enter the kingdom of God!"	[21] And he said, "All these I have kept from my youth." [22] When Jesus heard this, he said to him, "One thing you still lack. Sell all that you have and distribute to the poor, and you will have treasure in heaven; and come, follow me." [23] But when he heard these things, he became very sad, for he was extremely rich. [24] Jesus, seeing that he had become sad, said, "How difficult it is for those who have wealth to enter the kingdom of God!"

Differences

These texts exhibit a number of small differences where one Gospel adds a detail not found in another. In addition, Luke lists the commandment against adultery before the commandment against murder (Luke 18:20), while Matthew and Mark have the reverse order (Matt. 19:18; Mark 10:19). But we have dealt with similar difficulties in our earlier discussions of chronological order (chaps. 17 and 18). None of the Gospels gives us an explicit commitment always to stick to a strictly chronological order. So there is no contrastive claim in the Gospels necessarily implying that Jesus said one commandment chronologically in front of the others.

The most notable difficulty lies in the opening lines. Mark and Luke have basically the same wording, "Good teacher, what shall I do to inherit eternal life?" (Mark 10:17; Luke 18:18). Jesus responded by picking up on the word "good": "Why do you call me good? No one is good except God alone" (Mark 10:18; Luke 18:19). Matthew, by contrast, puts the word "good" with "good deed": "Teacher, what *good deed* must I do to have eternal life?" (Matt. 19:16). Jesus's response differs in a corresponding way: "Why do you *ask me about what is good*? There is only one who is good" (Matt. 19:17).[1]

---

[1] For extended discussion, see D. A. Carson, "Redaction Criticism: On the Legitimacy and Illegitimacy of a Literary Tool," in *Scripture and Truth*, ed. D. A. Carson and John D. Woodbridge (Grand Rapids: Baker,

Alternatives

Commentators over the centuries have suggested several explanations. We will consider a few.

Augustine says, "Accordingly, the best method of disposing of it is to understand both these sentences to have been uttered, 'Why callest thou me good?' and, 'Why askest thou me about the good?'"[2] This is possible. But is it the only possibility?

John McClellan[3] has followed the Byzantine family of Greek manuscripts, which have in Matthew 19:16–17 the wording: "'Good teacher, what good deed must I do to inherit eternal life?' And he said to him, 'Why do you call me good? No one is good except God alone.'" This textual variant essentially eliminates the most prominent differences between Matthew and the other two accounts. The word "good" appears twice in the young man's question: "Good teacher" and "good deed." It results in an easy harmonization. On some occasions, imperfections in textual transmission may explain difficulties in the copies that we now have. But we should not automatically prefer a particular textual reading just because it is useful for harmonization. We need to weigh which reading represents the original, that is, the autograph of Matthew.

While Byzantine manuscripts offer the reading that McClellan prefers, other Greek manuscripts have the wording that we have reproduced above for Matthew 19:16–17. These manuscripts are of better quality. We may also observe that scribes have a tendency when copying to introduce harmonizations like the one that appears in the Byzantine text family in this case. A scribe's memory of the expression "Good teacher" in the parallels in Mark and Luke may have interfered in the process of copying, and a scribe may have ended up accidentally inserting the extra word "good" by confusing the passage in Matthew with its parallels. Because scribes sometimes smoothed out difficulties, the more difficult text is the one more likely to represent the original. We may conclude that the original of Matthew probably did contain the more difficult wording.

As a final possible solution to the difficulty, we have the following comment from Johann Bengel: "A good man gives good instruction concerning the good, John vii.12."[4]

1992), 131–37; Ned B. Stonehouse, *Origins of the Synoptic Gospels: Some Basic Questions* (Grand Rapids: Eerdmans, 1963), 93–112.

[2] Augustine, *Harmony of the Gospels*, in vol. 6 of *NPNF*1, 2.63.123.

[3] John Brown McClellan, *The New Testament of Our Lord and Saviour Jesus Christ, a New Translation . . .*, vol. 1 (London: Macmillan, 1875), 659–60.

[4] Johann A. Bengel, *Gnomon of the New Testament*, 2 vols. (Philadelphia: Perkinpine and Higgins, 1860), 1:235.

Wording and Intention

Bengel's short comment might appear at first to brush over the differences. But I believe it is insightful; it opens the door to further reflection. In fact, the rich man's concern, at the level of underlying intention, necessarily embraces several dimensions. (1) He sought good instruction, beyond what he already knew, or he would not have come to Jesus. (2) His act of seeking implies that he thought Jesus was a good teacher. And (3) the content of his question concerned what to do in order to inherit eternal life. In this question he sought for Jesus to give him a specification of good deeds that he should do. Whatever the exact, verbatim wording of his question or questions—for he may have posed more than one—all three foci (1–3) belong to his purpose. All three Gospels articulate aspects of his purposes.[5]

It is possible that the young man asked a whole series of questions and that each Gospel has selected only one. Whether the young man actually uttered a series of questions or one question only, he had complex intentions, which included many dimensions. As usual, there are no quotation marks in the original. What we have are three reports of what the young man said. But we do not obtain information as to whether any of the reports gives us a verbatim transcript. The Gospel writers may choose if they wish to express the content and substance of what was said without giving the exact words. They may also express that substance selectively. As Ned B. Stonehouse argues:

> It is obvious therefore that the evangelists are not concerned, at least not at all times, to report the *ipsissima verba* [exact words] of Jesus. And on this background one must allow for the possibility that Matthew in his formulation of 19:16, 17 has not only been selective as regards subject matter but also that he used some freedom in the precise language which he employed. The singular [i.e., distinctive] use of the adjective "good" might then be a particularly clear example of his use of that freedom.[6]

William Hendriksen has similar comments about this incident.

> [The differences] do not change the substance of the story. They indicate that each Gospel-writer had his own style. A document can be fully inspired and inerrant without being pedantically precise. The evangelists are not reeling off a recording. What each of them is doing is reproducing the happening in his own

---

[5]Note the remark of Stonehouse, "But it is by no means evident that Matthew says anything that is not implicit in the Marcan account" (Stonehouse, *Origins of the Synoptic Gospels*, 101).
[6]Ibid., 108–9. It is worthwhile to consider Stonehouse's fuller discussion, 93–112, which includes the quote earlier reproduced in chap. 9 above.

characteristic manner. For this we should be thankful. It makes the combined account that much more interesting. Besides, it is surely not to be supposed that *all* the words of Jesus spoken at each occasion were written down. It is entirely possible that in the course of the conversation with the young man, the latter, in addressing the Lord, used both forms of address, "Teacher" and "Good Teacher." And so also in connection with the other slight differences: an evangelist has the perfect right to substitute a synonym for the actual word that was spoken, as long as this synonym conveys the same meaning.[7]

What the Gospels do in these instances accords with the truthfulness of God. There are no quotation marks in the original, and the Gospels are not claiming to give us exact words concerning what was said earlier. They are claiming to give us the meaning. Their wording is exactly what God says in giving us each Gospel. As usual, we can rely on each Gospel without having to reconstruct some hypothetical wording *behind* the Gospels.

Distinctive Emphases

Matthew chooses to emphasize the young man's focus on good deeds, which the young man wants to hear about in order to know the path to inherit eternal life. Mark and Luke focus more on his hope that Jesus as a "good teacher" might satisfy his desire. Both elements belong to the young man's total intentionality. It is legitimate in addition for each Evangelist to choose to emphasize what fits in with a larger theme in his Gospel as a whole. After all, the coming of the kingdom of God through Jesus and his ministry presents us with *many* concerns, all of which are aspects of the total picture. God through the Evangelists may choose to emphasize one aspect in any one Gospel.

Matthew, according to God's design, has a particular concern for the commandments of God, as is visible in the important discussions in Matthew 5:17–48; 19:3–9; 23:2–3; 28:20, and other passages. The emphasis on "good deed" in Matthew 19:16 strengthens the ties with this larger theme and thereby encourages us to notice the relationship to these other passages and to absorb this particular meaning, which actually belongs to the episode with the rich young man, but might otherwise not be so easily noticed.

Stonehouse, in commenting on this passage, observes the benefits of carefully studying the differences as well as the commonalities among the three Gospels: "Moreover, the rather detailed observations and judgments

---

[7]William Hendriksen, *Exposition of the Gospel according to Matthew* (Grand Rapids: Baker, 1973), 724. Hendriksen also directs readers to Stonehouse, *Origins of the Synoptic Gospels* (725n692).

concerning the agreements and divergences in the three forms of the story serve . . . to enhance our understanding of the passage as a whole. "[8]

Jesus's Response to the Young Man

There might still seem to be a difficulty with Jesus's response. According to Matthew, Jesus says, "Why do you ask me concerning what is good?" In Mark and Luke the wording runs, "Why do you call me good?" The two wordings differ notably, and their meanings differ. Each wording is an appropriate response to the antecedent question from the rich young man, given within its own narrative. But the wording in Mark and Luke does not fit the question in Matthew, nor does the wording in Matthew fit the question in Mark and Luke. How do we understand what the Gospels present us?

In all three Gospels Jesus's initial response takes the form of a rhetorical question. The question does not really expect the rich young man to answer immediately. Jesus is rather asking him to reflect on what he really wants, and what his initial question or questions may presuppose. Jesus then continues with a statement. In Matthew he says, "There is only one that is good." Mark and Luke have, "No one is good except God alone." These two wordings are effectively paraphrases of one another. It is difficult to say which is closer in its details to being a word-for-word copy of what Jesus said. He may have spoken to the young man in Aramaic, in which case the Greek is already a translation. The translation, with either wording, conveys what he meant. So there is no discrepancy.

There remains the rhetorical question: "Why do you ask me about what is good?" (Matt. 19:17) and "Why do you call me good?" (Mark 10:18; Luke 18:19). Once again, we cannot be certain which of the two wordings corresponds in a more word-for-word fashion to what Jesus spoke, probably in Aramaic. It is always possible that Jesus responded to the young man with a more extensive discourse than what any of the Gospels has provided. All three may have condensed or summarized. Jesus may have posed both the question in Matthew and the one in Mark in exactly those words. We do not know. All three Gospels are intent on giving accurately the meaning of what was said. And the meaning may include intentions of Jesus that were implicit rather than explicit in the exact wording.

There is still an apparent difference in meaning. With the one wording, Jesus asks the young man to reflect on what he intends and desires and presupposes about "what is good." With the other wording, he asks the young man to reflect on what he thinks about Jesus as a teacher, and why

---

[8]Stonehouse, *Origins of the Synoptic Gospels*, 93.

he chooses to describe Jesus as good. But, as Bengel notes, the two concerns are deeply related to one another. If the young man should ask himself about one, he should also ask himself about the other. Hence, even if the young man asked only a single question, Jesus may have given an extended response in which he made explicit inquiries to the young man, inquiries that explored both issues. Or Jesus may have given only a short response. But in that short response, within a single rhetorical question, we can still see implicitly a challenge in both directions: concerning the young man's attitude toward "what is good" and toward Jesus as allegedly a reliable (and therefore "good") teacher.

Further Reflections on Language

Language contains implications and reveals intentions. These intentions include not only the intentions that a speaker chooses to express most explicitly and directly, but also subtler, less direct concerns that only further reflection may reveal. Moreover, verbal communication is in many situations interactive. No one sentence stands alone. And no one monologue stands alone, but belongs to a larger dialogue that is going somewhere. The particular monologues have intentions to move beyond themselves toward larger personal goals.

Such is certainly the case in Jesus's interchange with the rich young man because, there is dynamic development in the interchange. One point in the dialogue leads to another. First, the young man raises the issue of the way to eternal life. That issue leads to the topic of keeping the commandments. Then the mention of the commandments leads to the young man's claim to have kept them. The young man's claim leads in turn to Jesus's challenge to give away his riches and to follow Jesus. Finally, Jesus's challenge leads to the young man's disappointment.

Given the rich potential of language and the obliqueness of rhetorical questions, we can see in either of the two wordings of the rhetorical questions larger intentions, which lead the dialogue forward. Both wordings are therefore expressions of aspects of Jesus's intentions and aspects of Jesus's challenge to the young man. They differ in their meanings because God chooses to highlight different aspects in the distinct narratives. And this highlighting harmonizes with the larger context, whether of Matthew, Mark, or Luke.

Linguistically speaking, the rhetorical questions have contrast, variation, and distribution (see chap. 8). The meanings in Matthew are distinguishable in some details from those in Mark and Luke. But these distinctions contribute to a larger picture in which Jesus's intention has several dimensions. The distinctive aspects in each Gospel contribute harmoniously to a total intention, for God's glory and man's salvation.

Each wording also contains variation. The sparseness of language allows that there may still be a range of possibilities concerning what was the exact, verbatim form of what Jesus said in Aramaic.

The distribution includes distribution in the context of a particular Gospel. The wording contributes to the themes of the Gospel in which it is set. Contrast, variation, and distribution as aspects of language, mirroring the Trinity,[9] function together in full communication. Jesus's intentions in this one interchange—intentions that are already rich in their implications—have ties with the context of many themes about the kingdom of God that come up throughout the Gospels. The meanings of the parts contribute the meaning of the whole. This whole meaning was intended by God from the beginning, and he intended that the dialogue between the young man and Jesus would contribute to that whole as it in fact does in each of the three Gospels.

---

[9]See chap. 8, and Vern S. Poythress, *In the Beginning Was the Word: Language—A God-Centered Approach* (Wheaton, IL: Crossway, 2009), chap. 19.

PART SEVEN

MORE CASES

28

RAISING JAIRUS'S DAUGHTER

Next we consider the accounts of the raising of Jairus's daughter. Here are the texts:

Matthew 9:18–26	Mark 5:22–43	Luke 8:41–56
[18] While he was saying these things to them, behold, a ruler came in and	[22] Then came one of the rulers of the synagogue, Jairus by name, and seeing him, he fell at his feet	[41] And there came a man named Jairus, who was a ruler of the synagogue.
knelt before him,	[23] and implored him earnestly, saying,	And falling at Jesus' feet, he implored him to come to his house,
saying,		[42] for he had an only daughter, about twelve years of age, and she was dying.
"My daughter has just died,	"My little daughter is at the point of death.	
but come and lay your hand on her, and she will live." [19] And Jesus rose and followed him, with his disciples.	Come and lay your hands on her, so that she may be made well and live." [24] And he went with him.	As Jesus went,
	And a great crowd followed him and thronged about him.	the people pressed around him.
[20] And behold, a woman who had suffered from a discharge of blood for twelve years . . . [vv. 21–22]	[25] And there was a woman who had had a discharge of blood for twelve years. . . . [vv. 26–34]	[43] And there was a woman who had had a discharge of blood for twelve years. . . . [vv. 44–48]

Matthew 9:18–26	Mark 5:22–43	Luke 8:41–56
	35 While he was still speaking, there came from the ruler's house some who said, "Your daughter is dead. Why trouble the Teacher any further?" 36 But overhearing what they said, Jesus said to the ruler of the synagogue, "Do not fear, only believe." [see v. 38]	49 While he was still speaking, someone from the ruler's house came and said, "Your daughter is dead; do not trouble the Teacher any more." 50 But Jesus on hearing this answered him, "Do not fear; only believe, and she will be well."
23 And when Jesus came to the ruler's house		51 And when he came to the house,
	37 And he allowed no one to follow him except Peter and James and John the brother of James.	he allowed no one to enter with him, except Peter and John and James, and the father and mother of the child.
	38 They came to the house of the ruler of the synagogue,	
and saw the flute players and the crowd making a commotion,	and Jesus saw a commotion, people weeping and wailing loudly. 39 And when he had entered, he said to them, "Why are you making a commotion and weeping?	52 And all were weeping and mourning for her,
24 he said, "Go away,		but he said, "Do not weep,
for the girl is not dead but sleeping." And they laughed at him.	The child is not dead but sleeping." 40 And they laughed at him.	for she is not dead but sleeping." 53 And they laughed at him, knowing that she was dead.
25 But when the crowd had been put outside,	But he put them all outside	
he went in	and took the child's father and mother and those who were with him and went in where the child was.	
and took her by the hand,	41 Taking her by the hand he said to her, "Talitha cumi," which means, "Little girl, I say to you, arise."	54 But taking her by the hand he called, saying, "Child, arise."
and the girl arose.	42 And immediately the girl got up and began walking (for she was twelve years of age), and they were immediately overcome with amazement. 43 And he strictly charged them that no one should know this, and told them to give her something to eat.	55 And her spirit returned, and she got up at once. [see v. 56] And he directed that something should be given her to eat.

Matthew 9:18–26	Mark 5:22–43	Luke 8:41–56
[26] And the report of this went through all that district.	[see v. 43]	[56] And her parents were amazed, but he charged them to tell no one what had happened.

All three texts contain in their middle an account of the healing of the woman with the flow of blood (Matt. 9:20–22; Mark 5:25–34; Luke 8:43–48). The table above has not reproduced the full text of this smaller episode; we concentrate on the healing of Jairus's daughter.

The Same Event?

The three accounts have so many detailed similarities that we can be confident we are dealing with the same event. Many of the differences involve mere omission or inclusion of some detail. They pose no difficulty. There remain two basic issues: the point at which Jesus excluded all but Peter, James, and John (Mark 5:37; Luke 8:51), and the question of when the daughter died.

Excluding the Multitude

First, Mark 5:37 and Luke 8:51 both indicate that Jesus permitted no one to come with him except Peter, James, and John. Luke adds, "and the father and mother of the child." It becomes clear later in Mark that the father and mother and "those who were with him" "went in where the child was" (Mark 5:40). We infer from the earlier information in Mark 5:37 that "those who were with him" were Peter, James, and John. So Mark and Luke agree about the composition of the group that went into the girl's room. The difficulty lies in the fact that in Mark the narrowing down to Peter, James, and John appears to have taken place while they were on the way to the house. In Luke it appears to have taken place when they arrived at the house and were about to go into the girl's room.

Most of the difficulty lies in a mental-picture theory of truth. To have a correct mental picture of this event, we would have to ascertain the one unique chronological point at which the narrowing of the group took place. But further thought shows that the situation is more complex.

Jesus could have asked the crowds and the other disciples not to accompany him while he was still at some distance from the house. He presumably anticipated that there would be mourners and commotion at the house already, even without the addition of further people. He avoided increasing the crowding by excluding most of the twelve apostles.

When Jesus arrived at the house, he would for similar reasons have dealt a second time with the problem of too many people. Only he and three disciples and the father and mother entered the room—no additional curious onlookers. There is no real incompatibility between Mark and Luke. They happen to focus on different points at which Jesus had to devote attention to the pressure, confusion, and distraction produced by too many people. Both narratives also allow us to see Jesus's concern for people who were hurting, not for making a "spectacle" that could be observed by a large group.

It could also be that Mark 5:37 mentions the narrowing down to Peter, James, and John proleptically. Maybe Mark mentions it slightly before mentioning the coming to the house in order, so to speak, to get that detail dealt with before going on to the more important action. I believe this is possible, since Mark does not become explicit or pedantic about exact chronological relations. However, it still seems to me more likely that Jesus undertook to narrow down the group before he arrived at the house. Given the likely circumstances, that would have been a kind thing to do for the sake of undistracted ministry and sensitivity to the parents and their daughter. We are dealing with what is more probable, given the nature of the situation.

Jairus and His Daughter's Death

The more challenging difficulty has to do with when the daughter died. In Matthew Jairus says, "My daughter has just died" (Matt. 9:18). In Mark and Luke we have two stages. First, Jairus asks Jesus to come because "my little daughter is at the point of death" (Mark 5:23). Next, while Jesus is saying his final words to the woman healed from her bleeding, someone comes from Jairus's house announcing, "Your daughter is dead" (5:35).

Here it may be useful to remember Matthew's tendency to compress material. We saw compression clearly in the opening genealogies. In this account of Jairus's daughter, Matthew's is the shortest of the three accounts, both in the number of verses and in the number of words. He has nine verses compared to twenty-two in Mark. Matthew omits the name Jairus. He mentions that the father is a "ruler," but omits the detail of what he is a ruler of—"a ruler of the synagogue." He omits the crowd around Jesus. He omits the second stage in which someone comes to say that the daughter has died. He omits the mention of Peter, James, and John. He omits the parents' going into the room with Jesus. He omits Jesus's direction to give the girl something to eat. He omits the charge to tell no one.

The collapse into one stage—the daughter has died—is in harmony with the kind of thing that Matthew indicates in his opening genealogy. It is compression. Calvin sees it clearly enough.

> He [Matthew] represents the father as saying, *My daughter is dead*, while the other two say that she was in her last moments, and that, while he was bringing Christ, her death was announced to him on the road. But there is no absurdity in saying that Matthew, studying brevity, merely glances at those particulars which the other two give in minute detail.[1]

Calvin says that Matthew is "studying brevity." I am offering "compression" as another label for the same thing, but one that ties in this episode with Matthew's genealogy and with a practice elsewhere in the Gospel of Matthew. Augustine's thinking is similar.

> It becomes necessary for us, therefore, to investigate this fact, lest it may seem to exhibit any contradiction between the accounts. And the way to explain it is to suppose that, by reason *of brevity* in the narrative, Matthew has preferred to express it as if the Lord had been really asked to do what it is clear He did actually do, namely, raise the dead to life. For what Matthew directs our attention to, is not the mere words spoken by the father about his daughter, but what is of more importance, his mind and purpose. Thus he [Matthew] has given words calculated to represent the father's real thoughts. For he had so thoroughly despaired of his child's case, that not believing that she whom he had just left dying, could possibly now be found yet in life, his thought rather was that she might be made alive again. Accordingly two of the evangelists have introduced the words which were literally spoken by Jairus. But Matthew has exhibited rather what the man secretly wished and thought. Thus both petitions were really addressed to the Lord; namely either that He should restore the dying damsel, or that, if she was already dead, He might raise her to life again. But as it was Matthew's object to tell the whole story *in short compass*, he has represented the father as directly expressing in his request what, it is certain, had been his own real wish, and what Christ actually did.[2]

Augustine is invoking the principle that a report may express a speaker's intentions rather than his exact words (chaps. 24–26).

---

[1] John Calvin, *Commentary on a Harmony of the Evangelists, Matthew, Mark, and Luke*, 3 vols., trans. William Pringle (Grand Rapids: Eerdmans, n.d.), 1:409–10; similarly D. A. Carson, "Matthew," in D. A. Carson, Walter W. Wessel, and Walter L. Liefeld, *Matthew, Mark, Luke*, vol. 8 of *The Expositor's Bible Commentary* (Grand Rapids: Zondervan, 1984), 230.

[2] Augustine, *Harmony of the Gospels*, in vol. 6 of *NPNF*1, 2.28.66 (italics mine).

Contrast and Variation

We can summarize what is going on in Matthew using the categories of contrast and variation that we developed in chapter 8. Mark and Luke, when they choose to take more space in giving their accounts, have the opportunity to provide various details. And each detail possesses contrast. It contrasts with an alternative where the detail is omitted. And it also contrasts with various hypothetical alternative wordings concerning details. For example, Jairus's early description "at the point of death" (Mark 5:23) is fairly specific. It contrasts with her being well, or mildly sick, or already dead. Mark 5:35 says that someone came from the house with the message that the daughter was dead. That contrasts with no one coming and with someone coming to announce that she was better. And so on. We should digest all these contrastive elements in the texts.

Matthew makes a choice to give us a compressed narrative. How much can a person say once he has chosen this kind of option? To illustrate the challenge, we can plot the alternatives in two dimensions (fig. 11). In the horizontal dimension we place the two main alternatives: to compress or to take more space. Obviously this is a simplification. There might be still other alternatives on a spectrum of complexity in several dimensions. But a simplified representation can still make the point. On a second, vertical axis we can plot the alternatives as to whether or not an account mentions two stages, with a gradual development from the daughter being at the point of death, to her being dead, and then to the announcement that she has died.

Figure 11. Narrative options: stages versus snapshot

	Compressed	Expanded
Two stages		
One compound snapshot picture of the daughter's condition		

If the narrative is going to unfold two distinct stages, there needs to be something that intervenes to differentiate them. In practice, this differentiation requires not only more specific information about timing of various events, but also the addition of a report to Jairus, so that Jairus comes to know of his daughter's death. So a commitment to narrating two stages leads to the inclusion of an explicit mention of people from Jairus's house who deliver the message to Jairus and to Jesus. Some complexity must be added to the narration.

Figure 12. Effect of compression

	Compressed	Expanded
Two stages	0	✓
Only one stage narrated	✓	✓

variational range; no contrast

contrast

But then, if a person has decided to give a compressed narrative, it does not really leave space for a full explanation. The narrator must be content with a summary. Hence, when we "intersect" the two dimensions, only certain alternatives are viable. In figure 12, ✓ marks options that remain viable, and 0 marks options that will not work.

It is *not* viable both to have two stages and to have a compressed account.

Now we are ready to observe the contrasts. In Mark's and Luke's expanded accounts, they have distinct options as to how they elaborate. If there were only one stage in the actual events, they could say so. If there were two stages, they could say so. The two kinds of narrative choice contrast with one another. In a compressed account such as Matthew's, one stage does not actually contrast with two. Compression reduces the number of options available. Hence, Matthew's account, which wraps together what in Mark and Luke are two stages in Jairus's interaction with Jesus, does not contradict Mark and Luke. He is not making a contrastive assertion that stands over against ("contrasts" with) a two-stage narration.

To make his point, Matthew must indicate somewhere that the daughter is dead and not merely sick. This he indicates in the compact summary of Jairus's interaction with Jesus.

I believe, along with Augustine and Calvin, that this approach offers a reasonable solution. It shows that there is no error in Matthew once we understand the constraints that he has chosen. Reckoning with the mental-picture theory of truth also shows why a person could be disturbed if he comes to the text with a wrong view of how language functions to communicate truth. The mental-picture theory would criticize Matthew because he produces a mental picture that lacks the details splitting the action into two stages. But that dissatisfaction is due to the deficiency in the mental-picture theory. There is no deficiency in Matthew.

Alternatives?

We should also consider some alternative explanations that have been offered. C. J. Ellicott thinks "that Jairus spoke from what his fears suggested, and that he regarded the death of his daughter as by that time having actually taken place."[3] Ellicott does not elaborate, but he may intend to imply that Jairus in his distress spoke both about his daughter dying and about his daughter being dead, the latter out of fear for the worst. Such a dual speech is far from impossible. People in distress and under pressure may blurt out a whole stream of words without regard for complete consistency. Each of the Gospels gives us a sparse account. It may be that Jairus's initial speech to Jesus was in its entirety much more elaborate than what we have in any one of the Gospel records.

John McClellan is more elaborate, offering us the following sequence: (1) Jairus made a first request, such as we have in Mark and Luke, indicating that his daughter was dying. (2) Jesus went toward the house. (3) Jairus made a second request, using the words of Matthew, because he now supposed that his daughter had died. (4) Jesus healed the woman with the flow of blood. (5) People came from the house with the message that the daughter had died. And so on.[4] This scenario is possible. But I believe that Calvin's and Augustine's explanations are simpler and more likely.

A Greek Word with Variation

We should consider an issue arising from a detail in Matthew 9:18. The ESV reads, "My daughter has just died." Rendered very woodenly, the Greek text comes out, "My daughter now finished/came-to-an-end." The key word in Greek is *eteleutēsen*, the aorist tense of *teleutaō*. *Teleutaō* means "*to come to an end*" or "*die*."[5] The Greek lexicon of Liddell, Scott, and Jones informs us further that its broader meaning is to *accomplish, finish*, or *come to an end*. It can be used in the expression, "finish the (one's) life."[6] The common Greek word for "die" in the New Testament is *apothnēskō*; *teleutaō* is less common. It appears to be a euphemism, much as we might say in English, "she passed

---

[3]C. J. Ellicott, *Historical Lectures on the Life of Our Lord Jesus Christ, Being the Hulsean Lectures for the Year 1859. With Notes, Critical, Historical, and Explanatory* (Boston: Gould and Lincoln, 1872), 180n2. Ellicott cites Augustine in his favor. But Augustine's account is slightly different, because he distinguishes between what Jairus said and what he thought. Ellicott thinks that Jairus literally spoke what we have in Matthew.
[4]John Brown McClellan, *The New Testament of Our Lord and Saviour Jesus Christ, a New Translation . . .* , vol. 1 (London: Macmillan, 1875), 439–41.
[5]Frederick William Danker, ed., *A Greek-English Lexicon of the New Testament and Other Early Christian Literature*, 3rd ed. (Chicago: University of Chicago Press, 2000); see also Henry George Liddell, Robert Scott, and Henry Stuart Jones, eds., *A Greek-English Lexicon* (Oxford: Oxford University Press, 1973).
[6]Ibid.

on," or "she breathed her last," or "she went to be with the Lord." The Bible also has the expression "sleep" as a euphemism for death (1 Thess. 4:15).

In the context of Matthew 9:18, *teleutaō* does not merely have the general meaning "finish." It must have its narrower, euphemistic meaning. It is talking about the girl's death. But it is doing so indirectly, as euphemisms do. Literally, the text says, "My daughter has now finished." "Finished her life" is what is implied. *Teleutaō* can be used in a context where someone is *in the process of dying*: "By faith Joseph, at *the end of his life* [literally, "while *finishing*"], made mention of the exodus of the Israelites . . ." (Heb. 11:22). But in Matthew 9:18 *teleutaō* is in the aorist indicative. It would not do to translate it "was finishing," but rather "finished." She has now "finished."

Still, the wording is not perfectly precise. Words always exhibit variation, that is, flexibility or range of meaning. "She has finished her life"—does that mean that she has died? Most of the time, yes, though the inference involves the interpretation of the euphemism. But could it mean that she has come to the end of her life in the sense that she has no more life to live but is at the point of death? I suspect—I cannot prove it in a matter of delicacy like this one—that there is some range of meaning here. The word is not perfectly specific. And why should we expect it to be? The ancient context did not have special apparatus from modern medical technology to determine the exact moment of death. Even with our technology, there is a region of uncertainty, since, for example, it takes some time for cells in the brain to die after the heart stops beating.

I suspect, then, that "she has finished (her life)" is not quite as definite as "she has died." It leaves a range, that is, variation, in a context suitable for that purpose. Matthew is not quite specific about timing in the details of the events, because in his compression he does not get into such details.

Benefits from the Three Narratives

What can we learn when we pay attention to the distinct ways of telling the story? All three Gospels clearly reveal Jesus's miraculous power, a power that even includes raising the dead. Mark and Luke, with their more extended narratives, can give us a sense of how Jesus supported Jairus's faith as the crisis deepened: "Do not fear, only believe" (Mark 5:36). Jesus gave Jairus more than he initially asked for. Matthew with his compression focuses on the main point more starkly. Jesus raised the dead.

We may underline a point that we have already made: God, as well as the human authors, has given us all three narratives. God wants us to absorb the distinctive emphases of each, as well as what is common.

29

BLIND BARTIMAEUS

We turn, finally, to the healing of blind men in the vicinity of Jericho. We have three accounts.

Matthew 20:29–34	Mark 10:46–52	Luke 18:35–43
	[46] And they came to Jericho. And as he was leaving Jericho with his disciples and	[35] As he drew near to Jericho,
[29] And as they went out of Jericho,		
a great crowd followed him. [30] And behold, there were two blind men	a great crowd,	
	Bartimaeus, a blind beggar, the son of Timaeus,	a blind man
sitting by the roadside,	was sitting by the roadside.	was sitting by the roadside begging.
and when they heard that	[47] And when he heard that	[36] And hearing a crowd going by, he inquired what this meant. [37] They told him, "Jesus of Nazareth is passing by."
Jesus was passing by, they cried out, "Lord, have mercy on us, Son of David!"	it was Jesus of Nazareth, he began to cry out and say, "Jesus, Son of David, have mercy on me!"	[38] And he cried out, "Jesus, Son of David, have mercy on me!" [39] And those who were in front rebuked him,
[31] The crowd rebuked them, telling them to be silent, but they cried out all the more, "Lord, have mercy on us, Son of David!"	[48] And many rebuked him, telling him to be silent. But he cried out all the more, "Son of David, have mercy on me!"	telling him to be silent. But he cried out all the more, "Son of David, have mercy on me!"
[32] And stopping, Jesus called them	[49] And Jesus stopped and said, "Call him." And they called the blind man, saying to him, "Take heart.	[40] And Jesus stopped and commanded him to be brought to him.

212

Matthew 20:29–34	Mark 10:46–52	Luke 18:35–43
and said, "What do you want me to do for you?" [33] They said to him, "Lord, let our eyes be opened." [34] And Jesus in pity touched their eyes,	Get up; he is calling you." [50] And throwing off his cloak, he sprang up and came to Jesus. [51] And Jesus said to him, "What do you want me to do for you?" And the blind man said to him, "Rabbi, let me recover my sight."	And when he came near, he asked him, [41] "What do you want me to do for you?" He said, "Lord, let me recover my sight."
and immediately they recovered their sight and followed him.	[52] And Jesus said to him, "Go your way; your faith has made you well." And immediately he recovered his sight and followed him on the way.	[42] And Jesus said to him, "Recover your sight; your faith has made you well." [43] And immediately he recovered his sight and followed him, glorifying God. And all the people, when they saw it, gave praise to God.

In addition, Matthew 9:27–31 has another account of healing the blind. But this healing appears not to be at the same time or location as the other accounts. It appears to be a distinct event.

Analysis

All three Synoptic Gospels place the event in the vicinity of Jericho. In all three it falls in a section just before Jesus's arrival in Jerusalem for his last days there. Moreover, there are striking similarities in detail. So we appear to be dealing with the same episode. Just as with many other episodes, there are small differences in detail. For example, Matthew says that Jesus "touched their eyes" (Matt. 20:34), while Mark and Luke record that he verbally declared their healing (Mark 10:52; Luke 18:42). I take it that he did both.

A more noteworthy difference is found in the fact that Matthew speaks of two blind men. Mark and Luke mention one. But in mentioning one, they do not make a statement in contrast to two. They do not say that there was *only* one. If two were healed, it implies that at least one was healed. As in the case of the Gadarene demoniacs (chap. 17), there is no error.

Finally, Matthew and Mark appear to say that the healing took place as Jesus was leaving Jericho (Matt. 20:29; Mark 10:46). Luke has Jesus coming near to Jericho (Luke 18:35). This difference is the most difficult.

Proposals

We find several proposals in commentaries. Here is Calvin:

My conjecture is, that, while Christ was approaching the city, the *blind man cried out*, but that, as he was not heard on account of the noise, he placed himself in the way, *as they were departing from the city*, and then was at length called by Christ. And so *Luke*, commencing with what was true, does not follow out the whole narrative, but passes over Christ's stay in the city; while the other Evangelists attend only to the time which was nearer to the miracle.[1]

Calvin uses the word "conjecture," indicating that though he is satisfied that his proposal is possible, he cannot be sure. There is not enough information in the Gospels themselves.

Craig Blomberg postulates a temporal gap between Luke 18:35 and 18:36.

Luke has probably just abbreviated Mark, as he does consistently elsewhere, leaving out the reference to the departure from Jericho. Mark, after all, begins his passage in agreement with Luke, by reporting that Jesus first came *to* Jericho, but his style is somewhat inelegant in stating, literally, that "they come to Jericho, and as he is going out of Jericho . . ." (Mark 10:46). Luke therefore improves the style by excising the latter clause, so that one must not press him to mean that the miracle narrated in 18:36–43 occurred immediately after the action of verse 35. Luke simply records Jesus' arrival, Mark presupposes his entrance into and exit from the town, which Luke omits, and then both describe the healing as Jesus was on his way out.[2]

Blomberg's full explanation depends on the assumption that Luke used Mark. If we do not make this assumption (see chap. 16), the point might nevertheless hold that Luke has not undertaken to supply all the details about location that are found in Mark—he has omitted details. Mark gives more details about location by mentioning both Jesus's entrance and his departure from Jericho. But Mark does so at the cost of some lack of smoothness: in Mark's account Jesus entered, only to depart in the next half verse without any mention of his having done anything while in the city (Mark 10:46). Matthew (20:29) omits the detail about entering Jericho and mentions only the departure. This omission results in a smoother and more compact narrative. But another difficulty is introduced, namely, that we are not given any indication that Jesus had previously come to Jericho. The preceding

[1]John Calvin, *Commentary on a Harmony of the Evangelists, Matthew, Mark, and Luke*, 3 vols., trans. William Pringle (Grand Rapids: Eerdmans, n.d.), 2:429. Louis Gaussen, *Theopneustia: The Plenary Inspiration of the Holy Scriptures: Deduced from Internal Evidence, and the Testimonies of Nature, History and Science*, rev. ed. (Chicago: Bible Institute Colportage, n.d. [1915]), 214, gives a similar explanation.
[2]Craig L. Blomberg, *The Historical Reliability of the Gospels*, 2nd ed. (Downers Grove, IL: InterVarsity, 2007), 170.

material in Matthew mentions that Jesus left Galilee and came to the region on the east of the Jordan (Matt. 19:1). Then the name Jericho appears for the first time in Matthew 20:29, where we find that Jesus was already there and was leaving.

Luke mentions only Jesus drawing near to Jericho, and not his leaving. Luke thus has more compactness than Mark. He also provides more continuity than Matthew: by telling us that Jesus was coming to Jericho, he gives us a smooth transition from the earlier stages of Jesus's journeying to Jerusalem (Luke 9:51).

According to Blomberg's interpretation, the blind man identified in Luke 18:35 was sitting by the roadside every day. In particular, he was sitting there at the time when Jesus first entered Jericho. So what Luke 18:35 records was completely true. Then Jesus's *encounter* with the blind man, described in verses 36–43, took place when Jesus was leaving the city, but Luke simply omits the detail about the passage of time.

Luke places the healing at Jericho, as evidenced by the information about the setting in 18:35. Verse 35 also supplies a larger chronological and geographical framework to indicate Jesus's movement toward Jerusalem for the final days before his crucifixion. But Luke does not say one way or the other whether there was a time gap between the entry in 18:35 and the healing in 18:36–43. In this respect, he leaves the details of chronology unspecified (there is remaining variation). So far, this interpretation has some appeal.

The situation is more difficult for Blomberg's interpretation because in the next passage, in Luke 19:1, Jesus is described as entering Jericho, where he meets Zacchaeus. Then, by Luke 19:28, Jesus has left Jericho. On a superficial reading, Luke seems to give a clear linear progression in location: drawing near in 18:35, entering in 19:1, and leaving either by 19:11 or by 19:28. Blomberg anticipates this objection and points out that Luke does not explicitly indicate a chronological order in 19:1. Could the narration of the healing in 18:36–43 be chronologically displaced? Blomberg provides possible reasons for a topical arrangement.[3] Blomberg's explanation seems to me still to contain some awkwardness. Yet it has something in its favor: Blomberg is saying that Luke contains no error, but omits details in transitions that would have allowed us to pin down an exact chronology.[4] Omission is not error.

---

[3]Ibid., 171.
[4]When we read Luke as a continuous narrative, ignoring Matthew and Mark, it may produce a *mental picture* of a purely linear chronological and geographical succession. But we have seen the difficulties in a mental-picture theory of truth (chap. 7).

William Hendriksen offers something more ingenious.

> While he was going out of the city he saw Zacchaeus up in the tree, and told
> that little publican to come down. So, with Zacchaeus he *re-entered* the city
> to lodge at the tax-collector's home for the night. According to the proposed
> solution it was during this re-entry of the city that the miracle took place.[5]

Hendriksen also considers the possibility that "Jericho" might refer to more
than one location. The site thought to be the location of Joshua's Jericho was
known at the time of Jesus.[6] But it is not clear whether it was occupied at the
time.[7] The main city of Jericho ("Herodian Jericho") was at a different site.
Archaeological investigation has found remains covering hundreds of acres.[8]
Hendriksen suggests that the one Gospel writer might refer to the old site for
Joshua's Jericho and another to Herodian Jericho. But this difference of reference would be plausible only if Joshua's Jericho was still occupied. Even if it
was not, the center of Jericho might conceivably be the Herodian palace, or
the main market place, or some other center, depending on one's point of view.
This range of options displays the phenomenon of variation that exists in all the
synoptic accounts. None are perfectly precise about the exact spot from which
Jesus was leaving or toward which he was drawing near. The variation allows
for differences in reference in the comparison of Luke with Matthew and Mark.

Hendriksen also considers the possibility that we might have more than
one episode of healing: one event as Jesus was entering and another as Jesus
was leaving. Augustine actually prefers this explanation.[9] Calvin, however,
rejects this possibility because of the impressive similarities between the
three accounts.[10] After considering the difficulties with proposed solutions,
Hendriksen concludes: "The best answer is, There is, indeed, a solution,
for this 'Scripture,' too, is inspired. However, *we do not have that solution!*"[11]

For myself, I prefer the conjecture that Luke was thinking in terms of a different city center from that which Matthew and Mark presuppose. But this too is no
more than a conjecture. God has not chosen to provide complete information.

[5]William Hendriksen, *Exposition of the Gospel according to Matthew* (Grand Rapids: Baker, 1973), 752.
[6]See Flavius Josephus, *The Jewish War*, with English translation by H. St. J. Thackeray (London: Heinemann; Cambridge: Harvard University Press, 1967), 4.8.3.
[7]D. A. Carson, "Matthew," in D. A. Carson, Walter W. Wessel, and Walter L. Liefeld, *Matthew, Mark, Luke*, vol. 8 of *The Expositor's Bible Commentary* (Grand Rapids: Zondervan, 1984), 435.
[8]R. A. Coughenour, "Jericho: III. Hasmonean and Herodian Jericho," in *The International Standard Bible Encyclopedia*, vol. 2, rev. ed., ed. Geoffrey W. Bromiley et al. (Grand Rapids: Eerdmans, 1982), 995–96.
[9]Augustine, *Harmony of the Gospels*, in vol. 6 of *NPNF*1, 2.65.126.
[10]"But all the circumstances agree so completely, that no person of sound judgment will believe them to be different narratives" (Calvin, *Harmony of the Evangelists*, 2:429).
[11]Hendriksen, *Matthew*, 752–53.

CONCLUSION

It is fitting in a way to stop with an instance (blind Bartimaeus) in which we do not have a clear answer. In doing so, we display the principle articulated in chapter 13: our knowledge is limited. Even the knowledge of the human authors of the Gospels was limited. We should trust what they wrote, because they wrote under the inspiration of the Holy Spirit, and God himself speaks in all that they wrote. Their writings have the same status as the Ten Commandments, "written with the finger of God" (Ex. 31:18; Deut. 9:10). We receive true knowledge from the Gospels. But this true knowledge is also incomplete knowledge. We are so created that we can know some things without knowing everything.

God so designed it. He gave us language. He rules over history. And in this language and history there operate the realities of contrast, variation, and distribution (chap. 8). Choices take place in verbal communication about how people communicate, what is their focus, and what are their goals. Verbal communication to us is always sparse, according to God's design. And verbal communication, through its mysteries as well as its clarities, serves to sanctify us and rebuke our pride (chaps. 14–15). A realistic respect for who God is and how wise he is encourages us to grow in appreciating how he uses the full resources of language when he speaks. He does not confine himself to the one-dimensional woodenness in communication that some critics of Scripture—and some defenders as well—have imprudently imposed.

It is fitting also, by admitting that we do not know all the details about Bartimaeus's healing, for us to underline the fact that God expects us to trust him because he is worthy of trust, not because we can first of all check things out according to our own standards. We ought not to seek assurance

Conclusion

in our own independently positioned intellectual or critical powers before we commit ourselves to God's care and submit to his voice. A pursuit of security through autonomous criticism presupposes autonomy. It is already intrinsically in rebellion against what we were created to be, children of our heavenly Father.

BIBLIOGRAPHY

Aland, Kurt, ed. *Synopsis of the Four Gospels: Greek-English Edition of the Synopsis quattuor evangeliorum* .... Stuttgart: German Bible Society, 1989.

——. ed. *Synopsis quattuor evangeliorum* .... 5th ed. Stuttgart: Württembergische Bibelanstalt, 1967.

Alexander, Loveday C. A. "Luke-Acts in Its Contemporary Setting with Special Reference to the Prefaces (Luke 1:1–4 and Acts 1:1)." DPhil diss., Oxford University, 1977.

Alford, Henry. *The Greek Testament* .... Vol. 1. 7th ed. London: Longmans, Green, 1898.

Andrews, Samuel J. *The Life of Our Lord upon the Earth: Considered in Its Historical, Chronological, and Geographical Relations.* Grand Rapids: Zondervan, 1954.

Archer, Gleason L. *Encyclopedia of Bible Difficulties.* Grand Rapids: Zondervan, 1982.

Augustine. *The Harmony of the Gospels.* In vol. 6 of *A Select Library of the Nicene and Post-Nicene Fathers of the Christian Church.* Series 1, edited by Philip Schaff, 65–236. Reprint, Grand Rapids: Eerdmans, 1979. This work is sometimes also called *Harmony of the Evangelists.*

Bahnsen, Greg L. "The Inerrancy of the Autographa." In *Inerrancy*, edited by Norman L. Geisler, 149–93. Grand Rapids: Zondervan, 1980.

Bauckham, Richard. *Jesus and the Eyewitnesses: The Gospels as Eyewitness Testimony.* Grand Rapids: Eerdmans, 2006.

Bavinck, Herman. *Reformed Dogmatics.* 4 vols. Edited by John Bolt. Translated by John Vriend. Grand Rapids: Baker, 2003–2008.

Beale, G. K. *Handbook on the New Testament Use of the Old Testament: Exegesis and Interpretation.* Grand Rapids: Baker, 2012.

Beale, G. K., and D. A. Carson, eds. *Commentary on the New Testament Use of the Old Testament.* Grand Rapids: Baker, 2007.

Bengel, Johann A. *Gnomon of the New Testament.* 2 vols. Philadelphia: Perkinpine and Higgins, 1860.

Berkhof, Louis. *Introduction to the New Testament.* Grand Rapids: Eerdmans-Sevensma, 1915.

Black, David Alan, and David R. Beck, eds. *Rethinking the Synoptic Problem.* Grand Rapids: Baker, 2001.

Blomberg, Craig L. *The Historical Reliability of John's Gospel: Issues and Commentary.* Downers Grove, IL: InterVarsity, 2002.

———. *The Historical Reliability of the Gospels.* 2nd ed. Downers Grove, IL: InterVarsity, 2007.

———. *Jesus and the Gospels: An Introduction and Survey.* 2nd ed. Grand Rapids: Baker, 2010.

———. "The Legitimacy and Limits of Harmonization." In *Hermeneutics, Authority, and Canon,* edited by D. A. Carson and John D. Woodbridge, 139–74. Grand Rapids: Zondervan, 1986.

Bock, Darrell L. *Luke.* Vol. 1, *1:1–9:50.* Grand Rapids: Baker, 1994.

Bromiley, Geoffrey W., et al., eds. *The International Standard Bible Encyclopedia.* 4 vols. Rev. ed. Grand Rapids: Eerdmans, 1982.

Bruce, F. F. *The New Testament Documents.* 2nd ed. London: Inter-Varsity, 1970.

———. "The Trial of Jesus in the Fourth Gospel." In *Gospel Perspectives: Studies of History and Tradition in the Four Gospels.* Vol. 1., edited by R. T. France and David Wenham, 7–20. Sheffield: JSOT, 1980.

Calvin, John. *Commentary on a Harmony of the Evangelists, Matthew, Mark, and Luke.* 3 vols. Translated by William Pringle. Grand Rapids: Eerdmans, n.d.

———. *The Gospel according to St John.* 2 vols. Translated by T. H. L. Parker. Edited by David W. Torrance and Thomas F. Torrance. Grand Rapids: Eerdmans, 1959.

Carson, D. A. *The Gospel according to John.* Grand Rapids: Eerdmans, 1991.

———. "Gundry on Matthew: A Critical Review," *Trinity Journal* 3 (1982): 71–91.

———. "Redaction Criticism: On the Legitimacy and Illegitimacy of a Literary Tool." In *Scripture and Truth,* edited by D. A. Carson and John D. Woodbridge, 115–42. Grand Rapids: Baker, 1992.

Carson, D. A., and Douglas J. Moo. *An Introduction to the New Testament*. 2nd ed. Grand Rapids: Zondervan, 2005.

Carson, D. A., Walter W. Wessel, and Walter L. Liefeld. *Matthew, Mark, Luke*. Vol. 8 of *The Expositor's Bible Commentary*. Grand Rapids: Zondervan, 1984.

Carson, D. A., and John Woodbridge, eds. *Hermeneutics, Authority, and Canon*. Grand Rapids: Zondervan, 1986.

———. eds. *Scripture and Truth*. Grand Rapids: Zondervan, 1983.

"Chicago Statement on Biblical Hermeneutics." International Council on Biblical Inerrancy, 1982. Reproduced in Norman L. Geisler, *Explaining Hermeneutics: A Commentary*. With exposition by J. I. Packer. Oakland, CA: International Council on Biblical Inerrancy, 1983, 19–25. Accessed July 12, 2011. http://www.bible-researcher.com/chicago2.html.

"The Chicago Statement on Biblical Inerrancy." International Council on Biblical Inerrancy, 1978. Reprinted in Carl F. H. Henry, *God, Revelation and Authority*. Vol. 4. Waco, TX: Word, 1979, 211–19. Also available at several Internet sites. Accessed July 12, 2011. http://www.bible-researcher.com/chicago1.html.

Coughenour, R. A. "Jericho: III. Hasmonean and Herodian Jericho." In *The International Standard Bible Encyclopedia*. Vol. 2. Rev. ed., edited by Geoffrey W. Bromiley et al., 995–96. Grand Rapids: Eerdmans, 1982.

Danker, Frederick William, ed. *A Greek-English Lexicon of the New Testament and Other Early Christian Literature*. 3rd ed. Chicago: University of Chicago Press, 2000.

Ellicott, C. J. *Historical Lectures on the Life of Our Lord Jesus Christ, Being the Hulsean Lectures for the Year 1859. With Notes, Critical, Historical, and Explanatory*. Boston: Gould and Lincoln, 1872.

Ellis, E. Earle. "New Directions in Form Criticism." In *Jesus Christus in Historie und Theologie*, edited by Georg Strecker, 299–315. Tübingen: Mohr, 1975.

ESV Study Bible: English Standard Version. Wheaton, IL: Crossway, 2008.

Eusebius. *Ecclesiastical History*. 2 vols. Translated by Kirsopp Lake. London: Heinemann; Cambridge: Harvard University Press, 1965.

Feinberg, Paul D. "The Meaning of Inerrancy." In *Inerrancy*, edited by Norman L. Geisler, 265–304. Grand Rapids: Zondervan, 1980.

Frame, John M. *Apologetics to the Glory of God: An Introduction*. Phillipsburg, NJ: P&R, 1994.

———. *The Doctrine of the Christian Life*. Phillipsburg, NJ: P&R, 2008.

———. *The Doctrine of the Knowledge of God*. Phillipsburg, NJ: P&R, 1987.

———. *The Doctrine of the Word of God*. Phillipsburg, NJ: P&R, 2010.

———. *Perspectives on the Word of God: An Introduction to Christian Ethics.* Phillipsburg, NJ: Presbyterian and Reformed, 1990. Reprint, Eugene, OR: Wipf and Stock, 1999.

France, Richard T. *The Gospel of Matthew.* Grand Rapids: Eerdmans, 2007.

———. "Inerrancy and New Testament Exegesis," *Themelios* 1 (1975): 12–18.

———. *Matthew: Evangelist and Teacher.* Downers Grove, IL: InterVarsity, 1989.

France, Richard T., and David Wenham, eds. *Studies in Midrash and Historiography.* Gospel Perspectives 3. Sheffield: JSOT, 1983.

Gaffin, Richard B., Jr. *God's Word in Servant-Form: Abraham Kuyper and Herman Bavinck on the Doctrine of Scripture.* Jackson, MS: Reformed Academic, 2008.

Gaussen, Louis. *Theopneustia: The Plenary Inspiration of the Holy Scriptures: Deduced from Internal Evidence, and the Testimonies of Nature, History and Science.* Rev. ed. Translated by David Scott. Chicago: Bible Institute Colportage: n.d. (1915).

Geisler, Normal L., ed. *Inerrancy.* Grand Rapids: Zondervan, 1980.

Goulder, M. D. *Midrash and Lection in Matthew: The Speaker's Lectures in Biblical Studies, 1969–71.* London: SPCK, 1974.

Green, Joel B. *The Gospel of Luke.* Grand Rapids: Eerdmans, 1997.

Gundry, Robert H. *Matthew: A Commentary on His Handbook for a Mixed Church under Persecution.* 2nd ed. Grand Rapids: Eerdmans, 1994.

———. *Matthew: A Commentary on His Literary and Theological Art.* Grand Rapids: Eerdmans, 1982.

Guthrie, Donald. *New Testament Introduction.* Rev. ed. Downers Grove, IL: InterVarsity, 1990.

Hendriksen, William. *A Commentary on the Gospel of John.* London: Banner of Truth, 1959.

———. *Exposition of the Gospel according to Luke.* Grand Rapids: Baker, 1978.

———. *Exposition of the Gospel according to Mark.* Grand Rapids: Baker, 1975.

———. *Exposition of the Gospel according to Matthew.* Grand Rapids: Baker, 1973.

Hodge, Archibald A., and Benjamin B. Warfield. "Inspiration," *The Presbyterian Review* 2 (April, 1881): 225–60.

———. *Inspiration.* With introduction by Roger R. Nicole. Grand Rapids: Baker, 1979.

Hodge, Charles. *An Exposition of the First Epistle to the Corinthians.* New York: Robert Carter & Brothers, 1882.

The Infallible Word: A Symposium by Members of the Faculty of Westminster Theological Seminary. 3rd ed. Edited by N. B. Stonehouse and Paul Woolley. Philadelphia: Presbyterian and Reformed, 1967.

Irenaeus. *Against Heresies*. In *The Ante-Nicene Fathers: Translations of the Writings of the Fathers down to A.D. 325*. Vol. 1. Edited by Alexander Roberts and James Donaldson. Grand Rapids: Eerdmans, 1979.

Josephus, Flavius. *The Jewish War*. 6 books. With an English translation by H. St. J. Thackeray. London: Heinemann; Cambridge: Harvard University Press, 1967.

Köstenberger, Andreas J. *John*. Grand Rapids: Baker, 2004.

Kruger, Michael J. *Canon Revisited: Establishing the Origins and Authority of the New Testament Books*. Wheaton, IL: Crossway, 2012.

Kuyper, Abraham. *Principles of Sacred Theology*. Grand Rapids: Eerdmans, 1968.

Lagrange, Marie-Joseph. *Évangile selon Saint Marc*. Corrected and augmented. Paris: Gabalda, 1947.

Liddell, Henry George, Robert Scott, and Henry Stuart Jones, eds. *A Greek-English Lexicon*. Oxford: Oxford University Press, 1973.

Longacre, Robert. *The Grammar of Discourse*. New York: Plenum, 1983.

McClellan, John Brown. *The New Testament of Our Lord and Saviour Jesus Christ, a New Translation . . . .* Vol. 1. London: Macmillan, 1875.

Merriam-Webster's Collegiate Dictionary. 11th ed. Springfield, MA: Merriam-Webster, 2008.

Moulton, James Hope, and George Milligan, eds. *The Vocabulary of the Greek Testament: Illustrated from the Papyri and Other Non-literary Sources*. Grand Rapids: Eerdmans, 1930.

Murray, John. *Calvin on Scripture and Divine Sovereignty*. Grand Rapids: Baker, 1960.

Packer, James I. *God Has Spoken: Revelation and the Bible*. Grand Rapids: Baker, 1994.

Plummer, Robert L. "Does the Bible Contain Error?" Chap. 4 in *40 Questions about Interpreting the Bible*. Grand Rapids: Kregel, 2010.

Poythress, Vern S. *God-Centered Biblical Interpretation*. Phillipsburg, NJ: P&R, 1999.

———. *Inerrancy and Worldview: Answering Modern Challenges to the Bible*. Wheaton, IL: Crossway, 2012.

———. *In the Beginning Was the Word: Language—A God-Centered Approach*. Wheaton, IL: Crossway, 2009.

———. *Redeeming Science: A God-Centered Approach.* Wheaton, IL: Crossway, 2006.

———. *Redeeming Sociology: A God-Centered Approach.* Wheaton, IL: Crossway, 2011.

———. "Reforming Ontology and Logic in the Light of the Trinity: An Application of Van Til's Idea of Analogy," *Westminster Theological Journal* 57, no. 1 (1995): 187–219.

———. *Symphonic Theology: The Validity of Multiple Perspectives in Theology.* Reprint. Phillipsburg, NJ: P&R, 2001.

Ridderbos, Herman. *Redemptive History and the New Testament Scriptures.* Phillipsburg, NJ: Presbyterian and Reformed, 1988.

Sanders, E. P., and Margaret Davies. *Studying the Synoptic Gospels.* London: SCM; Philadelphia: Trinity Press International, 1989.

Silva, Moisés. "Ned B. Stonehouse and Redaction Criticism (Part I)," *Westminster Theological Journal* 40, no. 1 (1977–1978): 77–88.

———. "Ned B. Stonehouse and Redaction Criticism (Part II)," *Westminster Theological Journal* 40, no. 2 (1977–1978): 281–303.

———. "Old Princeton, Westminster, and Inerrancy," *Westminster Theological Journal* 50, no. 1 (1988): 65–80.

Stonehouse, Ned B. *Origins of the Synoptic Gospels: Some Basic Questions.* Grand Rapids: Eerdmans, 1963.

———. *The Witness of the Synoptic Gospels to Christ: One Volume Combining the Witness of Matthew and Mark to Christ and the Witness of Luke to Christ.* 2nd. ed. Grand Rapids: Baker, 1979.

Strauss, Mark L. *Four Portraits, One Jesus: An Introduction to Jesus and the Gospels.* Grand Rapids: Zondervan, 2007.

Van Til, Cornelius. *A Christian Theory of Knowledge.* Philadelphia: Presbyterian and Reformed, 1969.

Vos, Geerhardus. *Biblical Theology: Old and New Testaments.* Carlisle, PA: Banner of Truth, 1975.

Warfield, Benjamin B. *Christology and Criticism.* New York: Oxford University Press, 1929.

———. *The Inspiration and Authority of the Bible.* Reprint. Philadelphia: Presbyterian and Reformed, 1967.

———. *Revelation and Inspiration.* New York: Oxford, 1927.

Wescott, Brooke Foss. *Introduction to the Study of the Gospels, with Historical and Explanatory Notes.* 6th ed. Cambridge/London: Macmillan, 1881.

Westminster Confession of Faith. 1646.

White, Kenneth J. "'A Voice Crying in the Four Gospels': A Guide to the Use of Harmonization as a Historiographic Tool with Special Emphasis on the Relationship of John to the Synoptics." MA thesis, Trinity Evangelical Divinity School, 1997.

Woodbridge, John D. *Biblical Authority: A Critique of the Rogers/McKim Proposal*. Grand Rapids: Zondervan, 1982.

General Index

Scripture Index

Genesis

1:3	175
1:28–30	175
1:31	49
2:4	68
3:4–5	79, 110
3:5	99
5	68
5:1	68
6:5	166
6:9	68
10	68
11:10–32	68
11:27	68
12:1–3	69
38	69

Exodus

20:15	28
31:18	217

Leviticus

16:5	31
16:15	31
16:16	31
16:21	31
25	143

Numbers

4:1–33	168

18:4–7	168
25:9	58

Deuteronomy

6:4–5	165, 166
6:5	164, 165, 166
6:16	179
9:10	217
29:4	170, 171
29:4a	171
29:29	137

Joshua

2:1	69

Ruth

1:4	69

2 Samuel

7:5–16	69
11	69
11:3	69
14:33	31
22	177

1 Kings

12:3	31
12:12	31

WORLDVIEW–BASED DEFENSE OF SCRIPTURAL INERRANCY

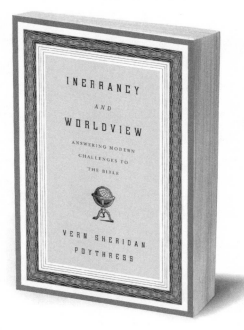

"A wide-ranging analysis that exposes the faulty intellectual assumptions that underlie challenges to the Bible from every major academic discipline in the modern university world. I think every Christian student at every secular university should read and absorb the arguments in this book."

WAYNE GRUDEM, *Research Professor of Bible and Theology, Phoenix Seminary*

"The book gets deeper into the question of inerrancy than any other book I know."

JOHN M. FRAME, *J. D. Trimble Chair of Systematic Theology and Philosophy, Reformed Theological Seminary, Orlando, Florida*

"Every new item that Vern Poythress writes is thoughtful, creative, and worth reading. This book is no exception. Besides its crucial contribution to his own subject in clarifying how it is that God communicates to us through the Bible, I think this basic idea will be fruitful for a good number of other topics as well. Thanks, Dr. Poythress, and thanks, God, for giving him to the church."

C. JOHN COLLINS, *Professor of Old Testament, Covenant Theological Seminary; author,* Science & Faith

---

Visit crossway.org for more information.